This Cookbook Belongs to

_____

THE WASHINGTON COOKBOOK

Published by SDH Company
PO Box 923
Spokane, Washington 99210

Cover Design by Nancy Starkman

Printed in South Korea

www.thewashingtoncookbook.com

INTRODUCTION

The Washington Cookbook is a fine collection of recipes gathered from all around the state of Washington.

Creativity and imagination are two important ingredients in the preparation of a great meal and also serve us well in our day to day lives. It is not coincidental that people who enjoy good food are the same ones most active in the pursuit of excellence in other areas as well. Washington's greatest resource is these people and the Evergreen State is fortunate to have so many.

Steven D Harvey
1982

A WORD ABOUT ORGANICS

We have been supporters of the organic movement for over 40 years. My parents were derided as *"Health Nuts"* in the 50's and 60's because they believed that food should not be produced the same way you produce cars and televisions. That wisdom has proven itself over the course of time. Good, natural, wholesome food is not produced in a factory or by using factory practices.

In supporting the organic philosophy, you can shop local and sustainable. This keeps money in your own area, supports local agriculture, helps to protect the environment, and of course you get to enjoy better tasting, more nutritious food. All of the recipes in this book can be prepared using organic ingredients and we urge you to do so whenever possible.

Steven D Harvey
2012

To the Artists...

My sincere thanks to the Washington artists whose works appear in this book: Glenn E. Emmons, Dennis Smith, Dan Jordan, Don Crook and Pat Powell. These drawings were commissioned exclusively for the Washington Cookbook.

TABLE OF CONTENTS

PIONEER

PIONEER STEW

1	pound ground beef
1/2	cup chopped onion
1/2	cup chopped green pepper
1	1-pound can whole kernel corn (2 cups)
1	1-pound can kidney beans (2 cups)
1	1-pound can tomatoes (2 cups)
2	teaspoons chili powder
1	teaspoon salt
1	cup shredded sharp cheddar cheese

Cook ground beef, onion and green pepper until meat is browned and vegetables are tender. Drain corn, beans and tomatoes. Add liquids, chili powder and salt to meat and cook until liquid is reduced to about half. Add corn, beans and tomatoes. Simmer 10 minutes. Stir in cheese and serve immediately. Serves 4.

MINCEMEAT

5	cups chopped cooked meat (neck of venison)
2-1/2	cups chopped suet
7-1/2	cups chopped apples (add apples just before cooking)
2-1/2	cups raisins
3	cups cider
1/2	cup vinegar
3	cups sugar or a little more
3/4	pound citron, finely chopped
	juice of 2 lemons
	juice of 2 oranges
1	tablespoon mace
2	tablespoons cinnamon
2	tablespoons cloves
2	tablespoons allspice
2	tablespoons nutmeg
3	cups liquor from beef or venison
1-1/2	cups brandy
	nuts

Combine all ingredients. Cook 1-1/2 hours then add brandy and seal in sterilized jars.

HAMBURG ROAST (1929)

1	pound finely ground beef round
2/3	cup bread, soaked in milk
1	slice onion, minced
1/4	cup onion, sliced
1	egg
	salt and pepper
	ginger
2/3	cup stewed tomatoes
2/3	tablespoon butter
2	hard boiled eggs

Squeeze milk from bread. Add to meat along with minced onion, uncooked egg (well beaten), and seasonings. Place hard cooked eggs in center of meat and roll meat over them. Add sliced onion and butter to stewed tomatoes and pour over meat roll in baking pan. Place in very hot oven for 5 minutes. Reduce heat and cook 20 to 30 minutes more, basting frequently with tomato sauce. Slice the roll crosswise when serving. Preparation time is about 30 minutes. Serves 2 to 3.

HAMBURGER SAUSAGE

5	pounds hamburger

Mix the following spices together and gradually add the hamburger while mixing with hands.

5	rounded teaspoons Morton's quick salt or curing salt
2-1/2	teaspoons garlic salt
2-1/2	teaspoons coarse pepper
1	teaspoon liquid smoke or hickory smoke salt
1-1/2	teaspoons medley pepper or season pepper
1	teaspoon (about) season salt
2-1/2	teaspoons mustard seeds

Mix in bowl, cover and refrigerate overnight. Next morning, mix with hands again and return to refrigerator. On the third day mix and shape into 2-1/2 inch rolls. Place on a broiler pan on lower oven rack. Set oven at lowest temperature (150 degrees). Bake for 8 hours turning every 2 hours. Let cool on paper. May be frozen.

HAMBURGER SALAMI

5	pounds hamburger
5	teaspoons Morton curing salt
2-1/2	teaspoons coarse ground pepper
2-1/2	teaspoons mustard seed
2-1/2	teaspoons garlic salt
5	teaspoons liquid smoke

Mix thoroughly. Cover and refrigerate for 3 days. Re-mix once each day. On the fourth day, roll into 1 pound logs. Place on broiling pan with rack and bake at 200 degrees for 8 hours. Cool, wrap in foil and keep in refrigerator or freeze.

ELLIE'S GASPACHIO

8	medium or large tomatoes
6	large bell peppers
4	small cucumbers
4	thick hard tack
5	hard boiled eggs

Put hard tack in bowl of water to soak until soft. Peel cukes and lay in salt water for an hour or more, then slice thin. Peel and slice tomatoes. Chop peppers fine. Keep all ingredients separate. Now make mayonnaise. Season very highly and mash into it through a coarse sieve, the eggs, (whites and all). Add about a teaspoon of Worcestershire sauce. Thin mayonnaise to the consistency of thin cream with the juice of your sliced tomatoes and add a little vinegar. If vinegar is strong, put a little vinegar in ice water to obtain right consistency. Now squeeze the 4 hard tack by hand, pressing until free of water. Break up a bit before placing in bottom of salad bowl. Make first layer of hard tack and cover lightly with mayonnaise dressing. Then a layer of tomatoes, cukes and peppers, lightly covering each with mayonnaise dressing. Alternate in this way until bowl is full. Save some green peppers for top layer. Be sure mayonnaise goes between each layer and especially on last layer before green peppers are sprinkled on top. Best to make a few hours ahead and place in refrigerator to allow mayonnaise to blend all through the salad. This was a great favorite of my Mothers, Mrs. J. M. Muldon. The above amount serves 12 plates or bowls. This is another old Southern recipe, although I never knew it to be made except in Pensacola, Florida, my old home or perhaps Mobile or New Orleans. The only problem you might encounter would be obtaining the thick hard tack. That was used by the fishing boats which would go out and stay for a month or two. It never seemed to spoil. I have some I brought from Florida well over 5 years ago and it is still O.K. It truly fits its name. It is hard as a rock and that is why it has to be soaked before making salad. The hard tack is about 4-1/2 to 5 inches round and 1/2 to 3/4 inch thick. Perhaps on the coast where fishing boats are found, there might be someone who knows about it. In this modern day, they probably don't need it!! I believe they are just made of flour and water. I do remember they were baked long and slow in an old brick oven. Maybe a hard thick water cracker could be used — just an idea. It is a truly wonderful salad!

MOTHER'S MAYONNAISE

8	tablespoons sugar
1/2	teaspoon dry mustard
1/2	teaspoon salt
2	rounded tablespoons flour
1	egg, slightly beaten
1/4	cup vinegar
1	cup milk
1	tablespoon butter

Mix dry ingredients in a saucepan. Add egg, vinegar and milk. Be sure to add vinegar before the milk to prevent curdling. Cook, stirring constantly till mixture is thick. Remove from heat, add butter and beat well. Refrigerate. This is good on cole slaw, roast pork (hot or cold) or just plain on bread and butter. My children loved it mixed with peanut butter when they were young.

POTATO CHIPS

The origin of potato chips can be traced to Moon Lake House, Saratoga Springs, New York in the year 1853. They were first known as Saratoga Chips and the recipe for making them appeared in the 1887 edition of the White House Cook Book.

SARATOGA CHIPS

Peel good-sized potatoes and slice them as evenly as possible. Drop them into ice water. Have a kettle of very hot lard, as for cakes. Put a few slices at a time into a towel and shake to dry the moisture out of them. Drop into the boiling lard. Stir them occasionally, and when of a light brown take them out with a skimmer. They will be crisp and not greasy. Sprinkle salt over them while hot.

HOMEMADE NOODLES

6	egg yolks
1	tablespoon water
	enough flour to make dough stiff enough to roll out

Mix all ingredients. If you do not have a noodle roller, then fold and cut with a knife. Put newspaper over back of chair and cover with a towel. Hang noodle ovals over them and let hang until almost dry.

PEARL'S HARVEST DAY NUT ROAST

2	cups chopped celery
2	cups chopped onions
1	cup chopped walnuts
2	cups fresh bread cut in little pieces
1/4	cup dried parsley (or more)
1	teaspoon salt
1	teaspoon sweet basil
1/2	teaspoon poultry seasoning
2	tablespoons chicken style seasoning
3	teaspoons ground flax seeds
8	tablespoons soyagen powder
1/4	cup oil
1-3/4	cups water

Mix all together. Bake in pan at 325 degrees for 45 to 60 minutes or until done. I made this in a restaurant. Very good.

HIGHLAND SCONES FROM MOM DUNN

2	cups flour
2-1/2	teaspoons baking powder
2	tablespoons sugar
5	tablespoons shortening
1/2	cup milk
1/2	teaspoon salt
2	eggs
	jam or marmalade

Blend shortening with sifted dry ingredients. Stir in milk and egg. Pat with hands to 1/4 inch thickness. Spread jam over half the dough. Cut in squares and then crosswise to form triangles. Brush with milk to give a rich brown glaze and bake in a hot oven 10 to 15 minutes.

SLICED GREEN TOMATOES

2-3	average-sized green tomatoes
3	cups cold water
2	tablespoons salt
2/3	cup flour
1/4	teaspoon pepper
1-1/2	cups butter

Wash green tomatoes. Slice "not too thin". Soak in cold water with salt for 10 minutes. Drain off salt water. Mix white pepper. Dip sliced tomatoes in flour mixture. Heat skillet on medium heat with butter or lard; fry until golden brown. Serve with lemon.

HOMEMADE CRACKERS

4	cups flour
2	tablespoons sugar
1	teaspoon salt
1/4	cup butter

Sift flour, sugar and salt. Cut in the butter until mealy and stir enough milk into this to make a stiff dough. Roll out to 1/4 inch thick on a lightly floured board. Cut to cracker size. Prick surface well and coat lightly with milk. Place on an ungreased cookie sheet and bake in a 425 degree oven for about 15 minutes or until lightly browned.

TOMATO MINCE MEAT

1-1/2	pints chopped tart apples
1	pint chopped green tomatoes
2	teaspoons cinnamon
1	teaspoon salt
1	teaspoon allspice
1	teaspoon cloves
1	pound raisins
1	cup suet
3	cups sugar

Peel and chop apples or grind. Mix all ingredients together. Bring to a rapid boil and simmer until thick. Pour into sterilized jars and seal.

DELICIOUS BEET GREEN PIE

Use your favorite flour pastry shell. Filling:

2	pounds beet greens, chard or fresh spinach, washed and coarsely chopped
1	onion, chopped
1	tablespoon butter
1	clove garlic, chopped (optional)

Topping:

1-1/2	cups grated mild yellow cheese
1/4	cup grated parmesan cheese
1/2	cup heavy cream with enough milk to make it pour easy or yogurt and dry milk with enough milk to thin
	salt and pepper

Filling: Saute beet greens and onions in butter until greens wilt somewhat, about 10 minutes. Pour into pie crust.

Topping: Spread cream mixture to cover the greens. Sprinkle cheese to cover evenly. Salt and pepper to taste. Bake 1/2 hour or until cheese melts and bubbles. Bake at 325 degrees.

MILD TOMATO RELISH

Grind:

30	ripe tomatoes
12	large sour apples
10	onions

Add:

1	quart vinegar
1	quart sugar
4	tablespoons mustard (add last)
4	tablespoons salt
1	teaspoon cloves
1	teaspoon allspice
1	teaspoon cinnamon
1/2	teaspoon ginger

Mix thoroughly. Cook over low heat one hour. Seal in quart or pint jars. Makes 7 quarts.

ELLIE'S WESTERN SALAD

Make the following about 4 hours ahead of time.

Garlic oil: Peel 2 pods of good size garlic and slice thin into 1/4 cup of Wesson oil. Let stand until ready to use, then remove garlic.

Croutons: A full pint. Cut French bread in 1/4 inch cubes and dry out in slow oven. Should be light brown in color. Can be made a day ahead.

Lettuce: 2 heads fair size, broken into pieces (not cut). Place in large bowl ready for salad mixing. I prepare this early in the day and put it in large Tupperware, keeps well.

Cheese: Put 4 ounces crumbled bleu cheese in a cup. Add enough shredded Parmesan cheese to make 1 cup. This you can fix ahead and keep in box.

In another cup, put 2 tablespoons lemon juice (more can be added if you like it tart). Add 1 tablespoon Worcestershire sauce and set aside.

1/2	teaspoon (full) salt
1/4	teaspoon (scant) black pepper
6	tablespoons Wesson oil
1	small raw egg
	coarse black pepper (for table)

Now for the last minute salad mixing. Sprinkle cheese over the lettuce. Next, drizzle 6 tablespoons oil over all. Then add 1/2 teaspoon salt and 1/4 teaspoon pepper. Now drop raw egg on top. Pour lemon juice and Worcestershire sauce onto egg and give salad a good tossing. Lastly, add croutons and pour garlic oil over them. Toss again lightly to mix and serve immediately or as soon as it is possible. Wonderful with steak or prime rib.

DUCHESS POTATOES (1929)

Use freshly boiled and mashed potatoes or some that are left over. Add to them a beaten yolk from 1 egg. Form mixture into balls, hearts or flat cakes and place in a greased pan. Brush with beaten egg white and brown in oven.

GRAN'S CORN CASSEROLE

4	eggs, beaten
1	can whole kernel corn (undrained)
1	can cream style corn
1	large can milk
1	bunch green onions or 1 small onion, diced
1	cup chopped celery
1	(2 oz.) jar pimiento (use liquid)
1/4	green pepper, chopped
2	cups sharp cheddar cheese, shredded
1/2	teaspoon garlic powder **or** 1 clove garlic, chopped
	salt and pepper to taste

Mix all together well. Place in large buttered casserole. Bake at 350 degrees until knife comes out of center clean.

BAKED SUCCOTASH (1929)

2	cups cooked or canned kidney beans
1-1/2	cups canned corn (cream style)
1	tablespoon green pepper, minced
1	egg, well beaten
1/2	teaspoon salt
1/8	teaspoon pepper

Combine ingredients and place in casserole. Bake in moderate oven for about 30 minutes.

VINEGAR PIE

2	cups boiling water
1/4	cup vinegar
1	cup sugar
3	tablespoons flour
3	eggs
1	teaspoon lemon flavoring
1/3	teaspoon salt
3	tablespoons sugar

Beat egg yolks until thick. Add 1 cup sugar, flour and salt. Add vinegar. Cook over hot water until thick and smooth. Add salt and flavoring. Pour into baked pastry shell. Cover with meringue made of egg whites and 3 tablespoons sugar. Bake in slow oven (325 degrees) for 20 minutes.

AGGIES POTATO SALAD

6	large potatoes, cooked in skins
2	pound carton small curd cottage cheese
2	medium onions, sliced and separated
1	cup real mayonnaise
	olive oil
	salt and pepper
	cayenne pepper

The day before, soak sliced onions in water, cover and refrigerate. Peel potatoes while warm. In a large bowl put a layer of sliced potatoes. Salt and pepper lightly, then add a layer of onions, cottage cheese and mayonnaise. Repeat as needed, ending with a layer of potatoes on top. Sprinkle lightly with cayenne pepper and cover top with olive oil. Refrigerate overnight. Toss before serving. This delightful salad comes from a dear old lady who lived in the Shepherd of the Hills country in Missouri.

POTATOES SUPREME

6	large potatoes
2	cups sour cream
1	bunch green onions, sliced (use some of the green)
1-1/2	cups sharp cheddar cheese, shredded
1	teaspoon salt
1/4	teaspoon pepper
1/2	teaspoon garlic powder
	paprika

Cook potatoes in jackets till tender. Cool, peel and shred into a large bowl. Stir in sour cream, onions, garlic powder, salt and pepper and 1 cup of cheese. Turn into greased 2 quart casserole. Top with remaining cheese and sprinkle with paprika. Cover and refrigerate several hours or overnight. Bake uncovered 30 to 40 minutes at 350 degrees till heated through.

ELLIE'S GRANDMOTHER'S WHITE FRUIT CAKE

2	pounds blanched almonds, sliced thin
3/4	pound butter
1	pound sugar
1	pound flour
	whites of 16 eggs, beaten, but not stiff
2	pounds citron, cut fine
2	fresh coconuts, grated fine **(use fresh)**
1	teaspoon soda
2	teaspoons cream of tartar, dissolved in 1/2 cup light cream
1	cup sherry

Cream butter and sugar well. Add citron, almonds and flour, then coconut and then whites of eggs. Flavor with sherry. Grease and flour loaf pans well. Bake at 300 degrees about 1 hour or until tested and straw comes out clean. Makes 3 loaf pans regular size or more smaller size. This makes a large quantity. I usually make one half of recipe using smaller pans. It is unusual and delicious, but I must warn you it does not keep like dark fruit cake due to fresh coconut. Do not use any other, as it doesn't work.

Half Recipe:

1-1/2	cups butter
2	cups sugar
4	cups flour
4	cups citron
4	cups almonds
3	cups fresh coconut, grated
8	egg whites
1/2	teaspoon soda
1	teaspoon cream of tartar, dissolved in 1/4 cup light cream
1/2	cup sherry

I am 80 years old and my hobby has been collecting cookbooks, especially personal ones. I have never seen this recipe or one even similar. Years ago, it was served with a glass of sherry when friends dropped in during the Christmas holidays.

SNOW CAKE (1929)

1/2	cup butter
2	cups sugar
3	cups pastry flour
2	teaspoons baking powder
1/2	teaspoon salt
1	cup cold water
4	egg whites
1/2	teaspoon almond flavoring
1/2	teaspoon vanilla

Cream butter and sugar. Sift flour, baking powder and salt. Add alternately with water to creamed butter and sugar. Fold in stiffly beaten egg whites and flavorings. Bake in three 9 inch layer cake tins at 375 degrees for 15 to 20 minutes. Put layers together with a boiled icing to which a dozen white marshmallows have been added.

SUNSHINE CAKE

11	large eggs, separated
1/8	teaspoon salt
2	teaspoons cream of tartar
1-1/2	cups sugar
1	cup cake flour
2	tablespoons orange juice
2	teaspoons vanilla extract
1	teaspoon lemon extract

In large bowl beat egg whites with cream of tartar. Just before stiff, add 1 cup sugar gradually. Add salt. Egg whites should form peaks. Sift flour once. Beat yolks in medium bowl until light in color. Add extracts and scant 1/2 cup sugar. Add 1/3 flour to egg yolks, beating at very lowest speed. Add 1 tablespoon orange juice. Mix slightly. Add another 1/3 cup flour. Beat only slightly. Add other tablespoon orange juice. Mix. Add last 1/3 cup flour. Don't beat much. Take some of the egg white and mix into bowl of yolks (with spoon). Lift spoon to get as much air in as possible, doing this with an up and down motion. Add this mixture back into bowl of remaining egg whites. Fold by lifting to get air inside. Mix so no white streaks can be seen. Put into non-greased angel food cake pan. Bake at 310 degrees for 1 hour and 5 minutes. Don't open oven till nearly done. Cake is done when finger pressed lightly on it does not leave an impression. Cool 15 to 20 minutes upside down. Cool thoroughly before covering to avoid sogginess. Cake is excellent after being frozen.

MOTHER'S WHITE CAKE

3	cups flour
1/4	teaspoon salt
3	teaspoons baking powder
2	cups sugar

Sift above ingredients together. Add 1/2 cup lard and mix till crumbly.

Add the following:

2	eggs, whole
1-1/2	cups milk
1	tablespoon of anise seed, pounded fine
1	tablespoon vanilla

Mix lightly till blended. Bake at 450 degrees for 45 minutes.

JEAN'S OLD TIME CINNAMON JUMBLES

Mix thoroughly:

1/2	cup soft shortening
1	cup sugar
1	egg

Stir in:

3/4	cup buttermilk
1	teaspoon vanilla

Sift together and stir in:

2	cups flour
1/2	teaspoon soda
1/2	teaspoon salt

Chill dough. Drop by teaspoonfuls on greased cookie sheet. Sprinkle with mixture of cinnamon and sugar. Bake until set, but do not brown. Bake at 400 degrees for 8 to 10 minutes. Can also add cinnamon sugar to mixture and bake in cake pans. This recipe has been in my family for many years. I always sent pans to the basketball and baseball teams of my daughter's high school.

ICE BOX FRUIT CAKE

1/2	cup sesame spread or 1/4 pound cold pressed butter
1/2	cup honey
1/3	cup pineapple or orange juice

2	cups dates, cut up
2	cups candied fruit
1/4	cup dried lemon or orange peel
1/4	cup candied cherries (green or red)
1	cup currants
1	teaspoon corriander (ground)

Mix ingredients and cover well. Let stand in refrigerator over night. Then add:

1	cup chopped nuts
4-5	cups granola crumbs

Mix all together and pack into small loaf pans. Makes 2 small loaves. Cover well and refrigerate for at least 2 days or 1 week or longer. Very Good!

POTATO OATMEAL COOKIES

1/2	cup grated potato (raw)
1/2	cup honey **or** corn syrup or corn syrup and molasses combined
1/4	cup melted shortening
1	egg, beaten
1	cup quick cooking oatmeal
1	cup flour
1	teaspoon baking powder
1/4	teaspoon soda
1/2	teaspoon salt
1/2	teaspoon cinnamon
1/4	teaspoon nutmeg
1/2	cup raisins
1/2	cup chopped nuts

Mix first 5 ingredients together. Mix all remaining ingredients with flour and combine with first mixture. Drop by spoonful onto greased baking sheet. Bake at 350 degrees for 15 minutes. Makes 2-1/2 dozen. These cookies are real moist and so good!

MEMORABLE CHOCOLATE POUND CAKE

1	cup butter
2	cups sugar
4	eggs
2	teaspoons vanilla
1	(4 ounce) bar German sweet chocolate, melted
3	cups sifted all-purpose flour
1	teaspoon salt
1/2	teaspoon baking soda
1/2	teaspoon cinnamon
1/2	teaspoon nutmeg
1	cup buttermilk

Cream together butter and sugar until light and fluffy. Add eggs, one at a time, beating well. Blend in vanilla. Add melted chocolate. Sift together flour, baking soda, salt and spices.

Add to creamed mixture, alternately with buttermilk. Pour into buttered 10 inch tube pan. Bake at 300 degrees for 1 hour and 30 to 35 minutes. Serve dusted with powdered sugar.

SOUR CREAM POUND CAKE

1/2	pound butter, softened
3	cups sugar
6	egg yolks, beaten
3	cups all-purpose flour
	pinch salt
1	carton (8 ounce) sour cream
1/4	teaspoon baking soda
6	egg whites, stiffly beaten
1	teaspoon vanilla extract
1	teaspoon almond extract

Cream butter and sugar. Add egg yolks. Combine flour and salt and sift three times. Combine sour cream and baking soda. Add flour and sour cream alternately to the creamed mixture. Fold in egg whites and flavorings. Spoon batter into a 10 inch greased and lightly floured tube pan or bundt pan. Bake at 300 degrees for 1-1/2 hours.

OLD FASHIONED PEACH COBBLER

1/2	cup butter
2	cups flour
1-1/2	cups sugar
1	tablespoon baking powder
1-1/2	cups milk
1	quart or can sliced peaches and juice

Place square of butter in a 9 x 13 inch pan; place in oven to melt. In mixing bowl, stir together flour, sugar, baking powder and milk. Mix all together. Put in pan with melted butter and stir to mix. Spread evenly in pan. Put peaches and juice over batter. Bake 1 hour at 350 degrees.

SPICED SUGAR WALNUTS

2	cups walnut halves or pieces
1	cup sugar
1/2	cup water
1	teaspoon cinnamon
1/2	teaspoon ginger
1/4	teaspoon mace
1/4	teaspoon salt
1	tablespoon butter
1/4	teaspoon ground orange peel

Place nuts in shallow pan. Toast about 15 minutes at 325 degrees until lightly browned. Cool. In 2 quart saucepan, combine sugar and spices. Add water. Heat to boiling, stirring till sugar dissolves. Cover and boil 3 to 4 minutes. Uncover and boil to 236 degrees F on candy thermometer or till a little dropped in cold water forms soft ball. Remove from heat and add butter and orange peel. Stir till mixture begins to lose gloss and is creamy (doesn't take long). Add nuts and stir to coat. Turn out on wax paper. Cool. Break apart and store in airtight container. Delicious!

INDIAN PUDDING

Mix in saucepan:

1/4	cup corn meal
1	cup water
1	teaspoon salt
2	cups milk

Bring to a boil, stirring constantly. Boil 10 minutes.

Mix together and blend in:

1	egg, well beaten
1/4	cup sugar
1/2	cup light molasses
1	tablespoon butter
1	teaspoon cinnamon
1	teaspoon ginger

Pour into buttered 1-1/2 quart casserole. Bake at 325 degrees for 1/2 hour, then stir in 1 cup milk. Bake 1-1/2 hours more. Serve with baked beans, etc. Serves 6.

NEVER FAIL TWICE COOKED DIVINITY

Stir 2 cups sugar into 1/2 cup water. Add 1/2 cup corn syrup and a dash of salt. Bring to a boil, (boil to 240 degrees) and slowly pour 1/3 of the syrup over 2 stiffly beaten egg whites beating constantly. Cook remaining syrup (to 265 degrees), and pour into first mixture. Stir well and cool 15 minutes. Stir once or twice, then add 1 teaspoon vanilla and 1 tablespoon melted butter. Drop from a teaspoon on wax paper.

OLD HARTFORD ELECTION CAKE

This recipe is over 100 years old.

5	pounds sifted flour
2	pounds butter
2	pounds sugar
3	gills distillery yeast (or twice the quantity of home brewed)
4	eggs
	gill of wine
	gill of brandy
1	quart sweet milk
1/2	ounce nutmeg
2	pounds raisins
1	pound citron

Rub the butter and flour together very fine. Add half the sugar, then the yeast and half the milk (hot in winter, blood-warm in summer). Add the eggs, then remainder of the milk and the wine. Beat well and let rise in a warm place all night. In the morning, beat a long time, adding brandy, rest of sugar, spice and fruit well floured. Allow to rise again until very light. Put in cake pans and let rise 10 or 15 minutes. Have the oven about as hot as for bread. This cake will keep for any length of time. Note: I should think so!

GRANDMA'S DROP DONUTS

2	eggs
1/2	cup sugar
1	tablespoon vegetable oil
1	cup milk
3	level teaspoons baking powder
1-1/2 to 2	cups flour (enough to make it stiff)
1	teaspoon vanilla

Combine above ingredients, adding enough flour to make dough stiff. Pour cooking oil in heavy pan until 4 to 5 inches deep. Add 2 tablespoons vinegar to prevent donuts from soaking up oil. Drop by tea-spoonful into hot oil and cook until brown. Donuts should rise to the top easily. If not, the oil is not hot enough. Roll in sugar.

WHITE CHRISTMAS PIE

Blend in saucepan:

1/2	cup sugar
1/4	cup flour
1	envelope Knox gelatin

Gradually stir in 1-3/4 cups milk. Cook on medium heat, stirring constantly. Boil 1 minute. If you prefer, cook in microwave for 7 minutes, stirring occasionally, with no danger of scorching. Place in cold water until slightly thickened. Blend in:

3/4	teaspoon vanilla
1/4	teaspoon almond flavoring

In mixing bowl beat:

3	egg whites
1/4	teaspoon cream of tartar
1/2	cup sugar

Beat 1/2 cup heavy whipping cream and fold into meringue, then into cooled gelatin mixture. Add 1 cup Angel flake coconut and pile into favorite pie crust. Chill. Sprinkle with additional coconut if desired.

BACON GREASE CAKE

2	cups sugar
1	cup bacon grease
1	pound raisins
1	teaspoon cloves or allspice
1	teaspoon cinnamon
2	cups hot water
1/8	teaspoon salt
2	teaspoons soda
3-1/2	cups flour
1	teaspoon vanilla extract
1/4	cup chopped nuts (optional)

Mix sugar, grease, raisins, spices, water and salt. Boil for 3 minutes. Add soda and beat well. Cool. Add flour, vanilla and nuts. Pour into greased and floured 9 x 13 inch pan. Bake at 350 degrees for 1 hour.

SCRIPTURE CAKE

(read Luke 14:15, the last part)

Oven: 325 degrees

3/4	cup Psalms 55:21a (1/2 cup shortening, 1/4 cup oil)
1	cup Jeremiah 6:20 (sugar)
3	of Isaiah 10:14 (eggs)
2-1/4	cups I Kings 4:22a (flour)
1	teaspoon I Corinthians 5:6 (baking powder)
	pinch of Matthew 5:13 (salt)
1/4	cup Judges 4:19b (milk)
1	tablespoon Judges 14:18b (honey)
1/4	teaspoon II Chronicles 9:9 (nutmeg)
1	teaspoon II Chronicles 9:9 (allspice)
2	teaspoons II Chronicles 9:9 (cinnamon)
1	teaspoon II Chronicles 9:9 (cloves)
1	cup II Samuel 16:1b (raisins)
1	cup Song of Solomon 2:13a (figs or dates)
1	cup Numbers 17:8 (almonds), chopped

Cream shortening, oil and sugar together. Add eggs one at a time. Proverbs 23:14 (beat) well. Sift and measure flour, baking powder and salt. Add alternately to sugar mixture with milk. Stir in honey and spices, then raisins, figs or dates and almonds. II Kings 4:5 (pour) into well greased vessels (loaf pans or a 9 x 13 inch pan) and Leviticus 24:5 (bake) for 45 minutes.

EDITH'S GRITTED BREAD

6	ears corn, creamed (uncooked)
1/2 to 2/3	cup flour
1	teaspoon salt
1	teaspoon baking powder

Mix together corn, salt and baking powder. Add flour to thicken. Turn into a well greased No. 8 cast iron pan. Bake at 350 degrees for 20 to 25 minutes or until golden brown. My folks were born and raised in North Carolina. Came to Washington State in 1903 and settled close to the Cowlitz River near Balflour Bar with Post Office at Ethel, Washington. I was one of their 11 children, next to the oldest, born September 25, 1904 at Ethel.

MINCEMEAT FRUITCAKE

Mix together:

2	cups mincemeat
1-1/2	cups chopped nuts
2	cups fruit mix
3/4	cup chopped dates

Sift into above mixture:

3-1/4	cups flour
1	cup sugar
1-1/2	teaspoons soda
1	teaspoon salt

Combine:

3	beaten eggs
3/4	cup salad oil
2	teaspoons vanilla

Blend into mixture. Bake at 300 degrees about 60 minutes or until done.

OLD ORIGINAL SEE'S FUDGE RECIPE

Place in a large sauce pan:

4-1/2	cups sugar
1	can Carnation milk

Bring to a boil and count 7 minutes from time it comes to full boil.

Remove from fire and pour over:

1	(8 ounce) jar marshmallow creme
3	packages of chocolate chips

Stir in 1 cup chopped nuts and 1/2 pound butter. Cream together well. Add 1 teaspoon vanilla. Pour into buttered 10 x 15 inch pan. Store in refrigerator.

BEV'S MOTHER'S CHOCOLATE PIE

Place in skillet and heat:

2	cups sugar
4	tablespoons Hershey's cocoa
4	tablespoons flour
6	eggs
1	cup water
1	pinch salt

Add:

1/4	cup butter or margarine
2	teaspoons vanilla

Stir till mixed well, comes to a boil and becomes thick. Pour into already cooked and prepared pie shell.

ON THE TRAIL

GLENN E. EMMONS ©1982

CATTLE DRIVE SOUP

1	pound soup bones
1	cup water
2	cups tomato juice
1/2	cup coarsely chopped onion, sauted in butter
1	tablespoon salt
1/4	teaspoon chili powder
2	bay leaves
1	cup diced celery
1	cup sliced carrots
1	cup diced potatoes
2	teaspoons Worcestershire sauce

Simmer, covered, for 2 hours with bones, water, tomato juice, onion and seasonings. Add vegetables; cover and simmer for 1 hour longer. Remove meat from bones and return to soup.

BRANDING IRON CHOWDER

1	pound soup bones
1	pound ground beef
2	cans kidney beans
1	large can tomatoes
1	quart water
1	large onion, chopped
1-1/2	teaspoons seasoned salt
1/2	teaspoon garlic powder
1/2	teaspoon thyme
1/4	teaspoon pepper
1	cup diced potatoes
1/2	green pepper, chopped

Brown ground beef; pour off fat. In large kettle, combine everything except green pepper and potatoes. Simmer, covered, 2 hours. Add green pepper and potatoes. Cook covered 15 to 20 minutes, until potatoes are tender.

SKILLET STEW

1	pound ground beef
1	(10 ounce) can beef consomme
1	pound can cream style corn
1	pound can lima beans
1	medium onion, chopped
3	large potatoes, diced
	salt and pepper to taste

Brown beef and onion in large skillet. Stir to chop meat into small pieces. Add consomme, potatoes, salt and pepper. Mix well. Cover and cook over low heat about 25 minutes or until potatoes are cooked. Add corn and beans, heating thoroughly. Stir often to keep potatoes from sticking.

CAMPFIRE STEW

4	carrots, quartered
1-1/2	cups chopped potatoes
2	medium onions, quartered
1	(16 ounce) can peas, drained
1/2	pound frankfurters, sliced diagonally
1	can condensed cream of celery soup
1	cup shredded cheddar cheese (sharp, preferably)

Add enough water to cover carrots, potatoes and onions. Cover; cook 10 minutes. Add peas and frankfurters. Continue cooking additional 5 minutes, drain. Stir in soup and cheddar cheese, heat, but do not boil.

CAMP SKILLET DISH

6	knackwurst sausages or frankfurters
2	tablespoons butter
1	can (16 ounce) sauerkraut
1	can (8 ounce) sliced peaches, drained

Brown sausages in butter in a 10 inch skillet over medium heat on grill or camp stove. Cook 8 to 10 minutes, turning occasionally. Stir in sauerkraut, with liquid, and top with peaches. Heat to a boil and then reduce heat. Cover and simmer until sauerkraut is hot, about 10 minutes.

MINESTRONE STEW

1-1/2	pounds beef, cut in 1 inch cubes
1/4	cup Italian dressing
1	(29 ounce) can tomatoes
1-1/2	cups water
1	teaspoon salt
1/4	teaspoon pepper
1-1/2	cups carrot chunks
1-1/2	cups sliced celery chunks
4	small onions, quartered
2-1/2	cups (6 ounces) spiral noodles, cooked, drained
	grated Romano cheese

Brown meat in dressing; add tomatoes, water and seasonings. Cover; simmer 1 hour. Add carrots, green beans and onions. Cover; simmer 15 minutes. Stir in noodles; continue cooking additional 5 minutes or until vegetables are tender. Sprinkle with cheese before serving.

CAMPFIRE CHILI

1	(16 ounce) can pork and beans
1	(16 ounce) can kidney beans, drained
1	(16 ounce) can green beans, drained
6	crisply cooked bacon slices, coarsely crumbled
1	(8 ounce) jar Jalapeno Pepper Cheez Spread
	chili powder to taste (optional)

Combine pork and beans, kidney beans, green beans and bacon; heat. Stir in pepper cheez spread, continue heating until hot.

INDIAN STEW

Cut 1/2 pound bacon in small pieces. Fry till brown in kettle. Add 1 cup sliced onions and cook until half done, but do not brown. Add 3 cups diced potatoes and 1/2 pound dried beef pulled into pieces. Cover with water and cook very slow for about 3/4 hour or longer as it improves with simmering. Add pepper to taste and salt if needed, but beef may be salty enough. Very good served with some kind of hot bread and plenty of celery, radishes and pickles. Cookies for dessert.

CAMPER'S MACARONI AND CHEESE

1-1/3	cups nonfat dry milk
1	tablespoon flour
1	tablespoon instant minced onion
1	tablespoon freeze dried chives
1	teaspoon salt
	dash cayenne pepper
3-1/2	cups water
7	ounces uncooked macaroni
2	cups shredded cheddar cheese
1	can (8 ounce) kidney beans

Mix dry milk, flour, onion, chives, salt and pepper in skillet. Stir in water and macaroni. Heat to boiling on grill or camp stove. Reduce heat and cover. Simmer 10 minutes, stirring occasionally. Add cheese to macaroni mixture, stirring until melted. Stir in beans with liquid. Cover and simmer until macaroni is tender, about 5 minutes.

COLUMBIA RIVER EGGS

1	(28 ounce) can stewed tomatoes
1/2	cup chopped green pepper
1/4	cup chopped green onion
1	cup celery, chopped
	bay leaf
	salt and pepper to taste

Prepare ahead of time the above ingredients. Simmer covered until vegetables are slightly tender. Cool and pour into heavy plastic bag (zip-lock). Chill.

1	(16 ounce) can peas
1	tablespoon water
3/4	cup corn bread crumbs
1	tablespoon cornstarch
1-1/2	cups cheddar cheese, grated
10	or more eggs

Combine made ahead tomato mixture and undrained peas in heavy skillet. Bring to boil. Blend water and cornstarch and stir into mixture. Remove bay leaf. Break eggs into skillet, one at a time. Cover and simmer for about 8 minutes or until poached the way you like them. Sprinkle with cheese and corn bread crumbs. Cover briefly and allow cheese to melt.

CAMPFIRE BURGERS

These can be made ahead and refrigerated. Take along for easy fireside fixin. Real good!

SPUDBURGERS

1	pound ground beef
1	cup shredded potatoes
1/4	cup chopped onion
1	teaspoon salt
	dash of pepper
	cheddar cheese slices
5	kaiser rolls, split
5	red onion slices
	mushroom slices

Combine meat, potatoes, chopped onion and seasonings. Shape into five patties. Grill both sides on greased grill to desired doneness. Top with cheese slices and heat until cheese melts. For each sandwich, cover bottom half of bun with patty, onion slice and mushroom slices. Serve with top half of bun.

CANTONESE BURGERS

1	pound ground beef
1	(16 ounce) can bean sprouts, drained
	soy sauce
1/2	teaspoon onion salt
	cheddar cheese slices
6	sesame seed buns, split
6	pineapple rings
	salad dressing
6	mandarin orange segments

Combine meat, bean sprouts, 2 tablespoons soy sauce and onion salt. Shape into six patties. Grill both sides on greased grill to desired doneness. Top with cheese slice and heat until cheese melts. For each bun, cover bottom half with patty, grilled pineapple ring brushed with soy sauce, salad dressing and orange segment. Serve with top half of bun.

TACOBURGERS

1	pound ground beef
1	cup crushed corn chips
1/4	cup chili sauce
	cheddar cheese slices
5	poppy seed buns, split
	chopped tomato
	chopped avocado

Combine meat, corn chips and chili sauce. Shape into five patties. Grill both sides on greased grill to desired doneness. Top with cheese slice and heat until cheese melts. For each sandwich, cover bottom half of bun with patty, tomato and avocado. Serve with top half of bun.

HAM AND CHEESE PIE

1	(16 ounce) container creamed cottage cheese
1	(16 ounce) container ricotta cheese
2	cups ham, cooked and diced
3	eggs
2	teaspoons Italian seasoning
2/3	cup grated Parmesan cheese
1/2	teaspoon salt
1/4	teaspoon pepper
	pie crust for two 2-crust pies
1	egg yolk, slightly beaten

Mix first 8 ingredients together, set aside.

Mix pastry together in 1 large ball, then divide into 2/3 and 1/3 size balls. On lightly floured surface roll large ball into 16-inch circle, about 1/8 inch thick. Fold circle into fourths and carefully lift into 10-inch springform pan; unfold. With fingers, lightly press pastry into bottom and sides of pan, trim edges of pastry to make it even with rim of pan. Brush pastry with some beaten egg yolk. Spoon cheese mixture into pastry-lined pan. Fold edges of pastry over filling; brush with some beaten egg yolk.

Roll remaining pastry ball into a 10-inch circle. With knife, cut design in pastry. Place pastry circle over filling in pan, pressing lightly around edges to seal. Brush top with remaining egg yolk. Bake pie at 375 degrees 1 hour or until knife inserted in center comes out clean. Cool pie in refrigerator until serving time.

SANDY'S COOK OUT MENU:

STUFFED HAMBURGER

Make 2 thin hamburger patties. Cut up pickles, onions and cheese. Mix together and salt and pepper to taste. Place between the 2 patties. Pinch edges of patties together. You can barbecue these or put in foil and cook on a campfire. Quick and easy.

OUTDOOR POCKET STEW

For each serving, make a patty of 1/4 pound ground beef. Place patty on a 12 inch square piece of double thickness heavy duty aluminum foil. Top with onions, potatoes, carrots and celery chunks. Sprinkle with salt and pepper. Seal foil securely. Cook directly on hot coals about 25 minutes, turning once. Eat stew directly from foil pocket.

ROASTED CORN

Remove husks and silks from sweet and tender corn. Place each ear on heavy duty aluminum foil. Add 1 tablespoon butter and 2 tablespoons water. Wrap securely in foil, twisting ends to make handle for turning. Roast on medium coals 10 to 15 minutes, turning once.

CHICKEN AND RICE MEAL IN ONE
(my favorite)

Take a piece of a fryer and place on top of 1/4 cup of rice on a piece of heavy duty aluminum foil. Add onion, celery and carrot chunks, seasoned salt and pepper. Add 1/4 cup water and seal. Place on campfire grill for 45 minutes, turning a few times. Really delicious and easy!

Tip: when going camping, take along some zip-lock bags. They are nice for mixing food in, so you don't need bowls. Add all ingredients in bag, zip shut and mix with hands. Good for pancakes, etc.

COW POKE BEANS

1	pound dried pinto beans
2-1/2	cups cold water
1/2	pound salt pork, cut up
1	medium onion, chopped
1	clove garlic, minced
1	(6 ounce) can tomato paste
1	teaspoon salt
1	teaspoon cumin seed
1/2	teaspoon marjoram

Wash and pick over beans. Put in mixing bowl, cover with water and soak overnight (or at least 2 hours). Next morning place beans and water in a Dutch oven and bring to a boil. Reduce heat and simmer for 1 hour. Stir in remaining ingredients, cover and simmer for 3 hours or until beans are tender. Add more water if necessary. Stir occasionally. Serve over rice, potatoes or hot cooked noodles with hot biscuits or corn bread.

CAMPFIRE SUPPER

1/3	cup oil
4	cups frozen hash brown potatoes
1	(12 ounce) can luncheon meat, cubed
1/3	cup chopped green onions
2	cups (8 ounces) shredded sharp cheddar cheese

Heat oil in skillet over medium heat. Add hash browns, meat and green onions. Cook 10 to 15 minutes or to desired brownness. Stir in cheese and heat until cheese melts.

WASHINGTON MOUNTAIN BREAD

4   cups whole wheat flour
1   cup water
1/2   cup honey
1/3   cup vegetable oil
3/4   cup brown sugar, packed
1/3   cup wheat germ
1/4   cup sesame seeds
1/4   cup molasses
3   tablespoons powdered milk
1-1/2 teaspoons baking powder
1-1/2 teaspoons salt

Mix all ingredients together until smooth. Pour into well greased 8 x 8 x 2 inch baking pan. Bake in pre-heated 300 degree oven for 1 hour or until bread starts to pull away from sides of pan. Cut into 16 squares and let stand uncovered overnight to dry a bit. Seal in plastic bag. This bread will keep for weeks. Does not need refrigeration.

DUTCH OVEN PACK BREAD

2   packages yeast
2-1/2 cups warm water
2   teaspoons salt
7-1/4 to
7-1/2 cups flour

Glaze for bread:

1   egg white
1   tablespoon water

Dough should be very stiff. Mix until dough does not stick to mixing surface or hands. Let rise twice in a dutch oven set in a pan of warm water. Second time it rises, punch down and make into two round loaves. Let loaves rise to double bulk on flat surface of foil over warm water. Cover with towel rung out of hot water.

Prepare dutch oven with a layer of thin flat rocks or one inch of small gravel. Place on fire to pre-heat. The lid should be heated with the oven. When bread is raised, set loaves on foil in pre-heated dutch oven. Put lid on and add glowing coals to lid. Using pliers to lift the lid, peek at bread every 15 minutes until done (approximately 45 minutes). Also, glaze the bread each time with the egg white and water mixture. A piece of paper towel or cloth works for glazing. High altitude bread is the best ever! Happy eating!

EASY CAMP BISCUITS

8   cups flour
2   teaspoons salt
1/4   cup plus 4 teaspoons baking powder
2   teaspoons cream of tartar
2   teaspoons sugar
2   cups shortening
1-1/2 cups powdered milk

Sift dry ingredients. Cut in shortening till mixture resembles coarse crumbs. Pack into coffee can or plastic bag. When the tent is up, add 1/2 to 3/4 cup water to 2 cups of mix. Mix well and drop one at a time onto lightly greased skillet. Bake covered until done. May be wrapped around a stick and toasted over coals. Dip in honey.

CHEESY SKILLET BISCUITS

6   ounces sharp cheddar cheese
2   cups flour
1   tablespoon baking powder
1   teaspoon salt
2   tablespoons chopped chives (dried)
3/4   cup milk
1/4   cup margarine, melted

Cut cheese into eight 2 x 1 x 1/2 inch slices. Combine dry ingredients. Stir in chives. Add milk and margarine, mixing just till moistened. Knead dough on lightly floured surface about 10 times. Pat dough out to a 12 x 9 inch rectangle.

Place cheese slices, equally spaced, on one half of dough. Fold dough over cheese and cut into 2 x 3 inch rectangles. Press edges together to seal. Place in well greased, hot 12 inch skillet. Cover and cook over low heat 10 minutes. Turn, cover and continue cooking 5 minutes or until golden brown.

BACON ROLLS

Use a slice of soft bread for each roll. Trim edge and put a small strip of cheese at one end. Roll and wrap with a strip of bacon. If bacon is very wide, cut in half lengthwise. Secure with a toothpick at each end. If you like, add a dash of Tabasco on the cheese before rolling. Will give a good flavor. When done outdoors, toast over open fire until bacon is crisp. For indoors use skillet or broiler and turn often until bacon is crisp.

OUTDOOR FRUIT DUMPLINGS

2	(#2) cans fruit pie filling
2/3	cup water
1	tube refrigerated cinnamon rolls (or make biscuit mix dumplings)
2	tablespoons butter

Mix fruit filling and water in large skillet or Dutch oven with tight lid. Bring to boil. Cut each roll (scissors work) into halves or quarters and drop into boiling mixture. Drop small lumps of butter over all. Cover and simmer 20 minutes. 8 servings.

FRANK AND MACARONI SALAD

1	(8 ounce) package bow tie egg noodles
1	(16 ounce) package frankfurters, cut into diagonal slices
1/2	small bunch celery, cut into bit size pieces
4	hard cooked eggs, sliced
2	medium tomatoes, cut into wedges
1/2	cup bottled oil and vinegar dressing with herbs and spices
1-1/2	teaspoons salt
1	teaspoon dill weed

Prepare noodles, drain well. In large bowl, toss noodles with remaining ingredients until well mixed; cover and refrigerate, tossing occasionally. Chill well.

PICKLED EGGS AND BEETS

2	(16 ounce) cans whole beets
2	cups white vinegar
3/4	cup sugar
2	tablespoons pickling spice
1-1/2	teaspoons salt
12	hard-cooked eggs

Drain liquid from beets, reserving 1-1/2 cups liquid. In 3 quart saucepan over medium heat, heat beet liquid, vinegar, sugar, pickling spice and salt to boiling. Reduce heat to low. Cover and simmer 10 minutes. In 2-quart jar, layer eggs and beets. Cover and let marinate in refrigerator at least 12 hours. Can be made up to a week ahead.

CORN IN HUSKS

Place 3 inches of water in a 12 quart pot and bring to boil over high heat. Add 12 medium ears of corn (leave husks and silk on). Heat to boiling. Reduce heat to medium, cover and cook 20 to 25 minutes until corn is tender. To serve, let each person pull back husks from corn, leaving attached at stem end. Wrap husks in paper bag to make handle. Dip into melted butter. Salt and pepper to taste.

KIDNEY BEAN-ZUCCHINI SALAD

3	tablespoons salad oil
3	medium zucchini, thinly sliced
2	medium onions, sliced
1	large green pepper, cut into 1-inch pieces
1	vegetable-bouillon cube or envelope
1	(15-1/4 ounce) can red kidney beans, drained
3	tablespoons white vinegar
2	teaspoons sugar
2	teaspoons salt
1/4	teaspoon pepper

In skillet over medium high heat, in hot salad oil, cook zucchini, onions, green pepper and bouillon cube until vegetables are tender crisp and bouillon cube is dissolved, about 5 minutes. Remove from heat, stir in kidney beans, vinegar, sugar, salt and pepper. Spoon mixture into large bowl. Cover and refrigerate until well chilled.

FRUIT LEATHER

2   cups fruit pulp (apple, peach, pear, strawberry, apricot, etc.)
1/2   cup sugar

If using fresh fruit, remove seeds and stems. Chop and cook, then puree in blender. Mix fruit and sugar together. Attach plastic wrap to cookie sheet with scotch tape. Mixture should be very thin (1/8 to 1/16 inch). Bake at 150 degrees until it looks like leather (won't stick when touched) for about 2 hours. Leave door slightly ajar for moisture to escape. When done, roll (in plastic wrap) into log.

SPICY PUMPKIN SEEDS

2   cups unwashed pumpkin seeds
1/2   teaspoon Worcestershire sauce
1-1/2   tablespoons melted butter
1   teaspoon salt

Mix all together in a shallow baking pan. Roast the seeds in a 250 degree oven for 1 hour. Shake pan several times to insure even browning. Roasted seeds can be placed in plastic bag or jar and stored in refrigerator.

WALKING SALAD

Carry with you on those long beach walks. Cut off the top of a large apple. Core out the center about 3/4 of the way down. Fill the hole with chunky peanut butter mixed with raisins. Replace the top of apple, put in a zip-lock bag and save until you are ready to eat.

HIKING SNACK

1   package sugared cereal
2   cups M and M's
2   cups salted nuts
2   cups raisins (or other dried fruits)

Mix together. Package in zip-lock bags to take hiking.

BARBECUED PEANUTS

3   cups salted blanched peanuts
1/4   cup barbecue sauce

In bowl, stir together peanuts and sauce until peanuts are evenly coated. Spread in shallow pan and bake in 300 degree oven, stirring occasionally, 10 to 15 minutes or until dry and separated. Cool in pan. Makes 3 cups. Store in airtight container or plastic bag. Will keep 1 to 2 months.

RAISIN-GRANOLA COOKIES

1-3/4   cups regular granola
1-1/2   cups all-purpose flour
1   cup butter, softened
3/4   cup sugar
3/4   cup packed dark brown sugar
1   teaspoon baking soda
1   teaspoon salt
1   teaspoon vanilla
1   egg
1   cup dark seedless raisins
1/2   cup unsalted peanuts, coarsely chopped

Measure all ingredients except raisins and peanuts into large bowl. Mixing at low speed, beat ingredients just until mixed. Increase speed to medium and beat 2 minutes, occasionally scraping bowl with spatula. Stir in raisins and peanuts until well blended. Drop by heaping teaspoon onto greased cookie sheet (about 2 inches apart). Bake at 375 degrees 12 to 15 minutes until lightly browned around edges. Store in tightly covered containers. Makes about 4 dozen.

ALMOND POPCORN SQUARES

1/4	cup popcorn kernels
2	tablespoons salad oil
1/4	cup butter
1	(10 ounce) package large marshmallows
1/4	teaspoon almond extract
1	(4-1/2 ounce) almonds, buttered, roasted and diced

Prepare popcorn per directions. Lightly butter a cookie sheet.

In 4 quart saucepan or Dutch oven, heat marshmallows and almond extract in hot butter till marshmallows melt, stirring frequently. Remove from heat. Add popcorn and almonds and stir till well coated. Immediately spoon mixture onto cookie sheet. With buttered hands, evenly and firmly press mixture into 13 x 9 inch rectangle. When cool, cut into 24 squares.

WILD GAME

MARINATED ELK ROAST

1   (6 to 8 pound) elk roast
      salt pork, thinly sliced
5   slices bacon
2   tablespoons garlic powder
2   cups dry red wine
2   bay leaves
      fresh ground pepper
      salt to taste

Make 1 inch deep slits across roast and force slices of pork into each slit. Rub roast with garlic powder, salt and pepper. Place in heavy duty foil in roasting pan and pour wine over meat. Add bay leaves and marinate in refrigerator 8 to 10 hours, turning occasionally. When ready to roast, arrange bacon slices over top and seal foil. Bake at 300 degrees for 2-1/2 to 3 hours. Uncover last 30 minutes to brown. Serves 8.

ELK IN WINE

2   pounds lean elk (1-1/2 inch cubes)
1/3   cup flour
4   medium onions
3   tablespoons cooking oil
1/4   teaspoon each salt and pepper
1/4   teaspoon each marjoram and thyme
1/2   cup beef bouillon
1/2   pound mushrooms
1   cup dry red wine

Brown onions in cooking oil in skillet and remove from pan. Saute meat in the drippings, adding more oil if necessary. Combine the flour and seasonings and sprinkle over the browned meat. Add the bouillon and wine. Simmer slowly for 3 hours, stirring occasionally. Add more bouillon and wine if needed. Add mushrooms and browned onions; cook one hour longer. Serve with rice. 6 to 8 servings.

ELK ITALIAN

2   pounds elk round steak
1/3   cup butter
1/2   cup mayonnaise
1   cup dry bread crumbs
3/4   teaspoon salt
1   teaspoon oregano
1/4   cup flour
1/4   teaspoon pepper
1   large onion, chopped
1   large green pepper, chopped
1   large jar spaghetti sauce with mushrooms
1   small can black olives, sliced
1/2   pound Mozarella cheese (or more)

Combine bread crumbs, salt, oregano, flour and pepper. Toss lightly. Spread whole round steak with mayonnaise and coat with bread crumb mixture. Melt margarine in skillet and quickly brown meat on both sides. Reduce heat to simmer. Add onion, pepper, olives and spaghetti sauce. Simmer about 45 minutes. Place cheese over meat. Cover and cook till melted. Remove meat to warm platter and surround with rice or spaghetti. Pour sauce over all.

BARBECUED ELK STEAK

1   thick sirloin elk steak
2   tablespoons butter
1   teaspoon salt
1   teaspoon dry mustard
1/4   teaspoon paprika
1/8   teaspoon pepper
1   teaspoon sugar
2   tablespoons salad oil
1   tablespoon catsup
1   teaspoon sugar
1   teaspoon salt
1   tablespoon Worcestershire sauce

Blend first 6 ingredients together. Rub this mixture well into steak. Make sauce of last 5 ingredients and brush part of it over steak. Broil steak 20 to 30 minutes to desired doneness. Leave oven door open and watch carefully. Turn once and brush frequently with remaining sauce.

WESTERN DINNER

2-1/2	pounds round steak (elk, moose or venison) cut in 1-1/2 inch cubes
2	cans cream of mushroom soup (or cream of chicken)
1	can mushrooms
2	bell peppers, cut in 1-1/2 inch pieces
3	onions, quartered
1/2	teaspoon thyme
2	teaspoons season salt
3	soup cans water
1	bay leaf
	salt and pepper

Lightly brown meat in oil. Reduce to simmer and add peppers, onions, mushrooms, soup, water and seasonings. Simmer at least 2 hours, adding more water if necessary. Serve over rice or potatoes.

SWEET AND SOUR ELK SPARERIBS

2	pounds elk spareribs, cut in 1 inch rib sections
	hot water
2	tablespoons oil
1/4	teaspoon salt
1/8	teaspoon pepper
3/4	cup sugar
1/4	cup flour
1-1/4	cups water
2/3	cup vinegar
1/2	cup soy sauce
1	onion, chopped
1	green pepper

Place ribs in large skillet; add enough hot water to cover. Bring just to boil, then reduce heat and simmer 5 minutes. Drain; dry thoroughly using paper towels. Heat oil in skillet. Add ribs; season with salt and pepper. Mix sugar and flour; sprinkle over browning ribs. Turn ribs often to prevent scorching. When ribs are well-browned, stir in remaining ingredients. Cover and simmer about 1 hour until ribs are tender. Yields 4 to 6 servings.

ELK SALAMI

4	pounds elk meat (ground)
2	cups water
1	tablespoon liquid smoke
1	pound pork (ground)
1-1/2	teaspoon garlic salt
1/2	teaspoon mustard seed
1	teaspoon onion salt
6	tablespoons meat curing salt
1/4	teaspoon pepper

Mix together elk and pork. Combine liquid smoke and water. Add to meat and mix well. Combine rest of ingredients and add to meat. Mix well by hand. Shape into rolls about 2-1/2 inches in diameter. Wrap each in heavy duty foil, closing tightly down center and on ends. Refrigerate for 24 hours. With fork, make holes through foil one inch apart on bottom of rolls (opposite fold). Place on rack in large shallow pan. Place pan of hot water on lower oven shelf to create steam. Bake rolls in center of oven at 325 degrees for 2 hours. Remove foil and set rolls on rack to drain and cool. Meat will be fairly pink on outside and inside. Wrap in foil. Can be kept in refrigerator about 10 days or in freezer about 1 month.

WILD GAME MARINADE

1/4	cup lemon juice
1/4	cup orange juice
1/2	cup honey
1/4	cup soy sauce (scant)
1	clove garlic (crushed)
1	teaspoon ground ginger
1	tablespoon grated orange rind
1/2	teaspoon pepper
1/4	cup pineapple preserves

Mix all together. Pour over ribs or roast of any game meat or beef. Let stand overnight, turning occasionally. Remove from marinade and barbecue over coals or in slow oven. 4 pounds of ribs will take about 1-1/2 hours.

STUFFED VENISON OR ELK STEAKS

Cut in serving pieces.

2   pounds venison or elk, cut 3/4 inch thick

Soak overnight in refrigerator in 1-1/2 cups milk. Try to turn a few times during the night or early morning. Drain meat and pat dry with paper towels. Cook 6 slices of bacon. Drain and save drippings. Crumble the bacon and set aside. With a sharp knife, carefully cut a pocket in one side of each meat piece. Mix the bacon with 1/3 cup green onion tops and stuff some into each pocket. Brown the steaks in the bacon drippings. Season with salt and pepper. Add 1/2 cup water, cover and simmer over low heat until tender, 45 to 60 minutes. Very good with venison or elk!

VENISON POT ROAST

1	(3 to 4 pound) venison roast
1/4	cup cubed salt pork or bacon
2-3	tablespoons butter
1-1/2	cups hot water
1	cup cider or apple juice
1	stalk celery, sliced
1	teaspoon parsley flakes
1/4	teaspoon thyme
1	teaspoon salt
1/4	teaspoon pepper
6	potatoes
6	carrots
6	onions
2-3	tablespoons flour

Make small cuts in roast. Insert salt pork (or bacon) cubes into cuts. Brown roast in butter. Add water, cider (or apple juice), celery, parsley and seasonings. Cover and simmer gently for 3 hours on top of stove or in 350 degree oven until meat is tender. If liquid gets too low, add water. About 1 hour before serving, add vegetables and cook until tender. Place meat and vegetables on platter. Thicken pan liquid with flour and serve gravy with roast. Yields 6 to 8 servings.

VENISON — HUNTER'S STYLE

3	pounds venison
	salt and pepper
2	tablespoons butter
1	onion, chopped
1	(1 inch) cube of ham, minced
2	bay leaves
2	sprigs thyme, crushed
1	tablespoon all-purpose flour
2	cups warm water
4	cups consomme
1/2	pound fresh mushrooms, chopped
	grated rind of 1 lemon

Cut venison into pieces 2 inches square. Salt and pepper generously. Heat butter in skillet and brown venison slowly. When almost brown, add onion and brown slightly. Add ham, garlic, bay leaves and thyme. Stir and simmer for 2 minutes. Add flour and cook a few minutes longer. Add warm water and bring to a boil. Add consomme, reduce heat and cook slowly for 1 hour. Season again according to taste and add mushrooms and lemon rind. Let cook 30 minutes longer. Serve on a very hot plate. 8 servings.

VENISON COCKTAIL MEATBALLS

1	pound ground venison
1/2	cup dry bread crumbs
1/3	cup minced onion
1/4	cup milk
1	egg
1	tablespoon snipped parsley
1	teaspoon salt
1/8	teaspoon pepper
1/2	teaspoon Worcestershire sauce
1/4	cup shortening
1	(12 ounce) bottle chili sauce
1	(10 ounce) jar grape jelly

Mix venison, bread crumbs, onion, milk, egg and next 4 ingredients. Shape into 1 inch balls. Melt shortening in large frying pan. Brown meatballs, remove from pan and drain. Heat chili sauce and jelly until jelly is melted. Add meatballs and stir until thoroughly coated. Simmer uncovered for 30 minutes. Serve warm. Makes about 4 dozen.

HUNTER'S BUCK STEW

6	pounds venison, cut into 1 inch pieces
1	pound onions, quartered
2-1/2	pounds potatoes, quartered
3	stalks celery, cut into large pieces
1	small bunch (about 6) carrots, peeled and cut up
1	can (28 ounce) tomatoes
	dry sherry
1	teaspoon garlic salt
1	teaspoon dried parsley
1	teaspoon sage
1/2	clove garlic
	salt and pepper to taste
1	teaspoon Italian seasoning
1/2	cup vegetable oil
1/3	cup butter or margarine

Marinate venison overnight in sherry. Drain and brown in 1/2 cup oil. Place in a large pot and season with garlic salt, parsley, sage, garlic, salt and pepper. Cover with water and simmer about 1-1/2 hours or until almost tender. Saute vegetables in butter until almost tender. Add vegetables to meat and continue to simmer 30 to 40 minutes more. Add Italian seasoning and simmer 15 minutes more until all vegetables and meat are tender. Elk or moose may be substituted for venison. Serves 8.

VENISON IN ONION SAUCE

1/4	cup flour
2-1/2	pounds boneless venison fillets
3	tablespoons fat or oil
3	large onions, sliced
1-1/2	teaspoons salt
1/2	teaspoon paprika
3/4	cup water
1	bay leaf

Sprinkle flour over meat. Brown in fat or oil and place in baking dish. Brown onion till golden brown. Add to baking dish. Add salt, paprika, sour cream, water and bay leaf. Bake at 350 degrees for 2-1/2 hours. Serves 6.

SWISS VENISON

1	clove garlic, halved
2	large onions, chopped
2	large venison steaks
1/2	teaspoon salt
	dash pepper
2	large cans tomatoes

Rub the bottom and sides of a Dutch oven with the garlic. Brown the steaks quickly. Add the chopped onion, salt, pepper and tomatoes. Simmer slowly for 2 hours.

VENISON SOUP

4-5	pounds venison neck bones
	water to cover
1	large onion, chopped
2	cloves garlic, chopped
1	large stalk celery, chopped
1	can stewed tomatoes
1	bay leaf
1/2	teaspoon Fines Herbs
3/4	cup yellow split peas
2	cups frozen mixed vegetables
3/4	cup small macaroni (salad type or small shells)
2	cups chopped cabbage
1	cup good dry red wine
	salt to taste
	leftover vegetables, chopped

Put neck bones in large pot with cold water to cover. Bring to boil and remove from heat. Remove neck bones and discard water. Rinse pot if necessary to remove all scum. Return bones to pot and cover with fresh water. Add onion, garlic, celery, tomatoes and seasonings. Bring to boil, reduce heat and simmer until meat can easily be removed from bones. Remove bones from broth. Strain broth through colander and return to pot. Mash vegetables through colander and add to broth. Add split peas and simmer while bones cool. Remove meat from bones and chop. Add to soup pot with frozen vegetables, macaroni, cabbage and wine. Salt to taste. Add any leftover vegetables you may have. Simmer until vegetables and macaroni are well done. Serve with crusty garlic bread. Serves 6 to 8.

VENISON CHILI

2	pounds venison
1/4	cup vegetable oil
1	cup chopped onions
2	cloves garlic, minced
1	large green pepper, cut in strips
3	tablespoons chili powder
2	tablespoons sugar
3-1/3	cups whole tomatoes
1	cup tomato sauce
1	cup water
1/2	teaspoon salt
1	tablespoon flour plus 2 tablespoons water (mix)
2	cups cooked kidney beans

Coarsely grind venison. Brown in hot oil in heavy pan. Add onions, garlic and green pepper. Cook about 5 minutes, stirring constantly. Add chili powder, sugar, tomatoes, tomato sauce, water and salt. Mix and let simmer about 1-1/2 hours. If thicker chili is desired, stir in flour and water paste and cook about 5 minutes till thickened. Add kidney beans just before serving and heat through.

VENISON MINCEMEAT

Approximately 4 pounds of "trim meat with the bones."

Cook this meat and refrigerate overnight in the meat broth. In morning, skim off the fat from the broth and grind the meat (with a coarse knife.)

To the ground meat, add:

3/4	pound beef suet (ground)
3	pounds of apples (peeled and ground)
2	pounds seedless raisins
1	12-ounce package currents
1	tablespoon salt
1	tablespoon cinnamon
1	tablespoon nutmeg
1	pound brown sugar
2	quarts cider (use some of the meat broth also along with the cider)

Combine all of the above ingredients in a large kettle and simmer for 2 hours, stirring frequently. Be sure that all of the ingredients are thoroughly mixed together. As the mixture simmers, season to the taste of the individual. (You may find that a certain season is more to your liking.) As the mincemeat cooks, it will thicken, and will appear to become quite thick when it is ready for the jars. (This mincemeat freezes very well.) Put into containers containing the exact amount for each pie. If it is canned (preferably quart jars) process for 60 minutes at 10 pounds pressure.

When making the pie, you may find that if 3 tablespoons of rum are added to the mincemeat as it is heated for the pie the flavor is greatly enhanced.

VENISON JERKY

1/2	teaspoon salt
1/3	teaspoon garlic powder
1/2	teaspoon black pepper
1	teaspoon Accent
1	teaspoon onion powder
1/4	cup Worcestershire sauce
1/4	cup soy sauce

Sauce for 1-1/2 pounds deer meat. Using meat half frozen (for easier slicing), slice in 1/8 inch strips with the grain, desired lengths. Cover with the above sauce and marinate overnight. Spread single layer on oven wire rack, using foil under to catch drippings. With the oven door cracked open and at the lowest temperature, bake for 6-8 hours. May be eaten immediately. Becomes dryer when cold.

VENISON JERKY

3	pounds lean venison
1	tablespoon salt
1	teaspoon garlic powder
1/2	teaspoon pepper
1/3	cup Worcestershire sauce
1/4	cup soy sauce
1	tablespoon prepared mustard

Cut venison into 1/2 inch wide and 1/4 inch thick strips. Mix all other ingredients and pour over the meat. Marinate overnight. Remove from marinade and dry with paper towels. Place in oven. In a gas oven the pilot flame will dry jerky in 4 days. In a 200 degree electric oven, leave in the oven until dry by feel.

PLANKED BEAR STEAK

Marinade:

1/3	cup vegetable oil
1	medium onion, chopped
3	carrots, chopped
1	stalk celery, chopped
3	cups beef bouillon
1	cup vinegar
8	black peppercorns
1	clove, whole
1	large bay leaf
1/2	teaspoon thyme
1	teaspoon marjoram
1	teaspoon salt
2	bear steaks, 1-1/2 to 2 inches thick

Saute onion, carrots and celery in oil until tender. Add remaining ingredients and simmer for 20 minutes. Trim fat from steaks, place in bowl and pour cooled marinade over meat. Refrigerate for two days, turning meat several times.

When ready to cook, drain and pat dry.

1/2	cup butter
1/2	cup chopped chives
2	tablespoons Dijon mustard
3	tablespoons tomato paste
1	teaspoon Worcestershire sauce
1	clove garlic, minced
	salt
	fresh ground pepper

Place butter in saucepan and melt over low heat. Add remaining ingredients and stir until well blended. Broil steaks, basting constantly with butter and chive mixture, until done. Serve steaks on plank, surrounded by mashed potatoes, corn niblets and tomato halves.

SOUR CREAM RABBIT WITH HERBS

1	large rabbit (or 2 small)
3	tablespoons butter
3	tablespoons olive oil
	salt
	pepper
	flour
4	medium onions, sliced 1/2 inch thick
2	cups beef bouillon
2	teaspoons tomato paste
1	tablespoon flour mixed with 2 tablespoons water
1/4 to 1/2	cup sour cream (to taste)
1	tablespoon chopped fresh parsley
2	tablespoons chopped fresh dill

Clean and cut rabbits into serving size pieces. Soak in salted water (1 to 2 hours for young rabbit, overnight if older). Remove meat and pat dry. Rub with salt and pepper and dust lightly with flour. Saute in heavy kettle in butter and oil until browned. Remove and set aside. Reduce heat and cook onions until golden. Pour in beef bouillon and cook on high heat for 5 minutes. Lower heat and add tomato paste, stirring for several minutes. Return rabbit to pan. Cover tightly and simmer until tender, at least an hour. Place cooked rabbit in heated serving dish. Add flour paste to liquid in pan and stir over medium heat till it thickens. Turn off heat and stir in desired amount of sour cream. Spoon some sauce over rabbit and sprinkle with parsley and dill. Serve remaining sauce in separate bowl.

ONE DISH RABBIT

1	rabbit, cut into serving pieces
1	teaspoon salt
1/8	teaspoon pepper
	flour
1/2	cup oil
2	medium onions, sliced 1/2 inch thick
4-5	small potatoes, quartered
1	can (28 ounce) tomatoes

Sprinkle rabbit with salt and pepper, roll in flour and fry in hot oil until lightly browned. In 2 quart casserole dish, place a layer of rabbit, onion and potatoes. Cover with tomatoes. Bake at 350 degrees for 2 hours. Serve with hot buttered biscuits. Serves 4 to 6.

SMOTHERED PHEASANT OR GROUSE

Flavor of this succulent bird is enhanced by vegetables. Garnish platter with tiny boiled carrots.

2	pheasant or 4 grouse (skinned, washed and quartered)
1	tablespoon salt
1/2	cup flour
2	tablespoons butter
1/4	cup chopped celery
1/4	cup chopped onion
2	tablespoons butter
1/2	cup boiling water

Mix flour and salt in a brown paper bag. Shake pheasant pieces in the bag, 2 or 3 at a time until coated. Melt 2 tablespoons butter in skillet. Saute celery, carrot and onion until tender. Place in a shallow baking pan. Add 2 more tablespoons butter to skillet and melt. Brown floured pheasant in skillet. Remove meat to baking pan, add water and cover with wax paper. Bake in pre-heated 350 degree oven for 1 hour or until meat is tender. Serve at once on a bed of wild rice. Spoon some pan juice over meat and rice. Yields 4 to 6 servings. So good!

PHEASANT OR GROUSE IN CREAM

(moist and delicately flavored)

1	pheasant or 2 grouse, cut up
1	small onion, chopped
1/4	cup butter
1	cup half and half cream
1	can (10 ounce) condensed cream of mushroom soup
1/4	teaspoon ginger
	salt and pepper

Roll pheasant in flour seasoned with salt and pepper. Saute onion in shortening. Remove and brown pheasant in same skillet. After browning, cover and place in pre-heated 375 degree oven to bake 35 to 40 minutes. Combine cream, soup and ginger. Add to pheasant last 10 minutes of baking time. Yields 3 to 4 servings.

ROAST GROUSE ON LIVER CANAPES

2	grouse salt
3	tablespoons minced scallions
1/2	teaspoon dried tarragon
1/4	cup butter, melted
4	strips bacon

Canapes:

	unsliced white bread
1/4	cup butter
	grouse livers (or chicken)
3	tablespoons chopped bacon
1/4	teaspoon salt
	fresh ground pepper

Sauce:

2	tablespoons minced scallions
1-1/2	cups beef bouillon
1	tablespoon butter

Season cavities of birds with salt, scallions, tarragon and half the butter. Truss the birds. Brush with remaining butter and place bacon over breasts and thighs. Roast in pre-heated 400 degree oven 30 to 40 minutes or until done, basting and turning frequently. Slice bread 1/2 inch thick and cut into rectangles the size of the grouse. Saute bread on both sides in hot butter. Chop liver and bacon very fine. Add seasonings. Spread on bread rectangles.

Arrange on broiler pan and set aside. Just before serving, broil for about 1 minute until sizzling. Remove all but 2 tablespoons of fat from the roasting pan. Add scallions and cook for 1 minute. Add the bouillon and boil rapidly, scraping up pieces until liquid reduces in half. Stir in butter. To serve, place grouse on top of hot canape and spoon sauce over top. Good with sauteed mushrooms.

ROAST PHEASANT

(with brown or wild rice stuffing)

Rice stuffing:

1	cup brown or wild rice
1	medium onion, finely chopped
1/2	cup diced celery and celery leaves
1	can (4 ounces) sliced mushrooms
1/4	cup butter
1	teaspoon salt
1/2	teaspoon ground marjoram
1/8	teaspoon pepper

Cook rice about 5 minutes less than directed on package. Cook onion, celery, celery leaves and drained mushrooms (save liquid) in butter until tender. Add to rice. Mix in seasonings. Add mushroom liquid as needed. The mixture should be moist and hold together very well.

Roast Pheasant:

3	pheasants
1/4	cup butter

Stuff pheasants with rice stuffing. Wrap each separately in aluminum foil. Bake in a slow oven (325 degrees) for 2 hours. Unwrap birds and brush with butter. Bake in hot oven (425 degrees) for 15 minutes or until browned. Prepare gravy from drippings. Season to taste. Yield: 8 to 10 servings.

ORANGE SAUCE (for game birds)

1	cup sugar
1/2	cup butter
1/2	cup frozen orange juice concentrate
1	(11 ounce) can mandarin oranges, drained
1/2	cup lemon juice,
	juice from fresh orange
	grated rind from orange
1	tablespoon Galliano

Bring orange juice concentrate, butter and sugar to boil. Add remaining ingredients. Heat through and serve. Excellent with duck or dove.

BASTED QUAIL

8	quail
	flour
	paprika
	salt
1	teaspoon Kitchen Bouquet
4	tablespoons butter

Split quail down back. Place in pan, cover with salted water and boil until tender, about 1-1/2 to 2 hours. Reserve this broth. Remove birds and place breast side up in a baking dish. Sprinkle with paprika. Add butter to 2 or 3 cups of reserved broth and gradually thicken with a flour and water paste to make gravy. Add Kitchen Bouquet for color and salt to taste. Pour gravy over birds and bake in pre-heated 350 degree oven until gravy bubbles (about 30 minutes). Baste several times while baking. Serves 4.

SANDY'S ROAST GOOSE

(old-time favorite of my Grandma's in Wisconsin)

Singe and remove pin feathers from goose. Wash very clean, using a soft brush with lukewarm water in which a little Ivory soap has been dissolved. Rinse with lukewarm water, then rinse well with cold water. Make sure the inside is clean. Wash and dry the goose inside and out. Place 1 unpeeled orange and 1 unpeeled, but cored apple in the inside of goose. Gash the orange 1/4 inch deep in the form of a cross. Tie legs to tail. Place the goose in a very hot oven (500 degrees) for 30 minutes. Remove from oven, take out the fruit and pour off excess fat. When cool, fill with stuffing and sew skin together. Dredge with 1/2 cup flour to which 1/4 teaspoon salt has been added. Place in a quick oven (450 degrees) for 30 minutes, until the flour is browned. Reduce heat to a slow oven (300 degrees) and finish baking, allowing 25 minutes to each pound. Baste every 10 minutes of the last half hour with 1 cup lukewarm water. By cooking goose or duck in this manner, all disagreeable or strong fat is removed.

SWEET AND SOUR DUCK

    5 or 6 pound duck
    salt and pepper
    flour

Sauce:

3   tablespoons butter
1   can (13-1/2 ounces) pineapple chunks, drained (reserve liquid)
2/3   cup reserved pineapple juice (if not enough juice, add water)
1/2   cup cider vinegar
3   tablespoons minced preserved ginger or one slice fresh ginger
1/4   cup water or duck broth
2   teaspoons soy sauce
2   tablespoons cornstarch
1   medium green pepper, cut into 1-inch squares
2   cups diced carrots

Rub duck with salt, pepper and a little flour. It may be left whole or split down the back and chopped across four times. Put it in a roaster and cook in a hot oven for 10 minutes, then turn down heat to 325 degrees for another 25 minutes. Drain off fat, add the broth or water, return to oven, cover and roast until tender, about 1 hour more. When done, drain off most of liquid from duck and set aside.

In skillet combine butter, soy sauce and ginger and simmer for about 2 minutes (until ginger gives off odor). Add green pepper and cook until tender. Add diced carrots, pineapple juice, vinegar and heat to boiling. Reduce heat, cover and simmer for about 2 minutes. Stir in pineapple chunks. Blend water and cornstarch and stir into skillet. Cook, stirring constantly until mixture thickens and boils. Boil and stir one minute. Serve duck chunks over rice topped with sauce.

QUAIL CASSEROLE

8-12   quail
        flour
        salt
1/3   cup butter
1/2   pound fresh mushrooms
        fresh parsley (or flakes), chopped
2   cups dry white wine

Split birds down back and dust lightly with flour and salt mixture. Melt butter in skillet and place birds skin side down. Saute until brown on both sides. Remove birds and place in casserole with lid. Add mushrooms and parsley. Pour in enough wine to half cover birds. Cover and bake in preheated 350 degree oven for 1 hour. Spoon wine gravy over birds. Serves 4 to 6.

SQUIRREL STEW

2   squirrels, quartered
2   teaspoons salt
1   cup canned tomatoes (or 1 can condensed tomato soup)
1   onion, thinly sliced
3   potatoes, thinly sliced
1   cup lima beans
1   tablespoon sugar
1   cup canned corn
1/4   pound butter
        salt and pepper to taste

Put squirrel pieces in deep kettle with 2 teaspoons salt and cover with water. Simmer till tender, about 1-1/2 hours. Remove squirrel pieces. Debone meat and cut into 1 inch pieces. Return meat to broth in kettle and add tomatoes, potatoes, onion, lima beans and sugar. Salt and pepper to taste. Cook until beans and potatoes are tender. Add corn and butter and cook 5 minutes more.

ALZORA'S ROAST RACOON

1. Check with nearest ranger to be sure you are obeying all laws.

2. Coon meat too near mating season is strong and stringy. Coons which have been living on fish or garbage have poor quality meat. Coons which have been living on your garden or upon our plentiful wild berries are VERY GOOD eating.

3. Coons have lots of fat in their tissues, so you pre-cook older coons and bring young ones to roast in very slow heat to brown them. It melts out its own fat for cooking in and you should not have to add extra fat in cookery unless you have a very young coon which has been living on Belle Isle grapes.

4. Use a very steady table for dressing and skinning your coon. Have a very sharp knife with a sharpening tool handy to re-edge it as you work. Reason: coons have small scent glands under the skin, along the spine and under the forelegs. DO NOT CUT INTO THESE GLANDS AS YOU SKIN!

5. Skin, dress and cool the meat as FAST as possible, cutting off all possible fat you see. Do not cure, age or hang coon meat. Freeze it as soon as it is well-chilled and bled.

Roast Racoon

Boil the skinned and dressed coon as soon as you have thawed the frozen meat. Use enough salted water to cover. Add 4 carrots (peeled), a large onion and 5 sticks of celery. Simmer for 30 to 60 minutes depending on size and age of coon. Older coons have more leathery ears and snouts if you are in doubt. Size of paunch is another indicator of age. Drain and pat the coon meat dry. Throw out the worn-out vegetables, but chill the stock, discard the fat and save the broth (for other recipes). You can broil young coons, or put cubes on skewers with pre-cooked onion alternated with apple and orange bits. Or you can roast a coon with apple-raisin stuffing (below). Put the stuffed coon in roaster on rack, adding a bit of apple juice to bottom of pan as needed. Roast at 350 degrees for 45 minutes per pound. If coon is old, cover the roaster with a lid, but uncover it during the last 1/2 hour of roasting, so as to brown it nicely. Any tart fruit stuffing is good, as the flavor is like dark meat of a turkey.

Apple-Raisin Stuffing

1/2	cup margarine (you presumably removed all coon fat) if young coon
2/3	cup raisins
3	big apples, unpeeled, but cored and diced
1	cup diced celery
	pinch of thyme
	pinch of marjoram
	shake of salt
	pepper to taste
	apple juice as needed to moisten during roasting

In deep skillet, cook celery in margarine so slowly that it is cooked without being browned. Add other ingredients and toss gently to mix. Makes about 3 pints.

TROUT AMANDINE

4-6	dressed trout
	salt and pepper
1	egg, beaten
1/4	cup light cream or milk
1/4	cup flour
2	tablespoons oil
2	tablespoons butter
1/4	cup slivered almonds
1/4	cup melted butter or margarine
2	tablespoons lemon juice

Bone trout if desired. Season with salt and pepper inside and out. Mix together the beaten egg and cream. Dip the trout in flour, then in the cream and egg mixture. Heat together the oil and 2 tablespoons butter. Fry trout in hot fat until golden and flakes easily, 8 to 10 minutes, turning only once. In another skillet, cook the almonds in the 1/4 cup melted butter till almonds are golden brown. Remove from heat and stir in lemon juice. Place trout on a warm serving platter, pour almond mixture over all and serve. Trout look real elegant with a few orange and lemon slices graced around them on parsley leaves.

BAKED STUFFED TROUT

1	large trout, 2-4 pounds, cleaned and sprinkled with salt
1/4	pound butter or margarine
1/2	cup finely chopped celery
2	tablespoons lemon juice
3	slices rye garlic bread, cubed
1	medium can hominy, drained and ground with bread
1	teaspoon sugar
1	teaspoon meat tenderizer
1	teaspoon sage
1	teaspoon poultry seasoning
1	medium onion, chopped
1	tablespoon diced dill pickle
2	tablespoons cashew nuts
2	tablespoons chopped black olives

Saute celery and onions in butter until transparent. Add rest of ingredients. Mix well together. If dry, moisten with enough milk to hold mixture together. Fill cavity of fish. Bake until done in 350 degree oven.

WILD FOODS

WASHINGTON HUCKLEBERRY DESSERT

1/2	pound graham crackers (crushed)
3/4	cup melted margarine
2	tablespoons sugar
2	packages Dream Whip
1	8-ounce package Philadelphia Cream Cheese
1 to	
1-1/2	quarts Washington huckleberries

Thicken the huckleberries as you would for a pie and sweeten. Set aside to cool. Mix melted margarine, graham cracker crumbs and 2 tablespoons sugar and form a crust in a 13 x 9 x 2 pan. Bake for 8 minutes and cool. Combine powdered sugar and cream cheese; mix well. Mix Dream Whip as directed on the package and add to the cream cheese and powdered sugar mixture. Pour cooled huckleberries over the crust and then spread the white mixture over the top. Chill and serve.

HUCKLEBERRY MARSHMALLOW DESSERT

16	graham crackers, crushed
1/4	cup melted margarine
1/4	cup sugar
24	marshmallows
1/2	cup milk
1/2	pint whipping cream
1	teaspoon vanilla
4	cups fresh huckleberries

Mix crackers, margarine, and sugar. Put half in 8-inch square pan. Bake at 375 degrees for 5 minutes. Melt marshmallows with milk in double boiler. Cool to room temperature. Do not allow to get too thick. Whip cream, add vanilla, then mix in marshmallow mixture. Put half over the graham cracker crust, then put all berries in.

Add rest of marshmallow mixture. Sprinkle with remaining graham cracker mixture and chill.

HUCKLEBERRY CREAM CHEESE PIE

1	9-inch baked pie shell
	3-ounce package Philadelphia Cream Cheese
1/2	cup powdered sugar
1	teaspoon vanilla
1	cup cream, whipped or
1	packaged Dream Whip, whipped

Cream the cheese, powdered sugar and vanilla. Add the whipped cream and put in pie shell. Put huckleberry filling on top of cream cheese mixture in pie shell. Chill several hours.

Filling:

2	cups huckleberries
1/2	cup water
1	cup sugar
2	tablespoons cornstarch softened in 1 cup cold water

Bring to boil; add cornstarch mixture and cook until thickened. Serve with whipped cream on top.

WILD HUCKLEBERRY PIE

1	quart huckleberries
3	tablespoons quick-cooking tapioca
1	cup sugar
1/4	teaspoon salt
	juice of 1 lemon
1	tablespoon butter
	pastry for two-crust 9 inch pie, unbaked

Mix berries with tapioca, sugar, salt and lemon juice. Roll out pastry. Use half to line pie pan and trim edges. Pour in the berries. Dot with butter. Use remaining pastry to cover pie. Moisten edges of pastry and flute to seal. Cut vents in top. Bake in preheated very hot oven (450 degrees) for 10 minutes. Reduce heat to 350 degrees and bake for 30 to 35 minutes longer. Sprinkle with additional sugar.

HUCKLEBERRY CAKE

1	cup sugar
1	cup sour cream
2	eggs
2	cups flour
1	teaspoon salt
1	teaspoon baking powder
1	teaspoon vanilla
2	cups clean huckleberries

Mix sugar, cream, eggs and vanilla together. Add dry ingredients, mixing well. Gently fold in huckleberries. Bake at 350 degrees, about 30 minutes. Serve with cream.

HUCKLEBERRY SALAD

1	6-ounce cherry Jello
1-1/2	cups boiling water
1	cup Hawaiian Punch
1	small can crushed pineapple
1-1/4	cups huckleberries
2	cups whipped dessert topping
1/2	cup chopped nuts

Dissolve Jello in boiling water; stir in punch. Chill until thick. Add fruits, whipped topping and nuts. Chill until firm.

SARVISBERRY PIE

4	cups fresh sarvisberries
1	cup sugar
3	tablespoons flour
	dash salt
1/2	teaspoon cinnamon
1/4	teaspoon nutmeg
	juice of 1/2 lime or 1/4 lemon
1	tablespoon butter

Line 9-inch pie plate with pastry. Combine fresh berries with sugar, flour and salt. Add cinnamon, nutmeg. Fill pie shell. Sprinkle with lime or lemon juice. Dot with butter. Adjust top crust. Bake in hot oven (400 degrees) 35 to 40 minutes. Serve warm.

CHOKECHERRY SYRUP AND JUICE

Put 12 pounds (or two gallons) of washed whole cherries through a food grinder. (This is a process that splatters juice badly, so if you have an outdoor table where it can be done, it will save much clean-up in the kitchen.) Put the cherries into a crockery or glass container and add two quarts of cold water and three ounces of tartaric acid. (This acid is obtained at a drug store and should be carefully weighed according to the amount of cherries. If you get it in bulk, three level tablespoons is one ounce.) Let the mash stand in a cool place for 48 hours.

Put small amounts of the mash into a cloth bag and squeeze out the juice. If a wooden fruit press is available, it saves much time and effort, but do not use any kind of a metal press. Strain the juice through a cloth two or three times until it flows through quickly. For the first straining, the cloth will need to be washed several times because there is a sediment that clogs the cloth. To make syrup, add one cup of sugar for each cup of juice, bottle and cork. The syrup must be kept in a cool place or it might ferment. (Note: this syrup is an uncooked product.)

It is also possible to heat the plain juice not quite to the boiling point, put into sterile jars and seal. Later any amount of sugar desired can be added.

The yield is at least as many cups of juice as you have pounds of cherries, but it is usually more and depends on the condition of the cherries. I have heard it said that cherries should not be gathered until after the first frost, but this is not correct and I like to gather the cherries when they are very dark but still plump.

The syrup is good on ice cream or on pancakes, or it can be diluted and Tab, lemon juice or gingerale added to "cut" the sweetness. If the plain juice is used for a drink for one cup of drink use 1/4 cup juice, 3/4 cup of water and about 2 tablespoons sugar. This is also good served in the winter as a hot drink. Put a small bag of spices in while heating it (stick of cinnamon, allspice, cloves).

CHOKECHERRY FRAPPE

Fill a glass with vanilla ice cream; add 1/4 cup syrup and 1/2 cup gingerale. Stir.

HOT SPICED CHOKECHERRY DRINK

Per Cup:

2	tablespoons syrup
1	tablespoon lemon juice
1/2 to	
3/4	water

Heat with bag of whole spices, cloves and cinnamon; remove spices when flavored enough.

CHOKECHERRY SYRUP

Cook cleaned ripe chokecherries in enough water to cover berries until cherries are soft. Strain juice through cloth. (Pulp may be rubbed through sieve and use to make jam.) For syrup: 7 cups prepared juice, 2 tablespoons pectin (Sur-Jel or Pen-Jel), 7 cups sugar. Mix pectin and juice and heat to rolling boil. Boil one minute. Add sugar and mix thoroughly. Bring to rolling boil and boil for one minute. Pour into sterilized jars and seal. Six pints.

DANDELION WINE

Quart dandelion flowers (not much green; less bitter). Gallon hot water.

Soak 24 hours, strain. Add 3 oranges and 3 lemons quartered. Add 1 pound raisins, 3 pounds granulated sugar (6-3/4 cups) and 1/2 cake fresh yeast. Let ferment 7-8 days. Strain. Put in jug till settled (at LEAST 6 weeks) and siphon into bottles. (While fermenting, stir 1-2 times daily with wooden spoon.)

DESERT TEA

Fill a gallon glass jar (plastic doesn't work) with water; add whatever weed or herb you like, such as mint, clover, pineapple weed, yarrow). Cover and set in the sun for 8 hours. Cool and add honey if you like. (Might also add: catnip, rose leaves and petals or strawberry leaves.)

FRESH GREEN CATNIP TEA

Collect fresh greens. Add young catnip leaves (1 cup to teapot or saucepan of boiling water (1-2 quarts). Boil one minute and steep for 5 minutes. Drink tea and eat greens with salt, pepper and butter. (Good for you!)

SALADS: FRESH GREENS OR FRUIT
BASIC WATERCRESS AND LETTUCE SALAD

To 1/4 head of lettuce, add 1 cup young watercress leaves. Top with your favorite salad dressing.

To this basic salad can be added various amounts of wild greens such as: 1 cup chopped chickweed, purslane, pigweed, lamb's quarters or sheep sorrel leaves and/or 1/4 cup chopped young mint, catnip, fan weed, shepherd's purse or tumbling mustard leaves, and/or small amounts (1 ounce) of watercress green pods or fanweed, shepherd's purse or tumbling buds, flowers, green pods and seeds.

MACARONI SALAD

Marinate 3 cups cooked macaroni in Italian Salad Dressing overnight. Next day add 3/4 cup of the chopped white tender bases of cattail leaves and/or the young tender white hooked roots of cattails.

To this salad you can add, if available, 1/2 cup chopped young watercress leaves, and/or 1/4 cup chopped young fanweed leaves or fanweed buds, flowers and young green pods.

CATTAILS WITH PEANUT BUTTER

Cut tender part of the base of the cattail leaves lengthwise and spread on peanut butter like celery.

CHICKWEED SALAD

2	cups chopped young chickweed greens
1	cup chopped young watercress leaves
1/4	cup chopped wild onion bulbs, leaves or flowers
1	ounce chopped buds, flowers and green pods of fanweed, shepherd's purse or tumbling mustard

Mix all ingredients and toss; add your favorite dressing.

DANDELION SALAD

Wash enough dandelions for four persons. Put salad in a bowl and add two chopped, hard-boiled eggs. In a skillet, fry 1/2 pound of minced bacon. When done, take the skillet from the fire and add to it one-third cup of wine vinegar and quickly pour over salad. Season with black pepper and salt. Add fresh watercress for an extra taste sensation.

When picking dandelions for these dishes, look for newly sprouted plants. Older dandelions have a tendency to become slightly bitter.

WILD FLOWER GARNISH

To brighten up an ordinary salad, simply garnish with fresh wild rose petals, wild violet blossoms, wild strawberry blossoms or tumbling mustard blossoms.

WILD GREENS

Most of the leafy greens — live sorrel, purslane, dandelion, pigweed, nettles or lamb's quarters could be cooked as much as you would spinach or chard. Wash thoroughly, but do not soak. The amount of water which clings to the leaves is almost sufficient if a cast aluminum or heavy pot is used, and 3-5 minutes boiling time in salted water.

FRESH PURSLANE PICKLES

1	cup white vinegar
2	cups of cold water
1/4	cup salt
1/2	teaspoon alum

Obtain two pint jars. Place in each jar on the bottom: flower of dill, clove of garlic and a small red pepper. Pack jars with fat, tender purslane stems, not too tight. Fill jars with liquid and seal. Store in a dark place for one month before using. Do not cook.

TRY A SOUFFLE!

3	tablespoons butter or margarine
3	tablespoons flour
1/2	teaspoon salt
1	cup milk
4	eggs beaten separately (separate yolk and white)
1	cup cooked, chopped or sieved greens
2	tablespoons grated cheese
	dash of cayenne
	a little grated onion
1-2	teaspoons dry mustard

Melt fat in heavy pan on top of double boiler. Add flour, salt, cayenne and blend. Pour in the milk. Cook and stir until mixture thickens. Add cheese, beaten egg yolks, mustard and spinach. Fold in beaten egg whites and pour into greased casserole. Bake in a 350 degree oven for 40 minutes or until knife inserted in center comes out clean. Put a few curls of butter on top and serve at once.

SAUCES

Most of the sauces suitable for broccoli or spinach could be used for wild greens:

Lemon butter: mustard-mayonnaise, browned butter (a little garlic, lemon juice and toasted, shredded almonds); white sauce; mock Hollandaise sauce (white sauce + egg yolk, butter, lemon juice); cheese sauce or just melted cheese and butter; vinaigrette sauce.

WILTED GREENS

2   quarts broken greens (torn) — (lamb's quarters, chickweed, dandelion, sheep sorrel, purslane, pigweed)
2   tablespoons chopped chives or green onion tops
3   tablespoons bacon fat
1/2   cup vinegar
1   teaspoon sugar
     salt and pepper

Sprinkle greens with chives. Heat fat; add vinegar, sugar, salt and pepper to taste; heat. Pour over greens; toss and serve at once. May add bits of pimiento or tomato, or sweet red peppers for color.

WILTED GREENS

(Use young chickweed, young dandelion leaves, lamb's quarters, red sorrel, purslane, pigweed or cow cabbage.)

Fry six or more strips of bacon quite well. Drain well and cut into 1/2 inch pieces. Toss lightly about 2 quarts or more of wild greens in warm frying pan in which about 2 tablespoons of fried bacon grease or drippings have been placed. Add 2 tablespoons vinegar, salt and pepper. Add bacon bits before serving. I do not wilt greens very much; just coat with bacon drippings and seasonings. Drain before serving. Some people like greens well wilted.

WILD GREENS WITH MUSTARD CREAM SAUCE

1/2   cup heavy cream - whipped
1/8   teaspoon salt
1-1/2   teaspoons prepared horseradish
1/4   teaspoon dry mustard
1   teaspoon vinegar

Fold into whipped cream, horseradish, mustard and vinegar. Set aside and chill. Use over hot cooked wild greens (young dandelion leaves, young nettles, pigweed, purslane, lamb's quarters, chickweed, cow cabbage). Garnish with hard boiled eggs and paprika.

WILD GREENS PIE

Use pigweed, lamb's quarters, sorrel, purslane, chickweed, nettles or dandelion greens, cow cabbage.

Crust:

Melt 1/4 cup butter or margarine in pyrex pie plate in low oven. Crush 30 soda crackers very fine (1 cup). Mix with melted butter in pie plate. Press to bottom and sides to make crust.

Filling:

Fill pie crust with 1 cup cooked greens. In sauce pan, beat 2 eggs (slightly), teaspoon salt (scant), dash of pepper, 3/4 cup milk. Place over low heat — do not boil. Pour while hot over greens. Top with 1/2 cup sharp cheese grated. Bake at 350 degrees for 30 minutes. Serve hot.

GREENS LOAF

(Use lamb's quarters, cow cabbage, pigweed, purslane, chickweed, nettles, dandelions).

Enough greens to make 2 cups after cooking; drain well.

2   tablespoons minced onion
1/4   teaspoon nutmeg
1/2   teaspoon each salt and pepper
1   cup sweet milk
2   cups bread or cracker crumbs — cut or mashed well
4   eggs

Beat cooked greens with egg beater until they are soupy. Add onion, nutmeg, salt and pepper, milk and eggs. Beat by hand just to mix. Fold in bread or cracker crumbs. Pour into a greased and floured loaf pan (8 x 8 x 2-1/2). Put in a pan of water in the bottom of oven. Bake about 50 minutes in 300 degree oven. Test with a cold knife. If it comes out clean, the loaf is done. Cut in squares and serve with lemon or catsup or tartar sauce.

CHAR-BROILED FISH DRESSED IN GREENS

1   10- 20-inch trout or other fish
2   cups red sorrel, purslane, lamb's quarters, watercress, chickweed, pigweed, dandelions or nettles (rhubarb stems should also work)

Clean trout; add salt, pepper, and garlic salt to stomach cavity. Wrap with greens on all sides (including inside). Wrap with aluminum foil thoroughly to prevent leakage. Bake or broil over fire, charcoal or in oven at 400 degrees to 1/2 hour for 10-inch trout — 45 minutes for 20-inch trout.

Eat greens and fish while still hot! Great camping combination dish!

WATERCRESS SOUP (FOR ONE)

Combine in blender and blend until smooth—about 1 minute—3/4 cup water, 1 chicken bouillon cube, or envelope of instant chicken broth mix, and 1/4 bunch watercress. Heat to boiling point and serve immediately or chill.

CREAMED WATERCRESS ON TOAST

Melt equal parts of butter and wholewheat flour in sauce pan (1/2 cup). Add chopped onion to taste (3/4 medium onion). Add salt and pepper. Add milk (about 4 cups). Simmer until thickened. Add parmesan cheese to taste (1 cup). Steam fresh watercress (save water for tea!) and add to sauce. Serve on toast or bread.

NETTLE GREENS

Nettles cooked in small amount of water (salted) 5 minutes with wild onions and 1 teaspoon bacon grease.

NETTLES WITH CREAM OF MUSHROOM SOUP

Cook nettles, strain, save juice. Mix juice with soup, fold in cooked nettles. Garnish with bacon and mint.

WILD RICE SOUP

1/2   cup wild rice (cooked)
2   (11 ounce) cans cream of chicken soup
2   (11 ounce) cans cream of mushroom soup
1   can chicken broth
4   cans water
1   onion, grated
1   carrot, grated

Heat all together, but do not boil. Add last: 1 cup sauterne, salt and pepper to taste. Serves 12.

STUFFED MUSHROOMS

1   pound fresh mushrooms
1/2   cup dry Parmesan cheese
1/4   cup margarine, melted
1   tablespoon green onion, chopped
1/4   cup dry bread crumbs

Clean mushrooms and remove stems. Mix all other ingredients and stuff mushrooms. Bake on cookie sheet at 350 degrees 15 to 20 minutes, until lightly browned. Baking time will vary depending on size of mushrooms. Serve hot on a heated plate. Can be cooked in microwave 3 to 4 minutes per dinner-size plateful and then browned lightly under broiler. Serves 10 to 12 as appetizers.

MATSUTAKE PICKLES (Armillaria ponderosa)

1/3   cup brown sugar
1/3   cup soy sauce
1/3   cup vinegar
      Matsutake mushrooms, sliced

Amounts may be varied according to the mushrooms you have. Combine first 3 ingredients in sauce pan and bring to a boil. Lower heat and simmer for 5 minutes. Meanwhile, clean and slice mushrooms very thin. Cook 20 minutes, then add to syrup. Continue simmering for 3 minutes. Pack in hot sterilized jars. Process 5 minutes.

RUSSULA BREVIPES PICKLES

1	pint white vinegar
1	cup granulated sugar
1	cup water
1	teaspoon celery seed
1	teaspoon ground tumeric
2-1/2	pounds mushrooms, cut into 1/4 inch slices
2	cups sliced onions
2	teaspoons salt

Combine first 5 ingredients with salt in saucepan. Bring to a boil, then simmer 10 minutes. Parboil mushrooms for 5 minutes. Add to syrup and continue simmering for 5 minutes. Continue simmering while quickly packing in one hot sterilized jar at a time. Fill within 1/2 inch of the top making sure the vinegar solution covers vegetables. Seal each jar at once. Process 5 minutes. Makes 3-4 jars.

CATTAILS-ON-THE-COB

Use as young cattail flowers as possible but they're still palatable after they turn brownish and start releasing pollen. Remove leaves. Drop in a pot of boiling water. Boil for 8-10 minutes. Drain well and serve with melted butter, salt and pepper. The water you cook them in will probably have turned yellow from pollen from the male flowers. Save it! It's full of pure pollen protein. Use it in a soup, or add a little salt and broth and drink it.

DEEP FAT FRIED DANDELION BLOSSOMS
(Dandelion Fritters)

Take 2 or 3 dozen fresh, young dandelion blossoms; cut off at the stem just under the blossom. Wash and take off excess water. Dip them into your favorite fritter batter. Fry in deep fat until golden brown. Serve with salt, pepper and melted butter or with maple syrup or honey.

DANDELION BLOSSOM CUSTARD
Select fresh yellow dandelion blossoms. Remove leaves and stems; wash enough to fill the bottom of a flat baking dish. Beat together six eggs, one cup milk and one teaspoon salt. Add chopped onion to taste and pour mixture over dandelion blossoms. Dot the top with butter and bake in oven at 375 degrees until eggs are set, or until a knife pushed into the dish comes out clean. As an option, imitation bacon crumbs can be used — sprinkled over the top before placing dish in oven. Dandelion blossom flavor has been compared to fresh, wild mushrooms. The dandelion greens can also be fixed as a cooked greens dish, although it's best to mix them with fresh or canned spinach.

FANWEED HERB CREAM CHEESE

Collect old, dried-up fanweed plants in the fall. Crush plants into a large pan. Run chaff and seeds through a flour sifter to separate seeds from large pieces of crushed plant. Blow off small pieces of chaff from seeds, carefully. Use 1 ounce of seeds to 8 ounces of cream cheese; crush seeds and blend into warm cream cheese (room temperature); chill and serve on crackers, celery, etc.

Fanweed seeds have a garlic flavor, and can be added to butter, dips, and other sauces. Fanweed also makes an excellent addition to home-made salami.

MOTHER'S MINT JELLY

3	cups fresh mint
3	cups water
2	tablespoons lemon juice
5	drops green food coloring
3-1/2	cups sugar
1/2	bottle pectin

Wash leaves and shred into small pieces. (Blender works great!) In a large pan bring water to boil, add mint and cook for two minutes; remove from heat and steep at least 10 minutes. Measure 1-1/4 cups strained juice into sauce pan and add 2 tablespoons strained lemon juice, food coloring and sugar. Place over low heat and bring to full boil for 1 minute stirring constantly. Remove from heat; take scum off with a metal spoon; pour into sterilized jars immediately. Seal with lids or paraffin. Store in cool place. Use as jelly or as a sauce for fish, wild game and other meats.

BERRY SWEET AND SOUR SAUCE

Use currants, gooseberries, strawberries, raspberries, huckleberries or buffalo berries.

Place 2 cups of berries in a quart saucepan. Add sugar or honey while mashing berries. (Amount of sugar or honey will vary, depending on berries used. For example, when using sweet berries, like raspberries, huckleberries, or strawberries, little or no sweetner may be added; but if using tart berries like gooseberries, currants or buffalo berries, as much as 1 cup or more sugar or honey may be desired.) Heat while adding sweetener. Sweeten until desired sour-sweet is obtained. Heat almost to boiling point. Pour in sterilized pint jars. Seal and process in boiling water for 5 minutes. Cool and store in dark place. After opening, refrigerate.

Take the berry sauce and use as it is on pork, game or mutton while frying, broiling or barbecuing, or strain out pulp and seeds through cheesecloth and use just the juice.

This is a basic sauce that has many other uses, when used with a little imagination. Don't be afraid to use it on salads, fish or other meats.

BUFFALO BERRY JELLY

To one quart of buffalo berry juice, add 1/4 cup lemon juice and 1 package powdered pectin, boil vigorously. Then add approximately 4 cups sugar and stir and bring to a boil again. Then boil 2 minutes and remove from fire. Skim if desired. Pour into glasses and jars and seal.

MINT SAUCE

Dissolve 1 tablespoon granulated sugar in 1/4 cup cider vinegar and 1/4 cup water. Add 1/4 cup chopped mint leaves and let stand 30 minutes in warm place. (May heat if desired.)

BROILED FISH COVERED WITH GOLDEN CURRANT-WILD MINT SAUCE

Go fishing. Catch two trout or other fish — 1 pound or more each. Fillet and place on cooking sheet. Season with salt, pepper and garlic salt.

GOLDEN CURRANT - WILD MINT SAUCE

Use fresh or dried currants (8 ounces). Cook with sugar or honey (no water) and mash into juicy pulp. In bowl, mix 1/4 cup finely chopped fresh or dried mint leaves with 1/2 cup sugar and 1 tablespoon finely grated lemon peel and 2 tablespoons finely grated orange peel. Let stand 1 hour. Mix with currants and stand by ...

Broil fish fillets. Cover with currant-mint sauce and serve.

BERRY SALAD DRESSING

Collect fresh greens for salad — collect 2 cups berries. Mash and add water and sugar or honey to obtain sweet-sour taste. Toss into salad. (Great salad dressing for camping.)

Berries that can be used include: huckleberries, currants, gooseberries, wild raspberries and wild strawberries and sarvisberries.

Greens that can be used include: pigweed, lamb's quarters, dandelions, purslane, sorrel, chickweed, cattails, watercress and mustard.

CAMP SWAMP BREAD

To make flour: collect horizontal cattail roots; peel, mash in water; after roots are crushed, get a bundle of them and tear them apart. Keep wringing till you have nothing left but what feels and looks like fiber. Strain water through cloth. Repeat until you have a white pulpy starch left. Dry and run through grinder.

To make bread:

1	large teaspoon baking powder
1/4	teaspoon salt
1/2	cup cattail flour

Mix in water until dough forms. Fry and serve hot.

CATTAIL WAFERS

Use cattail flour obtained as in Cattail Swamp Bread recipe, above.

Add teaspoon vanilla. Sift and then measure 3/4 cup cattail flour and 1 cup all-purpose flour. Mix while adding flour alternately with 1/2 cup milk. Form into small flat wafers. Bake at 350 degrees until done.

CATTAIL POLLEN DUMPLINGS IN SWEET ONION SOUP

Combine:

2/3	cup cattail pollen and flowers
1/4	cup wheat germ
1/2	cup cracker meal
1/4	cup powdered milk
1/2	cup flour
2	teaspoons baking powder
1/2	teaspoon salt

Add:

1 egg plus water to make 1/2 cup and 2 tablespoons melted oleo. Drop from wet spoon into simmering soup.

Soup: Saute sweet onions until tender. Add broth, seasoning. Simmer.

GOOSEBERRY AND CATTAIL POLLEN MUFFINS

2	tablespoons pollen + enough white flour to make 1/2 cup
3/4	cup wholewheat flour
2	teaspoons baking powder
1/2	teaspoon salt
2	teaspoons cinnamon or to taste
1/2	cup milk
1/2	cup gooseberries (about)
1	egg
1/4	cup melted butter, margarine or oil
1/2	cup sugar or firmly packed brown sugar
3	tablespoons milk

Combine the 2 flours, baking powder, cinnamon, salt. Make a well in the center. Lightly beat the egg. Stir in the remaining ingredients. Pour all at once into flour well. Stir just to moisten ingredients. Batter should look lumpy. Grease muffin cups or use paper liners. Fill each cup 2/3 full. Bake at 375 degrees about 25 minutes. Makes about 9.

CURRANT MUFFINS

1/2	cup currants
1	cup sifted flour
3/4	cup sifted wholewheat flour
1/4	cup sugar
2-1/2	teaspoons baking powder
3/4	teaspoon salt
1	well-beaten egg
3/4	cup milk
1/3	cup salad oil or melted margarine

Sift dry ingredients into bowl; make well in center. Combine egg, milk and oil. Add all at once to dry ingredients. Stir quickly just till dry ingredients are moistened. Add the currants. Fill greased muffin pan about 2/3 full. Bake at 400 degrees for 25 minutes. Yield 12 muffins.

OATMEAL CURRANT SQUARES

1/4	cup butter or margarine
1	cup firmly packed brown sugar
1	egg, beaten
1	teaspoon vanilla
1/4	cup sifted flour
	confectioner's sugar
1	teaspoon baking powder
1/4	teaspoon salt
3/4	cup rolled oats
1	cup dried currants
1/2	cup walnuts, chopped

Melt butter with brown sugar in saucepan over low heat. Stir until sugar is dissolved. Cool slightly. Stir butter-sugar mixture into beaten egg. Add vanilla/Sift flour, baking powder, and salt into egg mixture with oats, currants and walnuts. Turn into a greased 8-inch square baking pan. Bake in moderate oven, 350 degrees, 25 minutes or until golden brown. Cool on wire rack. While still warm, cut in squares. Sprinkle lightly with sugar. Store in covered container.

HERB BREAD
(Onion Watercress)

Any yeast bread recipe. Add 1/2 cup watercress and 1/4 cup chopped wild onion to yeast bread mixture before adding flour. Then continue following bread recipe. NOTE: Any greens can be used in breads. Some of the most flavorful are red sorrel, fanweed, tumbling mustard, shepherd's purse, or watercress.

HUCKLEBERRY PANCAKES

2	cups flour
1/2	teaspoon sour milk
2	eggs
1/2	teaspoon soda
1	teaspoon baking powder
2	tablespoons shortening
2	tablespoons sugar

Use your favorite pancakes mix if you wish. 1/2 cup to 1 cup huckleberries, depending on how many you can find. A few will flavor a lot of batter.

Sift flour, salt, soda, sugar and baking powder together in a bowl. Beat eggs lightly and stir in milk. Combine liquids and dry ingredients plus shortening and stir only enough to blend. Fold in huckleberries and drop by spoonsful on hot griddle. Turn only once.

BUFFALO BERRY CAKE

1	cup shortening
3	cups sugar
4	eggs, well beaten
3	cups applesauce (unsweetened)
5	cups flour (1/2 fine-ground wholewheat)
1	teaspoon salt
2	teaspoons cinnamon
2	cups buffalo berries
1	cup chopped nuts

Lightly flour berries and nuts. Fold into mix (grease and flour pan). Pour into large loaf size cake pan. Bake at 325 degrees for 1 hour 10 minutes. For variation replace 1/2 cup applesauce with 1/2 cup apricot pulp. Also, other nuts and seeds.

ELDERBERRY MUFFINS

1	egg
1/4	cup vegetable oil or melted shortening
1/2	cup sugar
1/2	teaspoon salt
1/4 to	
1/2	cup reconstituted sweetened elderberries
1/2	cup milk
1-1/2	cups sifted flour
2	teaspoons baking powder

Beat egg with fork. Stir in milk and oil. Blend dry ingredients, fold in elderberries, stir until just blended. Batter will be lumpy. Bake 20 to 25 minutes. Oven 400 degrees. Grease bottom of muffin cups. Makes 12 muffins. (Elderberries can be used fresh or dried. To dry elderberries, dry in oven overnight at 150 degrees or less. Reconstitute by boiling with sugar or honey.)

WILD RASPBERRY QUICK BREAD

In mixing bowl add:

1	cup wild raspberries
1	cup boiling water
1	teaspoon soda

Mix, now add:

1	cup sugar
3	tablespoons oil
1	egg and mix

In separate 4-cup measuring bowl blend: 1 tablespoon pollen from cattail head when green or starch from cattail roots (grounded or pounded). Fill to 2-cup level with flour. Add 1 teaspoon baking powder. Combine all ingredients and beat thoroughly. Bake at 350 degrees for 1 hour. Makes 1 loaf.

PIGWEED SEED GARNISH FOR ROLLS, BREADS

Gather old dried-up pigweed plants in fall with heavy gloves. Crush plants into large container. Run chaff and seeds through a flour sifter to separate seeds from large pieces of crushed plants. Blow off small pieces of chaff from seeds carefully. Use seeds to garnish breads like you would use poppy or sesame seeds. Also can be used to write on cookies.

PIGWEED-CHEESE CRACKERS

1/2	pound aged cheddar cheese, grated
1/2	cup butter
1/2	teaspoon salt
1-1/4	cups flour
1	ounce pigweed seeds

Combine all ingredients and work together until smooth. (Hands work best for mixing). Shape into a roll and wrap in waxed paper. Chill. Slice like refrigerator cookies and place on buttered cookie sheets. Bake in a 350-degree oven for 10 minutes or until lightly browned and done.

BREADS

MOM'S BREAD

4	ounces warm water
2	tablespoons yeast
4	ounces oil
10	cups fairly hot water
3	hands full of salt
2/3	cup sugar
	flour

Mix warm water and yeast and set aside. In large bowl, mix oil, hot water, salt and sugar. Use slotted spoon to stir with. Add large sifter of flour. Beat until not lumpy. Add a little more flour. Beat again until not lumpy. Add yeast mixture. Stir it in. Add more flour until you can't stir it.

Clean off the spoon with flour over dough. Knead in as much flour as possible. Put flour in bottom of pan under half the dough and start kneading around. When you think you have enough flour, stick your finger in the dough. If it sticks, knead in more flour. Knead until good and smooth. Let rise until twice in size. Knead down and let rise again until double in size. Grease pans. After the bread has risen in pans, preheat oven to 400 degrees. Put bread in for 12 to 15 minutes. Reduce heat to 300 degrees and bake for 45 minutes. Check every 15 minutes for doneness. You may have to turn pans around. When you think it is done, take it out of the oven and thump the top. If it sounds hollow it's done. Grease bread. Makes 6 loaves and 30 buns.

LAZY WAY DINNER BREAD

Place in this order in mixing bowl:

1	packet active dry yeast
2-1/2	cups flour
2	tablespoons sugar
2	tablespoons salad oil
1-1/4	teaspoons salt
2	eggs
1	cup hot milk

Beat 3 minutes. (Batter will climb beaters; just push down with rubber spatula). Turn into well-greased 9 x 5 x 3 pan. Cover; let rise in warm place 30 minutes or until light. Bake at 350 degrees for 30 to 35 minutes or until deep golden brown. Remove from pan and serve immediately. If possible, slice with electric knife. This is ready for the table in about 1 hour and 10 minutes. Makes 1 loaf.

HOMEMADE BREAD AND ROLLS

1	package dry yeast
1-1/4	cups warm water
1	teaspoon salt
1/2	cup sugar
3-1/2	cups plain flour
1/4	teaspoon butter
	dash cinnamon
1/4	cup milk
1/4	cup brown sugar

Bread: dissolve yeast in water. Add sugar and salt. Mix well. Add flour and knead until not sticky. Let rise in greased bowl about 1 hour. Knead down once. Let rise 1-1/2 hours. Shape into loaves in greased bread pans. Bake at 350 degrees for 40 to 45 minutes or until browned. Brush butter on top.

Rolls: use the same dough recipe, but don't knead first time as long. Dough should be a little sticky. After first rising, press out round. Spread with butter and sprinkle with cinnamon, a little milk and brown sugar. Cut into round rolls and place in a greased pan. Let rise for 1-1/2 hours. Bake at 375 degrees for 30 to 35 minutes or until browned. Remove and brush butter over rolls. Yields 4 servings.

DILLY BREAD

1	package yeast
1/4	cup warm water
1	cup creamed cottage cheese
1	egg, beaten
2	tablespoons sugar
2	tablespoons instant minced onion
1	tablespoon butter (melted)
3	teaspoons dill seed
1	teaspoon salt
1/4	teaspoon soda
2-1/4 to 2-1/2	cups flour

Mix by large wooden spoon and by hand to finish adding the flour. Let rise until double in bulk; punch down; put in pan size 8-1/2 x 4-1/2 x 2-1/2. Let rise again; brush top with butter and sprinkle salt lightly on top of loaf. Bake at 400 degrees for 40 minutes. Yields 1 loaf.

SHREDDED WHEAT BREAD

2-3/4   cups boiling water
3   large shredded wheat biscuits
1   teaspoon salt
2   teaspoons shortening
1/2   cup molasses
1   package dry or compressed yeast
1/4   cup lukewarm water
8-1/4   cups (about) sifted flour

Pour boiling water over shredded wheat biscuits in large bowl. Add salt, shortening and molasses. Cool to lukewarm. Sprinkle yeast over 1/4 cup lukewarm water. Let stand for 5 to 10 minutes or until thoroughly dissolved. Add yeast to biscuit mixture. Mix well. Add flour gradually, mixing until dough is soft and easy to handle. Turn out onto lightly floured board. Knead until smooth. Shape into small balls and place in greased bowl. Brush with melted fat and cover with towel. Let rise in warm place until doubled in bulk. Turn out onto lightly floured board. Knead until elastic. Divide and shape into 3 loaves. Place in 9 x 5 x 3 inch loaf pans and brush with melted fat. Cover and let rise until double in bulk. Bake at 400 degrees for 45 minutes or until done. Makes 3 loaves.

LYNDA'S SUPER OATMEAL BREAD

2   cups quick rolled oats
1/2   cup molasses
1   teaspoon salt
1/4   cup melted butter
2   cups water
2   packages active dry yeast
1/2   cup lukewarm water
5-1/2   cups flour
1   cup raisins (optional)

Combine oats, molasses, salt and butter. Stir in 2 cups water. Sprinkle yeast on 1/2 cup lukewarm water and stir to dissolve. Add yeast and 2 cups flour to oat mixture. Beat until smooth. Stir in raisins. Gradually add remaining flour to make soft dough. Turn onto floured board and knead 8 to 10 minutes. Place in greased bowl and turn dough to grease top. Cover and let rise in warm place until doubled (about 1 to 1-1/2 hours). Divide dough in half, shape into loaves and place in two 9 x 5 x 3 inch loaf pans. Let rise till doubled. Bake at 375 degrees 35 to 40 minutes or until done. Remove from pans and cool on rack. My boys ask for this bread every morning toasted with their breakfast.

ANADAMA BREAD

1-1/2   cups water
1   teaspoon salt
1/3   cup cornmeal (coarse preferred)
1-1/2   tablespoons shortening
1/3   cup molasses
1   package dry yeast
1/4   cup warm water
4   cups sifted flour
2   tablespoons melted butter
   cornmeal for topping

In medium saucepan, bring to boil 1 cup of water and the salt. Mix cornmeal into remaining water and stir into boiling water. Continue boiling and stir in shortening and molasses. Pour into large bowl and cool to lukewarm. Dissolve yeast in 1/4 cup warm water and then add to cornmeal mixture. Beat in flour to make a soft dough. Turn onto floured board and knead till smooth and elastic, adding only enough flour to keep from sticking. Place in greased bowl, turn to coat top, cover and let rise till double. Punch down. Turn out and divide in half. Shape each half into 14 balls about 1 inch in diameter. Make 2 rows of 5 balls each in two greased loaf pans. Place remaining 4 balls down middle. Brush with melted butter and sprinkle with cornmeal. Let rise till double. Bake at 375 degrees about 35 minutes.

RYE BREAD WITH DARK KARO

(makes 4 loaves)

1-1/2   cups boiling water
1   cup dark Karo
1   cup buttermilk
1   stick oleo
2   eggs
1   tablespoon salt
4   tablespoons sugar
3   packages dry yeast
2   cups rye flour
7-1/2   cups white flour

Mix oleo, boiling water, sugar, salt and Karo syrup. Let cool. Add beaten eggs, buttermilk and rye flour. Then stir in yeast and last the white flour. Let rise until doubled. Punch down and let rise again. Mold into 4 loaves. Let rise in pans until doubled in bulk and bake at 350 degrees for about 45 minutes.

HIGH PROTEIN BREAD

2	packages active dry yeast
1	teaspoon sugar
1/2	cup warm water (105-115 degrees)
2	cups milk
1	cup creamed cottage cheese
1/4	cup butter or margarine
1	tablespoon salt
1	tablespoon honey
3	cups stoneground whole wheat flour
1/2	cup rye flour
1/4	cup wheat germ
3	cups all-purpose flour (about)

Dissolve yeast and sugar in 1/2 cup warm water; set aside. Scald milk; stir in cottage cheese, 1/4 cup butter, salt and honey. Cool to lukewarm. Stir whole wheat flour, rye flour, wheat germ and cheese-milk mixture into yeast. Beat until smooth. Mix in enough all-purpose flour to make dough easy to handle. Turn dough onto lightly floured board. Knead until smooth and elastic, about 10 minutes. Place in greased bowl; turn greased side up. Cover; let rise in warm place until double, about 1 hour. Punch down dough; divide in half. Roll each half into rectangle 18 x 9 pan. Roll up, beginning at short sides. With side of hand, press each end to seal. Fold ends under loaves. Let rise until double, about 1 hour. Heat oven to 375 degrees. Place loaves on low rack so that tops of pans are in center of oven. Pans should not touch each other or sides of oven. Bake until deep golden brown and loaves sound hollow when tapped, about 1 hour. Cover loaves with aluminum foil at least 20 minutes if loaves get too brown. Remove from pans. Brush loaves with soft butter. Cool on wire rack. Makes 2 loaves.

ENGLISH MUFFIN BATTER BREAD

2	packages active dry yeast
2	tablespoons sugar
1	cup warm water (about 110 degrees)
	cornmeal
1	teaspoon salt
5	cups (about) all-purpose flour
1-1/2	cups warm milk (about 110 degrees)
1/2	teaspoon baking soda (dissolved in 1 tablespoon water)

In a large bowl, combine yeast and sugar in the water. Let stand 15 minutes or until puffy. Meanwhile, generously grease the insides of three 1-pound coffee cans and the underside of their plastic lids. Sprinkle cans and lids with cornmeal and shake off excess. Set aside. With an electric mixer, gradually beat the salt, 3 cups of the flour and 1 cup of milk into the yeast mixture. Add alternately and beat well after each addition. Then add soda-water mixture and beat well to blend. With a heavy-duty mixer or spoon, beat in the remaining 1/2 cup milk and enough of the remaining flour (1-1/2 to 2 cups) to make a stiff heavy dough that is too sticky to knead. Spoon dough equally into coffee cans and top with lids. Let rise in a warm place until lids pop off, about 45 to 60 minutes. Carefully remove the lids. Place cans upright on rack and bake at 375 degrees for 25 to 30 minutes or until tops are well browned and sides and bottoms are golden. (Slide one out of can to test.) Slide loaves out of cans and stand upright on wire racks to cool. Store airtight and keep at room temperature or in refrigerator up to 4 days. May be frozen.

FRENCH ONION BREAD MIX:

1	cup water and 1 tablespoon yeast

Then add:

1/4	cup oil
1/2	tablespoon garlic powder
2	cups whole wheat flour
1	large onion and fresh garlic, chopped fine
1/2	teaspoon onion powder
1	cup white flour
1/2	cup brown sugar
1	teaspoon salt
4	teaspoons dill (more if desired)

Combine all ingredients except flour. Stir well. Gradually add the white flour. Beat well to develop the gluten. Gradually beat in the whole wheat flour until stiff. Knead. Form loaves or rolls. Bake in oiled pans for 45 to 60 minutes at 350 degrees.

ONION AND GARLIC BREAD

2   packages active yeast
1/2   cup warm water (105 -115 degrees)
1/4   cup brown sugar
1/4   cup shortening + 2 tablespoons lecithin
1   tablespoon salt
1-1/4   cups warm water
3   cups whole wheat flour
1   large onion, chopped fine
3-4   small garlic pieces, chopped fine
4-5   cups white flour

In large mixing bowl, dissolve yeast in 1/2 cup warm water. Stir in brown sugar, shortening, salt, onion, garlic, 1-1/4 cups warm water and whole wheat flour. Beat until smooth. Mix in 4 or 5 cups white flour, enough to make dough easy to handle. Knead until smooth and elastic, about 10 minutes. Cover and let rise double in size. Punch down and make two loaves. Place in bread pans and let rise again. Bake at 350 degrees for about 40 minutes.

ITALIAN BREAD

4-1/2
to
5-1/2   cups unsifted all-purpose flour
1   tablespoon sugar
1   tablespoon salt
2   packages dry yeast
1   tablespoon soft margarine
1-3/4   cups very warm water (120 to 130 degrees)
        cornmeal
        peanut oil
1   egg white
1   tablespoon cold water

In large bowl, thoroughly mix 1-1/2 cups flour, sugar, salt and undissolved yeast. Add margarine. Gradually add warm water to dry ingredients and beat 2 minutes at medium speed of electric mixer, scraping bowl occasionally. Add 3/4 cup flour. Beat at high speed 2 minutes, scraping bowl. Stir in enough additional flour to make a stiff dough. Turn out onto lightly floured board and knead until smooth and elastic, about 8 to 10 minutes. Cover with plastic wrap, then a towel. Let rest 20 minutes. To make loaves: divide dough in half. Roll each half into an oblong 10 x 15 inches.

Beginning at the wide side, roll up tightly and pinch seam to seal. Taper ends by rolling gently back and forth.

To make rolls: Divide dough into 6 equal pieces. Roll each piece into an oblong 5x8 inches. Beginning at wide side, roll up tightly and pinch seams to seal. Taper ends.

Place on greased baking sheets sprinkled with cornmeal. Brush dough with peanut oil. Cover loosely with plastic wrap. Refrigerate 2 to 24 hours. When ready to bake, remove from refrigerator. Uncover dough carefully and let stand at room temperature 10 minutes. Make 3 or 4 diagonal cuts on top of each with razor blade or sharp knife. Bake at 425 degrees 15 minutes for rolls, 20 minutes for loaves. Remove from oven and brush with egg white mixed with cold water. Return to oven and bake 5 to 10 minutes longer, until golden brown.

BETSY'S POCKET BREAD

5-6   cups flour (part whole wheat flour may be used)
1   tablespoon sugar
2   teaspoons salt
1   package yeast
2   cups water (120 to 130 degrees)

In large bowl, mix 2 cups flour, sugar, salt and yeast. Add tap water. Beat 2 minutes. Add 3/4 cup flour. Beat 2 more minutes. Add more flour and knead 8 to 10 minutes. Place in greased bowl. Cover and let rise until doubled, about 1 hour. Punch down. Turn out on lightly floured board. Cover and let rest 30 minutes. Remove middle rack in oven. Place iron skillet on lowest rack. Pre-heat oven to 400 degrees. Divide dough into 16 balls. Roll one or two at a time to 1/8 inch thickness. Place directly on iron skillet. Bake about 2 minutes or until it puffs up. Flip with turner and bake 45 seconds more. Cool on wire rack. Repeat with remaining balls. Using unbleached flour works the very best.

BAGELS

1	package dry yeast
2	teaspoons salt
	sugar
4 to	
4-1/2	cups flour
1	cup potato water (left from boiling potatoes)
2	tablespoons salad oil
3	eggs

Combine yeast, salt, 2 teaspoons sugar and 1-1/2 cups flour in large bowl. In 1 quart saucepan over low heat, heat potato water and salad oil until very warm (120 to 130 degrees). With mixer at low speed, gradually beat liquid into dry ingredients until just blended. Increase speed to medium and beat 2 minutes, occasionally scraping bowl with spatula. Beat in 2 eggs and 1/2 cup flour (or enough to make thick batter). Continue beating 2 minutes, occasionally scraping bowl. Stir in enough flour (about 2 cups) to make a soft dough. Turn onto lightly floured board and knead until smooth and elastic, about 10 minutes, adding more flour while kneading. Shape dough into ball and place in greased bowl. Turn dough over to grease top. Cover with moist towel and let rise in warm place until doubled, about 1-1/2 hours. Punch dough down. Turn onto lightly floured board and cut dough into 16 pieces. Cover with moist towel and let rest for 20 minutes. Roll each piece into an 8 inch long strip. Form a ring by moistening one end with water and sealing firmly to the other end. Place rings about 2 inches apart, on 2 greased cookie sheets. Cover with moist towel and let rise in warm place about 30 minutes. (Dough will not double in volume.) Pre-heat oven to 425 degrees. In a 12 inch skillet over high heat, bring to boil about 1 inch of water and 2 tablespoons sugar. Reduce heat to medium and drop rings, a few at a time, into simmering water. Cook 3 minutes, turning once. Remove rings to paper towels. Drain, then place on cookie sheets. Beat remaining egg slightly and brush over rings. Bake 20 to 25 minutes until browned. Cool 5 minutes on wire rack. To serve, cut in half horizontally and toast. Spread with butter or cream cheese. Makes 16.

WHOLE WHEAT AND WHITE BREAD

5-1/2	cups white flour
2	packages dry yeast
2-1/4	cups warm water
1/4	cup oil
1/4	cup honey or molasses
2	tablespoons sugar
4	teaspoons salt
2	eggs, room temperature
1-1/2	cups whole wheat flour
1/4	cup sunflower seeds

Measure 2-1/2 cups white flour in large bowl. Add yeast; blend. Measure water, oil, honey, sugar and salt in pan. Blend and heat until warm (120-130 degrees), stirring constantly. Pour into flour mixture and add eggs. Beat 1/2 minute at low speed, scraping bowl. Beat 3 minutes at high speed. Stop mixer. Stir in whole wheat flour and sunflower seeds. Then add white flour to form soft dough. Turn and knead. Cover; let rise till doubled, 1 hour. Punch down. Cover and wait 10 minutes. Grease pans and form loaves. Cover and let rise 1 hour. Brush with egg white and sprinkle sesame seeds on top. Bake 35 to 45 minutes at 375 degrees.

WHOLE-WHEAT BREAD

1-3/4	cups milk
2	teaspoons salt
1/3	cup olive oil
1/2	cup water
1/3	cup honey
2	eggs
2	cakes of yeast
6	cups whole-wheat flour

Scald milk and cool slightly. Add salt, oil, honey, water, eggs and dry yeast. Mix well. Sift flour and add to mixture. Add enough flour to make the dough the consistency of cake. Let it stand for 15 minutes. Sift and add more flour until it is too thick to stir with a spoon. Work the dough with your hands, adding more flour until the dough is not sticky. Put dough into an oiled bowl and let it rise until it is double in size (about 45 minutes). Divide the dough into 2 pieces and shape into loaves. Place in buttered loaf pans. Cover and let rise until double. Bake for 1 hour at 350 degrees.

WHOLE-WHEAT HAMBURGER ROLLS

2	cups hot milk
1/4	cup butter
1/8	cup honey
2	teaspoons salt
2	packages dry yeast
1/4	cup lukewarm water
5-6	cups whole-wheat flour
1	egg
	sesame seeds

Heat milk and add butter, honey and salt. Dissolve yeast in lukewarm water and add milk mixture to it. Add half of the flour and heat it. Add rest of flour and mix with a wooden spoon. Turn out onto a floured board and knead 8 to 10 minutes. Place dough in a buttered bowl, cover and let rise until double. After first rising, knead down and roll dough to 1/2-inch thick. Cut with a 3-inch cutter. Place rolls on buttered cookie sheet. Brush rolls with beaten egg and sprinkle sesame seeds on top of rolls. Cover with a towel and let rise for an hour. Bake at 350 degrees for 12 to 15 minutes.

CINNAMON ROLLS

3/4	cup milk (scalded)
1/2	cup melted butter
1/2	cup sugar
1	teaspoon salt
2	packages dry yeast
1/2	cup warm water
4-1/2	cups flour
2	eggs

Dissolve yeast in warm water. Add sugar, salt, eggs, milk and margarine. Add dry ingredients. Knead. Let rise 1-1/2 hours. Punch down. Roll out dough 16 x 8. Spread with 1/2 cup butter and sprinkle with 1 tablespoon cinnamon plus 1 cup sugar. Sprinkle with 1/3 cup raisins. Roll up as a jelly roll. Cut in 1-inch slices. Place in two 9 x 9 x 2-inch greased pans. Let rise 30 minutes. Bake at 375 degrees 20 minutes. Frost. Makes 32 rolls. Rolls may be frozen.

FEATHERLIGHT ROLLS

1/4	cup margarine
1/3	cup sugar
1	teaspoon salt
3/4	cup hot potato water
1	egg, beaten
1/4	cup warm water
1	package dry yeast dissolved in warm water
1/2	cup mashed potatoes
4-1/2	cups flour

Mix together margarine, sugar, salt and hot potato water. Cool to lukewarm. Blend in all other ingredients and knead 8 to 10 minutes (until smooth). Let raise until double in size (2 hours). Make 24 small balls. Raise again and brush with melted butter before and after baking. Bake at 375 degrees for 15 to 20 minutes or until light brown on top.

EASY OVERNIGHT ROLLS

1	package dry yeast
1/4	cup warm water
1/2	cup oil
1	cup evaporated milk
1/2	cup sugar
1	teaspoon salt
1/2	teaspoon soda
2	well beaten eggs
4	cups flour

Dissolve yeast in warm water. Add oil, milk, sugar, salt, soda and eggs. Whip well and add flour. Let stand overnight, covered on counter top. Next morning, dump dough out onto lightly floured board and divide in half. Shape each half into 12 rolls and place in well greased muffin tins. Let rise covered, several hours or overnight. Bake at 350 degrees 12 to 14 minutes. Makes 2 dozen rolls.

COTTAGE CHEESE PINWHEEL ROLLS

1	package dry yeast
1/4	cup warm water
3-1/2	cups (about) flour
1/4	cup sugar
1/2	teaspoon salt
1/2	cup butter
1	pint creamed cottage cheese
1	egg, beaten
	pecan filling

Dissolve yeast in warm water. In large bowl, combine 2-1/2 cups flour, sugar and salt. Cut in butter until mixture resembles corn meal. Mix in cottage cheese, egg, dissolved yeast and enough remaining flour to make a soft dough. Cover with damp cloth and let rise in warm place until doubled, about 1 hour. Punch down and let rest 10 minutes. Roll out to 12 x 16 inch rectangle on lightly floured board. Spread pecan filling over dough. Roll up like jelly roll and slice into 1 inch rolls. Place cut side down in greased pan and let rise in warm place till doubled. Bake at 375 degrees about 20 minutes.

SOURDOUGH STARTER (Herman)

Sprinkle 1 package or 1 tablespoon yeast into 2-1/2 cups warm water in large glass bowl. Gradually stir in 3 cups unsifted flour, then beat until very smooth. Cover with towel and place in warm place for 24 hours to ripen. Mixture should then be bubbly. Store in tightly covered glass container in refrigerator. Mixture will keep several weeks.

To Make Batter: blend 2 cups warm water and 2 cups unsifted flour into above sourdough mixture. Beat till smooth. Cover with towel and place in draft free warm place overnight.

To Make Pancakes: Measure 4 cups batter. Refrigerate the remainder to use another time (as starter). Add 1 egg, slightly beaten to the 4 cups sourdough batter. Add 1/4 cup milk and 2 tablespoons oil. Beat until smooth. Add 2 tablespoons sugar. Just before frying, add 1 teaspoon soda and 1/2 teaspoon salt and stir just until blended. Fry on hot griddle and serve with syrup.

CRUSTY BROWN SOURDOUGH ROLLS

2	packages dry yeast
1	cup warm water
4	teaspoons sugar
2	teaspoons salt
2	tablespoons melted margarine
6-1/2	
to 7	cups flour
3	egg whites, beaten stiff
3/4	cup sourdough mash

Egg Wash: 1 egg white and 1 tablespoon water.

Sprinkle yeast on water; stir to dissolve. Add sourdough mix, margarine and dry ingredients. Add egg whites. Knead 5 minutes. Let rise 1 hour. Punch down. Let rise 1/2 hour. Shape into rolls. Put on greased sheet. Brush with egg wash. Let rise 20 minutes. Bake 10 minutes at 400 degrees. Brush with egg wash. Bake 10 minutes more. Best to bake over boiling water (in pan on lower shelf) for crispy crust. Makes 3 dozen. Rolls may be frozen.

RYE BREAD

1/4	cup brown sugar
1/4	cup molasses
1	tablespoon salt
2	tablespoons margarine
1	cup boiling water
1	package dry yeast
1/4	cup warm water
3	cups rye flour
3 to	
3-1/2	cups flour
3	tablespoons caraway seeds
1/2	cup sourdough mash
1	teaspoon grated orange peel

Sprinkle yeast on 1/4 cup water. Stir to dissolve. Pour boiling water over margarine, brown sugar, molasses and salt. Mix to dissolve. Cool. Add rye flour and yeast mixture and sourdough. Add caraway and orange peel. Add flour. Knead. Let rise two hours. Punch down. Let rise 10 minutes. Shape into 2 loaves. Let rise on greased sheet for 1-1/2 hours. Bake at 375 degrees for 25 to 30 minutes. (For hard crust, brush with egg wash as in roll recipe.)

SOURDOUGH CINNAMON ROLLS

1/2	cup milk
1/8	cup honey
2	teaspoons butter
2-1/2	cups unbleached flour
1	teaspoon baking soda
1/2	teaspoon salt
1	cup starter
1/2	cup raisins
1	cup raw brown sugar
2	tablespoons cinnamon
1/8	cup cream
2	tablespoons melted butter

Scald 1/2 cup milk; stir in 1/8 cup honey with 2 teaspoons butter and cool to lukewarm. Sift 1 cup flour with 1 teaspoon baking soda and 1/2 teaspoon salt. Add to milk, beating with a wooden spoon until smooth.

Beat in one cup starter and 1-1/2 cups flour to make an easy-to-handle dough. Knead on lightly floured board until smooth. Put in oiled bowl and turn to coat top of dough. Cover with a towel and let rise until double. Punch down and roll into 1/4-inch thick rectangle. Brush melted butter on dough. Combine 1/2 cup brown sugar and 2 tablespoons cinnamon and sprinkle on dough. Roll up and cut into 1-inch pieces. In bottom of pan, place 1/2 cup brown sugar and 1/8 cup cream. Place cinnamon rolls on top of cream and brown sugar. Let rise until double and bake at 375 degrees for 15 to 20 minutes.

SOURDOUGH BREAD

1	cup starter
2	cups lukewarm water
2-3	cups flour
1/4	cup sugar
1/4	cup salad oil
2	teaspoons salt

Mix these ingredients in a bowl. Cover with a cloth and let set overnight in a warm place. In the morning add 1 package yeast, dissolved in 2 tablespoons warm water. Add enough flour to make a stiff dough; turn the dough onto a well-floured board and knead for 15 minutes. Return it to an oiled bowl, cover with a cloth and let rise until double, 3 hours. Turn out onto floured board; knead a few minutes and shape into 2 loaves. Let rise (covered with a cloth) until double, about 2 hours. Bake at 375 degrees for 40 minutes.

SOURDOUGH CHOCOLATE CAKE

1	cup thick sourdough starter
1	cup sugar
1/2	cup shortening
2	eggs
1	cup evaporated milk
1	teaspoon vanilla
1	teaspoon cinnamon
3	(1-ounce) squares semi-sweet chocolate
1/2	teaspoon salt
1-1/2	teaspoons soda
2	cups flour

Cream sugar and shortening until light and fluffy. Beat in eggs one at a time. Stir in sourdough starter, milk, vanilla, cinnamon and melted chocolate. Beat with rotary beater 2 minutes. Blend salt and soda together until smooth. Sprinkle over batter and gently fold in. Fold in flour until batter is smooth. Pour into greased and floured cake pans. Bake at 350 degrees for 25-30 minutes. Cool and frost with Chocolate Sour Cream Frosting.

Chocolate Sour Cream Frosting

1	6-ounce package semi-sweet chocolate pieces
1/4	cup butter
1/2	cup sour cream
1	teaspoon vanilla
1/4	teaspoon salt
2-1/2 to 2-3/4	cups powdered sugar

Melt chocolate and butter. Blend in all other gradually with the powdered sugar until spreadable.

SOURDOUGH CORNBREAD

1	cup starter
1	cup corn meal
1/2	cup flour
4	tablespoons sugar
1/2	cup buttermilk
2	eggs (beaten)
1-1/2	teaspoons salt
1/4	cup bacon drippings
3	thick slices bacon (fried crisp)
2	teaspoons soda
2	tablespoons minced onions

Combine and mix the liquid ingredients. Beat into this the dry ingredients for about 1/2 minute. Fold in the onions and crumbled bacon. Pour into a medium-sized baking pan. Bake at 350 degrees for 35 to 40 minutes or until done.

SHARE HERMAN WITH A FRIEND

Record Herman's feeding instructions and cake recipe.
Remove sheet and give with 1 cup Herman to a good friend.

HERMAN

On the day you get Herman, you must feed him:

1	cup flour
1/2	cup sugar
1	cup milk

Remember, feed on the 1st day and the 5th day.

Keep Herman refrigerated in a large and loosely covered dish. Stir him every day because Herman grows!

On baking day (10th day), measure out 1 cup Herman for yourself and feed him.

Then, measure out 1 cup for a friend and give along with Herman's letter.

Put the 2 remaining cups into a large mixing bowl and add:

2	cups flour
2	eggs
1	cup sugar
1/2	cup oil
1/2	teaspoon cinnamon
1/2	teaspoon soda
1/2	teaspoon baking powder
1	cup raisins (and - or) nuts

Pour into greased and floured 9 x 13 inch pan and add topping.

Topping:

1	tablespoon flour
1	tablespoon cinnamon
1/2	cup brown sugar
1/2	cup melted butter

Pour over dough and swirl with a fork.

Bake at 350 degrees 30 to 40 minutes. Glaze after baking if desired.

Glaze:

1/4	cup butter
1/4	cup brown sugar
2	tablespoons milk

Boil 3 to 4 minutes and spoon over cake.

Say goodnight Herman.

EVELYN'S PINEAPPLE-PECAN LOAF

3/4   cup light brown sugar
1/4   cup shortening
1   egg
2   cups sifted all-purpose flour
1   teaspoon baking soda
1/2   teaspoon salt
3   ounces (1/3 cup) frozen orange juice, thawed
1   can (8-3/4 ounce) crushed pineapple
1/2   cup chopped pecans

Cream together sugar and shortening. Add egg and beat well. Sift together flour, soda and salt. Alternately add dry ingredients and orange concentrate to creamed mixture, stirring after each addition. Stir in undrained pineapple and pecans. Turn into well greased 8-1/2 x 4-1/2 x 2-1/2 inch loaf pan. Bake at 350 degrees for 50 to 60 minutes. Remove from pan and cool on rack. This delicious bread took a second place red ribbon in the 1977 Cowlitz County Fair, Longview, Washington. This bread is very good toasted for a mid-morning coffee break. It is also a very good bread to serve for a special holiday meal.

CINNAMON BREAD

6-1/2
to
7-1/2   cups flour
6   tablespoons sugar
1-1/2   teaspoons salt
2   packages yeast
1   cup milk
3/4   cup water
1/3   cup margarine
2-3   eggs
1/2   cup sugar (save for later)
2   teaspoons cinnamon (save for later)

Mix in large bowl, 2 cups flour, sugar, salt and yeast. Combine milk, water and margarine in saucepan. Heat to 120 to 130 degrees. Add to dry ingredients. Beat 2 minutes. Add eggs and 1/2 cup more flour. Beat 2 minutes more. Stir in enough flour to make a stiff dough. Knead 8 to 10 minutes. Place in greased bowl. Cover. Let rise until double (about 35 minutes). Punch down and divide in half. Roll each half to a 14 x 9 inch rectangle.

Mix 1/2 cup sugar and 2 teaspoons cinnamon together. Divide mixture in half and sprinkle over dough. Beginning with 9 inch end, roll up jelly roll fashion. Shape into loaves and place in 2 greased 9 x 5 x 3 inch pans. Cover and let rise about 35 minutes. Bake at 375 degrees 30 to 40 minutes. Cool on wire rack.

RAISIN BROWN BREAD

1   cup buttermilk
1   egg
3/4   cup molasses
2   tablespoons melted shortening
1   cup dark or golden raisins
3/4   cup corn meal
3/4   cup whole wheat flour
1-1/2   cups sifted flour
1-1/2   teaspoons salt
1-1/2   teaspoons soda
1   teaspoon baking powder

Stir buttermilk into lightly beaten egg. Add molasses and shortening and set aside. Combine raisins with corn meal and whole wheat flour. Resift flour with salt, soda and baking powder into raisin mixture. Add buttermilk mixture to dry ingredients and stir until all of flour is moistened. Turn into greased loaf pan 10 x 5 x 3 inches in size. Bake at 350 degrees 50 minutes. Let cool in pan 10 minutes. Turn out onto wire rack to cool completely. Makes 1 loaf.

CARROT BREAD

1	cup vegetable oil
2	cups white sugar
2	cups grated carrots
3	eggs
3	cups flour
1/4	teaspoon baking powder
1	teaspoon salt
1	teaspoon baking soda
1	teaspoon cinnamon
1	cup chopped pecans
1	(8 ounce) can crushed pineapple, drained

Beat eggs till foamy. Add oil, carrots and sugar. Beat well. Sift together flour, baking soda, salt, baking powder and cinnamon. Add to egg mixture and blend well. Stir in nuts and pineapple. Divide batter and place in 2 greased and floured loaf pans. Bake at 350 degrees about 1 hour, or until done. Cool.

DATE LOAF

Pour 1 cup boiling water over:

1-1/2	cups chopped dates
1/2	cup butter
1	cup brown sugar
	grated rind of 1 lemon

Stir in:

1	cup chopped nuts
1-1/2	cups sifted flour
1-1/2	teaspoons baking powder
1/2	teaspoon salt

Stir only until flour is blended. Pour immediately into greased and floured loaf pans. Bake at 350 degrees for 50 to 60 minutes (mini pans 40 minutes). Cool and remove from pans.

GREEN TOMATO BREAD

2-1/2	cups flour
2-1/2	teaspoons baking powder
1	teaspoon soda
1/2	teaspoon salt
1	cup brown sugar
1	tablespoon cinnamon
1	teaspoon nutmeg
1/4	teaspoon ginger
1	tablespoon molasses
3	tablespoons honey
1/2	cup oil
1	cup ground, undrained green tomatoes
2	eggs
1	teaspoon vanilla
1/2	cup chopped nuts

Mix dry ingredients. Add rest of ingredients and beat well. Spoon into 2 greased and floured pans. Let batter rest 10 minutes. Smooth tops of loaves and make an "I" indentation along center from end to end. Bake at 350 degrees for 45 to 50 minutes or until done.

PUMPKIN SPICE BREAD

1/2	cup flour
1/2	teaspoon baking powder
1	teaspoon baking soda
1/2	teaspoon salt
1	cup (packed solid) pre-spiced pumpkin
1/2	cup oil
2	eggs
1/3	cup water
1-1/2	cups 40% bran flakes cereal
1/3	cup chopped nuts

In large mixing bowl, beat pumpkin, oil, eggs and water until well blended. Stir in 40% bran flakes and nuts. Add flour, baking powder, baking soda and salt. Stir just until combined. Spread batter evenly in a greased 9 x 5 x 3 inch loaf pan. Bake at 350 degrees about 55 minutes or until toothpick inserted at center comes out clean. Let cool 10 minutes before removing from pan. Cool completely before slicing.

PUMPKIN BREAD

3-1/3	cups flour
3	cups sugar
2	teaspoons soda
1-1/2	teaspoons salt
1	teaspoon cinnamon

Sift dry ingredients in a large bowl.

Add:

1	cup salad oil
2	cups pumpkin
1	cup chopped nuts
4	eggs
2/3	cup water

Stir well and pour into 3 loaf pans that have been greased and floured. Bake in 350 degree oven for 1 hour 15 minutes.

PUMPKIN BREAD

1/2	cup butter (soft)
2	cups pumpkin
1-1/2	cups sugar
1/2	cup brown sugar
2-1/2	cups flour
1/2	teaspoon salt
2	teaspoons soda
3/4	teaspoon cinnamon
3/4	teaspoon cloves

Mix together all ingredients. Pour into 2 greased bread pans. Bake at 350 degrees for 1 hour or until toothpick inserted in center comes out clean. 1 cup of nuts or raisins may be added.

OLGA'S PEANUT BUTTER BREAD

1	cake yeast
1	cup warm milk
1/4	cup sugar
1/3	cup peanut butter
1	beaten egg
1-1/2	teaspoons salt
3 to	
3-1/2	cups sifted flour

Make a sponge as follows: Put yeast into milk, add 1 tablespoon of the sugar; stir in 1 cup flour. Cover bowl and set aside until the sponge is light and full of bubbles. Mix together peanut butter, egg, salt, and remaining sugar. Add to the sponge. Stir in remaining flour and mix until the dough follows the spoon around the bowl. Turn dough onto a lightly floured board, knead until smooth and elastic. Place in a greased bowl. Grease surface also, and cover. Let rise in a warm place 85 to 90 degrees, until doubled. Punch down and let rise a second time. Mold into a loaf and place in a greased baking pan. Let loaf rise until double in size. Bake in a moderately hot oven, 375 degrees about 10 minutes. Reduce heat to 350 and continue baking until bread is well browned. Remove from pan at once and cool. Brush top with butter. This is a tender bread, even the crust. The dough is waxy to knead.

FLUFFY PEANUT BUTTER BREAD

2-1/2	cups sifted flour
4	teaspoons baking powder
1/2	teaspoon salt
3/4	cup peanut butter
1/2	cup sugar
1	egg
1	teaspoon vanilla
1/4	cup water

Heat oven to 350 degrees. Mix all ingredients together. Pour into one or two greased baking pan(s). Bake 1 hour. Enjoy hot or cold!

BANANA BREAD

5	large ripe bananas
4	eggs
1	cup margarine or butter
2	cups sugar
4	cups flour
2	teaspoons soda
1	teaspoon salt
1	cup chopped walnuts

Beat bananas until liquid. Combine with eggs and set aside. Cream together butter and sugar until fluffy. Add banana mixture and blend. Add sifted dry ingredients and stir until smooth. Fold in nuts. Pour into 2 well greased loaf pans. Bake at 350 degrees for 40 to 45 minutes or until done.

KONA INN BANANA BREAD

1	cup margarine
2	cups sugar
6-7	ripe bananas, mashed
4	eggs, well beaten
2-1/2	cups sifted flour
1	teaspoon salt
2	teaspoons soda

Cream margarine and sugar thoroughly. Add bananas and eggs. Sift dry ingredients. Blend into creamed mixture, but do not overmix. Pour into ungreased loaf pans. Bake at 350 degrees for 50 to 55 minutes.

BANANA NUT BREAD

1/2	cup butter
1	cup sugar
2	eggs
2	mashed bananas
1	cup nut meats
2	cups flour
1	teaspoon soda
1	teaspoon salt

Cream butter and sugar. Add eggs and mashed bananas. Add dry ingredients and nuts. Bake in loaf pan at 350 degrees for 1 hour.

ZUCCHINI BREAD

3	eggs
2	cups sugar
2	cups ground zucchini
1	cup oil
2	teaspoons vanilla
3	cups flour
1	teaspoon salt
1	teaspoon soda
2	teaspoons cinnamon
1/2	teaspoon nutmeg
1/4	teaspoon cloves

Beat all ingredients together. Beat 2 minutes. Pour into greased and floured 9 x 5 inch pans. Bake at 375 degrees 55 to 60 minutes.

LIGHT ZUCCHINI BREAD

3	whole eggs
3/4	cup oil
1-1/2	cups sugar
1	teaspoon lemon peel (powdered)
1/4	teaspoon vanilla
2	cups grated zucchini (can be firm flesh of very large one, peeled if peeling is tough)
2-1/2	cups unsifted flour (more if zucchini has more moisture)
3/4	teaspoon salt
1/2	teaspoon cinnamon
1/4	teaspoon ginger
1	teaspoon soda
2	teaspoons baking powder
1/2	cup nuts, chopped

Beat eggs; add oil and sugar; beat well. Add flavoring and zucchini; beat. Mix dry ingredients together. Add nuts and stir in. Mix well. Bake in small loaf pans or oiled (size #2) cans at 350 degrees for 1 hour. Cool in cans until bread will remove easily, then cool on wire rack. Note: This freezes well and is an ideal way to use up those monsters. You may need more flour if using small or medium size zucchini that have more moisture. If using very large zucchini, discard center pulp. The firm flesh is not extra moist, but perfect for this recipe.

SPIDER BREAD

1	cup cornmeal
3/4	cup flour
1	tablespoon baking powder
1/2	teaspoon soda
1/2	teaspoon salt
2	tablespoons sugar
1	egg, slightly beaten
1	cup buttermilk
4	tablespoons melted shortening or oil or butter

Sift together cornmeal, flour, baking powder, soda, salt and sugar. Mix together egg, buttermilk and butter. Stir the mixed liquids into flour mixture to make a batter. Generously oil a 9 inch cast iron skillet or 8 inch square pan and heat until very hot. Spoon in batter. Bake in a pre-heated 400 degree oven for 18 to 20 minutes until bread is puffy and tests done. Serve with butter.

BEER BREAD

3	cups self-rising flour
1/2	cup sugar
1	bottle light beer

Mix self-rising flour and sugar in large mixing bowl. Pour one bottle light beer over dry ingredients and mix together. Pour into greased bread pan. Bake in pre-heated 350 degree oven for 55 to 60 minutes. Makes one loaf. Note: when cooled, bread can be sliced or torn into chunks. Delicious when heated in microwave for 30 seconds and topped with melted butter.

ITALIAN SAUSAGE BREAD

1	loaf frozen bread dough
1	package medium Italian sausage
1/2	cup sliced onions
2	eggs
1/2	teaspoon Italian seasoning
1-1/2	cups shredded Mozarella cheese
1	tablespoon grated Parmesan cheese

Defrost bread. Brown sausage with onions, drain and set aside. Beat eggs and set aside enough for brushing on top of bread. Add seasoning and cheeses to beaten eggs. Stir. Roll out bread dough to a 6 x 20 inch rectangle. Spoon sausage onto 1/2 of rolled dough. Spoon cheese and egg mixture on top of sausage. Roll dough and seal edges by pinching together.

Brush remaining egg on top and sprinkle with Parmesan cheese. Let rise for 1 hour. Bake at 350 degrees for 20 to 30 minutes.

PIZZA BREAD

1-1/2	cups baking mix
1	cup shredded cheddar cheese
3/4	cup chopped pepperoni
1	egg
1/4	cup milk
1	teaspoon Italian seasoning
2	tablespoons Parmesan cheese

Heat oven to 400 degrees. Grease 9 x 1-1/4 inch pie plate. Mix baking mix, half the cheese, 1/2 cup pepperoni, egg, milk, seasonings and Parmesan cheese. Spread in plate. Sprinkle with remaining cheddar cheese and pepperoni. Bake until pick comes out clean from center, about 20 minutes. Serve while hot.

RUBY'S MUFFINS

1-1/2	cups brown sugar
2/3	cup vegetable oil
1	egg
1	cup sour milk
1	teaspoon salt
1	teaspoon baking soda
1	teaspoon vanilla
2-1/2	cups flour
1-1/2	cups diced fruit (rhubarb is very good)
1/2	cup chopped nuts

Pre-heat oven to 375 degrees. Beat brown sugar, oil and egg in bowl until fluffy. Add milk and dry ingredients. Mix slightly until moistened. Add fruit, nuts and vanilla. Mix, put in baking cups and add topping. Bake until inserted toothpick comes out clean, about 30 minutes.

Topping:

Mix together 1/2 cup sugar and 1 tablespoon butter.

SALLY LUNNS

2	eggs, separated
2	cups flour
1/2	cup sugar
1	teaspoon salt
3	tablespoons melted butter
3	teaspoons baking powder
1	cup cream

Cream the sugar and egg yolks, then cream with the butter. Beat until fluffy. Add a little flour sifted with the baking powder and salt. Add rest of flour alternately with cream. Lastly, fold in stiff egg whites. Bake at 375 degrees for 25 to 30 minutes in well buttered muffin tins. Makes about 16 large tender muffins.

WHEAT GERM MUFFINS

1-1/2	cups sifted all-purpose flour
1/4	cup sugar
2	teaspoons baking powder
1	teaspoon salt
1	cup wheat germ
1	egg, well beaten
3/4	cup milk
1/4	cup butter, melted
1/4	cup light molasses

Sift flour, sugar, baking powder and salt into medium bowl. Stir in wheat germ. Combine egg, milk, melted butter and molasses in another bowl. Add all at once to flour mixture, stirring lightly just until liquid is absorbed. (Batter will be lumpy.) Spoon into 12 greased muffin-pan cups and bake at 400 degrees 20 minutes, or until nice and brown. Remove from pan at once. Serve hot with butter and jam.

BRAN AND BEER MUFFINS

1	cup whole bran cereal
1	cup beer
1	egg
1/4	cup honey
1/4	cup soft shortening
1	cup sifted all-purpose flour
3	teaspoons baking powder
1/2	teaspoon salt

Combine bran cereal, beer, egg, honey and shortening in mixing bowl. Beat well and set aside. Sift together flour, baking powder and salt. Add to bran mixture stirring only until combined. Fill greased 2-1/2 inch muffin cups 3/4 full. Bake at 400 degrees 25 minutes. Makes 8 muffins.

BUTTERMILK BRAN MUFFIN MIX

2	cups 100% bran
4	cups all-bran cereal
2	cups boiling water
1	cup shortening
3	cups white sugar
4	eggs, beaten
1	quart buttermilk
5	cups flour
5	teaspoons soda
1	teaspoon salt

Add boiling water to 100% bran. Cool. Cream shortening, sugar, eggs and buttermilk. Add soaked bran. Sift flour, soda and salt. Add to dry bran. Mix with liquid mixture. Batter may be stored in refrigerator for several weeks. Bake desired number of muffins at 400 degrees for 20 minutes.

BRAN MUFFINS

1/2	cup unbleached flour
1/2	cup whole wheat flour
1-1/2	cups miller's bran
1	teaspoon soda
1/2	cup raisins
1	egg
3/4	cup milk
1	teaspoon vanilla
1/2	cup honey
2	tablespoons melted butter **or** oil

Mix the dry ingredients together in a bowl with the raisins. In another bowl, beat the egg and mix with the milk, honey and butter. Add to the dry ingredients and blend. Bake at 375 degrees for approximately 25 minutes in well greased muffin pans. Makes 10 average size muffins. (If oil is used instead of butter, add a little salt.) Delicious!

BRAN MUFFINS

1-1/4	cups all-purpose flour
3	teaspoons baking powder
1/2	teaspoon salt
1/2	cup sugar
2-1/2	cups 40% bran flakes cereal
1-1/4	cups milk
1	egg
1/3	cup soft shortening **or** vegetable oil

Stir together flour, baking powder, salt and sugar. Set aside. Measure 40% bran flakes and milk into mixing bowl. Stir to combine and let stand 1 to 2 minutes until cereal is softened. Add egg and shortening. Beat well. Add dry ingredients to cereal mixture, stirring only until combined. Portion batter evenly into 12 greased 2-1/2 inch muffin cups. Bake at 400 degrees for about 25 minutes or until golden brown. Serve warm.

ORANGE TEA MUFFINS

1	cup nuts, ground
1	cup raisins, ground
1-1/2	cups flour
1	cup sugar
1/2	cup butter
1	cup buttermilk
1	teaspoon soda
2	eggs, well beaten
1	teaspoon vanilla
	juice of 1 orange
	rind of 1 orange

Roll ground nuts and raisins in 1/2 cup of flour. Mix remaining ingredients and add to raisin mixture. Cook in tiny muffin tins at 350 to 375 degrees until done.

SUGARY JAM MUFFINS

1/2	cup shortening
1/2	cup sugar
1	egg
1/2	cup milk
1-1/2	cups flour
1-1/2	teaspoons baking powder
1/2	teaspoon salt
1/2	cup walnuts

Cream shortening and sugar. Add egg and milk. Stir in flour, baking powder, salt and walnuts. Divide the batter in half. Spoon equal portions of half the batter into 12 large (2-1/2 inch) or 24 small (1-3/4 inch) well greased muffin cups. Top each with 1 teaspoon jam. Spread equal portions of remaining batter over jam. Bake at 350 degrees until golden brown — 35 minutes for large, 25 minutes for small. Let cool in pan about 5 minutes, then turn out. Serve plain with butter or roll each in melted butter (1/2 cup), then in cinnamon flavored sugar (1/2 cup).

BLUEBERRY MUFFINS

1	cup sugar
1/4	cup oil
1	cup milk
1/2	teaspoon salt
1/2	cup shortening
2	eggs
4	teaspoons baking powder
2-2/3	cups flour

Mix all ingredients well. Add 2 cups of blueberries which have been coated with flour. Fill greased muffin tins 3/4 full. Sprinkle sugar on top and bake at 375 degrees for 15-20 minutes.

BUTTERMILK BISCUITS

2	cups sifted flour
3	teaspoons baking powder
1/2	teaspoon salt
1/4	teaspoon soda
5	tablespoons shortening
1	cup buttermilk

Sift flour, baking powder, salt and soda. Cut in shortening till mixture resembles coarse crumbs. Add buttermilk, all at once, and stir till dough follows fork around bowl. Turn out and knead 1/2 minute. Roll 3/8 inch thick and brush with melted fat. Fold over and cut double biscuits. Bake on ungreased cookie sheet in very hot oven (450 degrees) 12 to 15 minutes. Makes 2 dozen.

TOMATO CHEESE BISCUITS

2	cups sifted flour
3	teaspoons baking powder
1	teaspoon salt
3	tablespoons shortening
1	cup grated American cheese
3	tablespoons chopped parsley or dry flake parsley
3/4	cup tomato juice

Sift flour, baking powder and salt. Cut in shortening. Add cheese and parsley. Mix well. Add tomato juice. Knead lightly on floured board for 30 seconds. Roll out 1/2 inch thick and cut. Bake at 450 degrees for 10 to 12 minutes. Note: if desired, add parsley and cheese to 2 cups prepared biscuit mix and add tomato juice instead of milk. Complete as in other recipe.

CHEESE TARTS

Mix together 1/2 cup butter, one 3 ounce package cream cheese and 1 cup flour. Press into small ungreased cupcake tins. Sprinkle finely chopped nuts over dough.

Then mix:

1-1/2	cups brown sugar
2	eggs
2	tablespoons melted butter
1	teaspoon vanilla
	pinch of salt

Mix together and pour into shells. Bake at 350 degrees for 25 minutes or till lightly browned.

CORN PUFFS

2	eggs
1	cup whole milk
2	cups whole kernel corn
6	tablespoons grated cheese
1/2	teaspoon salt
1/4	teaspoon paprika

Beat eggs until light. Add milk, corn, salt and paprika. Oil or spray with non-stick film, 6 custard cups and fill. Place in shallow pan of hot water. Add a tablespoon of grated cheese to each cup. Bake in moderate oven.

FRENCH DOUGHNUTS

1	cup milk
1/2	cup shortening
1-1/4	cups flour
4	eggs
1/2	teaspoon salt

Boil liquid with shortening and salt. Add flour, sifting by handfuls. Stir constantly until the mixture stirs away from the pan edge like thick paste. Add unbeaten eggs one at a time, beating the mixture smooth each time. Drop by small spoonfuls into deep hot fat.

DROP DOUGHNUTS

1	egg
1/3	cup sugar
1	teaspoon vanilla
1/2	cup milk
1/3	cup flour
2-1/2	teaspoons baking powder
1/4	teaspoon salt
1	tablespoon butter, melted

Beat egg 1 minute. Add sugar, butter, vanilla and milk. Beat 30 seconds. Add sifted dry ingredients. Drop teaspoons of batter into hot grease and fry until brown. Drain. Glaze if desired.

Glaze:

1	cup sifted powdered sugar
1/3	cup boiling water
1/2	teaspoon vanilla

Combine all ingredients. Dip warm doughnuts into mixture. Yields 1-1/2 dozen.

OATMEAL WAFFLES

2	cups quick oats
1	teaspoon salt
1	tablespoon buckwheat flour
1/4	cup almonds (ground)
2	tablespoons oil
1/2	cup soy milk powder

Mix above ingredients with approximately 2 cups water to obtain desired consistency.

CHOCOLATE WAFFLES

1-1/2	cups sifted flour
1-1/2	teaspoons baking powder
1/2	teaspoon salt
3/4	cup sugar
2	egg yolks, well beaten
1/2	cup milk
1/2	cup melted butter or other shortening
2	squares unsweetened chocolate, melted
1/2	teaspoon vanilla
2	egg whites

Sift flour once. Measure, add baking powder, salt and sugar and sift again. Combine egg yolks and milk. Add to flour mixture, beating until smooth. Combine shortening and chocolate. Add to batter and blend. Add vanilla. Beat egg whites until they will hold up in moist peaks. Stir quickly but thoroughly into batter. Bake in hot waffle iron. Serve hot, topped with scoops of vanilla ice cream. Makes four 4-section waffles.

MAIN DISHES

WASHINGTON BEEF SUPPER

2	pounds beef for stew, cut in 1 inch cubes
	salt and pepper
2	large onions, sliced
2	tablespoons olive or vegetable oil
1	jar (4-1/2 ounce) whole mushrooms
4	medium potatoes, pared and thinly sliced
1	can (10-1/2 ounce) condensed cream of mushroom soup
3/4	cup milk
3/4	cup dairy sour cream
1	teaspoon salt
1/4	teaspoon pepper
2	cups (8 ounce) shredded cheddar cheese cracker crumbs or fine dry bread crumbs

Season meat with salt and pepper. Cook and stir meat and onions in olive oil in large skillet over medium heat until meat is brown and onions are tender. Pour off oil. Drain mushrooms, reserving liquid. Add enough water to mushroom liquid to make 1 cup. Stir mushrooms and liquid into meat and onions. Heat to boiling. Reduce heat, cover and simmer 2 hours. Heat oven to 350 degrees. Pour meat mixture into 13-1/2 x 8-3/4 x 1-3/4 inch baking dish. Arrange potatoes over meat. Mix soup, milk, sour cream, 1 teaspoon salt and 1/4 teaspoon pepper. Pour over potatoes and sprinkle with cheese. Bake uncovered 1 hour. Sprinkle with cracker crumbs if desired. Bake uncovered until potatoes are tender and crumbs are brown, 20 to 30 minutes.

MICHELLE'S STEAK SUPPER IN FOIL

1-1/2	pound chuck steak, 1 inch thick
1	envelope onion soup mix
4	medium carrots, quartered
4	stalks celery, cut into sticks
3	medium potatoes, quartered
2	tablespoons butter
1/2	teaspoon salt

Tear a 2-1/2 foot length of 18 inch wide foil. Place meat in center and sprinkle with soup mix. Cover with vegetables, dot with butter and sprinkle with salt. Fold foil over and seal securely to hold in juices. Place on baking sheet and bake in pre-heated 450 degree oven for 1-1/2 hours. Serves 4.

BILL'S BEER STEAK

2	pounds round steak
1	medium onion, diced
2	teaspoons parsley
4	tablespoons flour
	garlic juice
	salt and pepper to taste
1	(11 ounce) bottle of beer

One hour before you begin recipe, take cap off bottle of beer, (to go flat). Cut steak into serving size pieces and add a few drops garlic juice to each piece. Combine salt and pepper with flour and roll meat in mixture. Brown both sides. Add onion, parsley and beer. Cover and simmer over low heat 1-1/2 to 2 hours until tender. Turn frequently. Thicken juice if desired. Additional liquid may need to be added. Serves 6.

EASIEST BEEF STROGANOFF

2	pounds round steak or stew meat, cut in small pieces
1	envelope dry onion soup
1	can cream of chicken soup
1	can water
1	tablespoon chopped parsley

Mix soups with water and marinate meat overnight or all day. Cook for 2 hours on slow heat in a heavy dutch oven or bake in a covered casserole for 2 hours at 325 degrees. Serve over rice, mashed potatoes or noodles. Serve with a crisp salad.

ROUND STEAK WITH RICH GRAVY

1-1/2	pounds round steak
1	(1-1/2 ounce) package onion soup mix
1/4	cup water
1	(10-1/2 ounce) can condensed cream of mushroom soup

Cut steak into serving size pieces. Place in slow-cooking pot. Add dry onion soup mix, water and mushroom soup. Cover and cook on low 6 to 8 hours.

CROWN ROAST BEEF AND VEGETABLES

3   pounds (or larger) cross rib roast
1   package dry onion soup mix
1   can cream of mushroom soup
3   cups potatoes, peeled and quartered
2   cups carrots, sliced
1   cup celery, diced
1/4   cup chopped green pepper (optional)

Place a large sheet of aluminum foil on a 15 x 12 x 2 inch cookie sheet. Place rib roast in center of foil. Sprinkle onion soup mix over top of roast. Pour undiluted cream of mushroom soup over the onion mix. Place vegetables around the roast. Pull foil tightly up and around roast, sealing completely. Pinch well so juices will be held in. Bake in 275 degree oven for 5 hours.

SAUCY STEAK SKILLET

1   pound beef round steak, cut in pieces
1/4   cup all-purpose flour
1   tablespoon oil
1   large onion, chopped
1   can (16 ounce) whole potatoes, drained (save liquid)
1/4   cup catsup
1   tablespoon Worcestershire sauce
2   tablespoons bell pepper flakes
1   teaspoon instant beef bouillon
1   teaspoon salt
1/2   teaspoon dried marjoram leaves
1/4   teaspoon pepper
1   package (10 ounce) frozen Italian green beans
2   ounces sliced pimiento, drained

Coat beef pieces with flour and pound in. Brown beef in oil in a 10 inch skillet and push to side. Cook and stir onion in oil until tender. Drain. Add enough water to potato liquid to make 1 cup. Mix liquid, catsup, Worcestershire sauce, pepper flakes, instant bouillon, salt, marjoram and pepper. Pour over beef and onion. Heat to a boil then reduce heat. Cover and simmer until beef is tender, 1-1/4 to 1-1/2 hours. Rinse frozen beans to separate. Add beans, potatoes and pimiento to beef. Heat to a boil then reduce heat. Cover and simmer until beans are tender, 10 to 15 minutes, 4 servings.

POT ROAST LIKE MOTHER NEVER MADE

Brown roast on both sides. Turn heat to simmer. Chop large onion fine and add to roast. Mix 1 heaping teaspoon of ginger with 1 cup of beer and pour over roast. Cover and let simmer for at least 2 hours. If liquid cooks down, add more beer as needed. When meat is about half done, add vegetables if desired. If liquid is not used for gravy, save to pour on left-over roast before storing in the refrigerator. Meat will be even better the next day.

BEEF STROGANOFF A LA ECONOMY

2   pounds chuck stewing beef
1   onion, chopped
4   tablespoons margarine
2   beef bouillon cubes
2   cups boiling water
1   pound mushrooms, sliced
1/2   cup sour cream
      salt and pepper to taste

Trim beef and pound it thin. Cut into 1 inch wide strips. Saute beef and onion in 2 tablespoons margarine. Dissolve bouillon cubes in water and add to skillet. Cover and simmer for 1 hour, adding more water if required. There should be only a small amount of water when cooked completely. Saute mushrooms in remaining margarine. Add to meat about 5 minutes before serving. Add sour cream and heat, but do not boil. Add salt and pepper to taste. Yields 6 servings.

MEAT LOAF

Mix:

2-3   pounds ground beef
2   eggs
20   crackers, crushed
1   onion, chopped
      dash garlic powder or garlic salt
      salt and pepper
1/2   cup milk

Place in a bread loaf pan. Bake at 350 degrees about 45 minutes.

CUBE STEAK PARMESAN

6	cube steaks
3	eggs
1-1/2	teaspoons salt
1/2	teaspoon pepper
1-1/2	cups fine dry bread crumbs
9	tablespoons grated parmesan cheese
1/2	cup olive oil
2	(8 ounce) cans tomato sauce

Combine eggs, salt and pepper. Beat well. Mix dry bread crumbs and 5 tablespoons Parmesan cheese. Dip steaks in egg mixture then in crumbs. Brown both sides in olive oil. Add tomato sauce and top with remaining Parmesan cheese. Bake uncovered at 325 degrees for 25 minutes. Serves 6.

CRAZY-OVEN STEW

1	can stewed tomatoes
1	can peas
1	tablespoon brown sugar
1/8	teaspoon pepper
1	tablespoon mixed herbs
3-1/2 to 4	pounds stew meat
1	can stewed onions
4	tablespoons instant tapioca
1	bay leaf
1	tablespoon salt
1/2	cup wine
6	carrots
1/2	cup bread crumbs

Combine all ingredients except bread crumbs. Bake in oven or crock pot for about 7 hours at 250 degrees. Sprinkle bread crumbs on top just before serving.

LASAGNA

1-1/2 to 2	pounds lean ground beef
1	large onion, chopped
1	clove garlic, minced
2	tablespoons olive oil
2	(15 ounce) cans marinara sauce
1	(15 ounce) can spaghetti sauce with mushrooms
1/4	teaspoon pepper
1	teaspoon salt
2	cans ripe olives, drained and chopped
1	can mushrooms, drained and sliced
1	pound Monterey Jack cheese, grated
1	pound Mozzarella cheese, grated
4	hard boiled eggs, sliced
1/4	cup grated Parmesan cheese
1	package lasagna, cooked

Saute meat, onion and garlic in olive oil. Drain off excess fat. Stir in marinara and spaghetti sauce, mushrooms and olives. Simmer 15 to 20 minutes. Layer in 13 x 9 inch baking dish. First layer: sauce, then noodles, cheese, eggs and Parmesan cheese. Repeat layers and top with sauce and cheese. Bake uncovered at 375 degrees for 30 to 40 minutes or longer. Let set out a few minutes before serving. Serves 10 to 12 or more.

CAULIFLOWER AND CORNED BEEF

1-1/2	cups milk
3	tablespoons flour
3	tablespoons butter
1	cup cheese
2	heads cauliflower
2	cans corned beef

Heat milk, flour, butter and cheese until thick. (You will have to double this sauce). Cook cauliflower in salt water until tender. Salt and pepper to taste. Mix all ingredients together and bake at 350 degrees for 30 minutes until bubbly.

PHILLIP'S CHILI

2	cups red beans (soak overnight)
1/2	cup ham and ham fat, cut up
	salt
1-1/2	pounds lean ground beef or ground round
1	medium onion, diced
2	stalks celery
1	small green pepper
1	can (12 ounce) tomatoes, whole or halves (stewed or cooked)
1	can (6 ounce) tomato paste
3	tablespoons thick catsup
1	teaspoon garlic powder
1-1/2	teaspoons Worcestershire sauce
1	tablespoon molasses (add more later if desired)
1-1/2	tablespoons chili powder
1	teaspoon pepper

Boil beans for 2 minutes. Add ham and ham fat and salt to taste. Simmer for a few hours. Brown ground beef and pour off excess grease. Add onion, celery and green pepper and simmer till tender. Add tomatoes, tomato paste and catsup. Add spices and rest of ingredients. Mix well and simmer 10 minutes. Drain 3/4 of water from beans. Mix sauce and beans together, simmer until hot. Season to taste.

MEAT BALLS AND ONION SOUP

1	pound hamburger
3/4	cup rolled oats
1	egg
1/2	cup milk
1	teaspoon salt
1/8	teaspoon pepper
1/4	teaspoon thyme
1/4	teaspoon marjoram
1/3	cup flour
2	tablespoons fat
1	can onion soup
1	soup can water

Combine all ingredients except flour, fat, soup and water. Make into 25 balls. Roll in flour and brown in fat. Add onion soup and water. Cook over low heat for 20 to 25 minutes. Mix remaining flour and 1/4 water to gravy. Blend until smooth. Yields 5 servings.

ZUCCHINI GARDEN CASSEROLE

4	medium ripe tomatoes, peeled and sliced

(To peel: dip tomatoes into boiling water, then into cold water. Peel from top to bottom.)

4	zucchini (about 1-1/2 pounds), sliced
2	teaspoons salt
1-1/2	pounds lean ground beef
2/3	cup long grain rice (uncooked)
2	tablespoons chopped parsley
1/4	cup chopped green pepper
1/4	cup chopped onion
1/4	teaspoon cinnamon
1/4	teaspoon allspice
1/4	teaspoon pepper
1	cup tomato juice
1	cup grated sharp cheddar cheese

Grease a 9 x 13 inch baking dish. Arrange half the tomatoes on the bottom. Arrange half the zucchini over tomatoes and sprinkle with 1/2 teaspoon salt. In a bowl, combine beef, rice, parsley, green pepper, onion, 1 teaspoon salt, spices and tomato juice. Mix until well blended and pat into casserole. Top with remaining zucchini and tomatoes and sprinkle with remaining 1/2 teaspoon salt. Cover and bake at 375 degrees for 1-1/2 hours or until vegetables are tender. Remove cover, sprinkle with grated cheese and bake about 15 minutes longer. Serves 4 to 6.

BEER BALLS

2	pounds ground beef
1	medium onion, finely chopped
1/2	cup oatmeal
2	eggs
1	cup tomato sauce
1/2	cup beer
	salt and pepper

Roll into balls about size of walnuts. Bake on cookie sheet at 350 degrees for about 20 minutes. Drain well.

Mix:

2	cups catsup
1	(11 ounce) bottle or can of beer
1/4	cup Worcestershire sauce
1/4	cup sugar
	salt and pepper

Mix all together and bring to a boil. Add meat balls and simmer in crock pot or other for 4 hours, stirring occasionally.

MEAL IN ONE

Brown:

1-1/2	pounds ground beef and
1/2	cup chopped onion

Add:

1	can cream of mushroom soup
1	can tomato soup
1/2	cup water
1	package (9 ounce) frozen green beans (cooked)
1	cup sliced carrots (cooked)

Pour into shallow baking dish. Spoon on and spread 3 cups mashed potatoes over top of casserole. Sprinkle with shredded mild cheese. Bake 30 minutes at 350 degrees. Good hearty meal, serve with salad for an easy menu.

HUNTER'S STEW

1	pound wide noodles
1	large can tomatoes*
1	can whole kernel corn*
4	small onions, chopped
1	small can mushrooms, drained
2	pounds ground beef
1	green pepper, chopped
1	package grated cheese

Brown meat, onion and green pepper. Mix together all juices and combine with rest of ingredients. Place in a baking dish, cover with the grated cheese and bake in a 350 degree oven until cheese is bubbly and brown. *Cook the tomatoes and corn together for awhile before mixing with rest of ingredients.

MEAT BALLS IN BUTTERMILK SAUCE

1	egg, beaten
1-1/2	pounds hamburger
1	small onion, finely chopped
1/3	cup celery (optional)
3	tablespoons green pepper, chopped
1	cup cooked rice
1	teaspoon salt
1/2	teaspoon pepper

Mix together and roll in balls. Place in casserole.

Sauce:

1	can mushroom soup
1	small can mushrooms (optional)
1	soup can of buttermilk

Mix well and pour over meatballs. Bake 1 hour at 350 degrees.

CABBAGE ROLLS

1	pound ground beef
1/4	cup fine chopped onion
1/3	cup raw rice
	salt and pepper to taste
	garlic (optional)

Mix above ingredients and form 5 to 6 balls for cabbage rolls. Choose cabbage with nice large leaves. Cut leaves from head and lay in a pan of hot water until limp enough to wrap around the meat, about 5 to 10 minutes. Place meat in leaves and roll up. Lay in a pan and add 1 can whole tomatoes or about 2 cups tomato juice. Add enough water to not quite cover the rolls. Salt and pepper, cover and stew until cabbage is done, about 1 to 1-1/2 hours.

BEEF AND BEANS

1	pound ground beef
2	cans (16 ounce each) pork and beans in tomato sauce
1 -1/2	tablespoons instant minced onion
1/3	cup chili sauce
1	tablespoon molasses
1	tablespoon mustard
1/2	teaspoon salt

Cook ground beef in skillet on grill or camp stove until light brown. Drain. Stir in remaining ingredients. Heat till bubbly, about 10 minutes.

EASY HAMBURGER CASSEROLE

1 to	
1-1/2	pounds hamburger
1	can cream of mushroom or cream of chicken soup
1	package dry onion soup
	Tater Tots (frozen)

Press hamburger into 13 x 9 inch pan. Sprinkle dry onion soup over hamburger. Pour soup over mixture. Cover with Tater Tots. Bake at 350 degrees for 1 hour.

MACARONI BEEF SKILLET SUPPER

1	cup elbow macaroni (cooked)
2	pounds lean ground beef
1	cup diced onion
1	clove garlic, mashed
2	tablespoons salad oil
1	can (8 ounce) tomato sauce
1	cup catsup
2	cans (4-1/3 ounce each) mushrooms
2	tablespoons Worcestershire sauce
1	teaspoon salt
1/2	teaspoon Italian seasoning
1/4	teaspoon monosodium glutamate
	dash of black pepper

Cook macaroni. Saute ground beef in salad oil with onion and garlic. Add tomato sauce, catsup, mushrooms, Worcestershire, salt, Italian seasoning and monosodium glutamate. Bring to a boil and add macaroni. Serves 6. With a green salad and fruit, makes a great meal.

WHIPPED HAMBURGERS

1	pound ground beef
2	tablespoons flour
1/2	teaspoon Worcestershire sauce
1/4	teaspoon pepper
1	teaspoon salt
1/2	onion, minced
	pinch thyme
	pinch marjoram
	pinch sage
1-1/4	cups diluted evaporated milk (little more milk than water)

Put meat in a large bowl and add all ingredients except milk. Whip the mixture with an electric beater. Add the milk slowly, beating constantly. When all the milk has been absorbed, cover bowl and let stand in refrigerator for a few hours. Drop in mounds on a hot greased skillet or griddle. Make bigger mounds if using for buns.

BEEF AND BEAN CASSEROLE

Brown 1-1/2 pounds hamburger

Add:

1	clove garlic, sliced thin
1-1/4	cups minced onion
1	chopped green pepper
1	teaspoon chili powder

Cook 5 minutes and remove from heat.

Add:

2	cups canned kidney beans
2	cups canned tomatoes
3/4	cup uncooked rice

Stir to blend well. Bake at 350 degrees for 1-1/4 hours or until rice is tender.

CRUNCHY EGG FOO YORK

1	pound hamburger or sausage

Brown, crumble and drain.

In medium bowl mix:

4	eggs, beaten
1	can bean sprouts, drained
1	small onion, diced or 1 bunch green onions, diced
2	tablespoons flour
1/2	teaspoon salt
	garlic powder (optional)

Stir in meat. Cook this mixture as patties. Stir mixture each time you spoon a patty on the grill. Also, spread patty out. Use a bit of cooking oil in pan if not teflon coated. Brown on each side and serve with sauce.

Sauce:

Dissolve a beef bouillon cube in 1 cup boiling water. In small cup mix:

2	tablespoons cornstarch
1	tablespoon soy sauce
2	tablespoons water
1/4	teaspoon ginger

Add to bouillon. Bring to a boil stirring constantly. Serve hot.

INDIVIDUAL MEAT LOAVES

1	pound ground beef
1	tablespoon horseradish
1	tablespoon dehydrated onion or onion flakes
1	teaspoon salt
1/2	cup mashed potatoes
2	beaten eggs

Mix first 5 ingredients together. Stir in 2 beaten eggs. Spoon into 12 small cupcake pans. Bake at 400 degrees for 20 minutes.

BEEF MACARONI CASSEROLE

1-1/2	pounds ground beef
1	tablespoon flour
1/2	envelope onion soup mix
1	(8 ounce) can tomato sauce
1	cup water
1	cup sweet and sour sauce
1	cup raw macaroni (cooked)
1/2	cup grated cheddar cheese (or more)

Brown meat in large skillet and drain off excess fat. Mix flour and soup mix together and stir into meat. Stir in tomato sauce, water and sweet and sour sauce. Let simmer covered about 5 minutes. Stir in cooked macaroni. Put in 3 quart casserole, sprinkle with cheese and bake about 15 to 20 minutes in pre-heated 400 degree oven. If you like, add a 4 ounce can of sliced and drained mushrooms. This is a simple dish, but well liked by men who do not like casseroles.

BEEF ENCHILADAS

2	pounds hamburger
1/2	cup chopped onion
1/2	cup green chilies
1	cup chopped mushrooms
1/4	teaspoon cumin
1/4	teaspoon chili powder
	salt and pepper to taste
2	packages enchilada sauce mix
	flour tortillas
1	pound (about) cheddar cheese

Brown the hamburger with the onions. Pour off any grease. Add the next 4 ingredients. Salt and pepper to taste. Mix the sauce according to directions. Pour 2 cups of sauce into the hamburger mixture. Fill each tortilla shell with hamburger mixture. Add grated cheddar cheese to each enchilada. Roll each one up and place in a greased and floured pan. Pour the rest of the sauce over the top. Sprinkle with any remaining cheese. Bake at 375 degrees for 20 minutes. Makes 10 large ones.

QUICK SLOPPY JOES

1-1/2	pounds ground beef
2	(6 ounce) cans tomato sauce
1	(6 ounce) can water
1	onion, thinly sliced
1	tablespoon chili powder salt and pepper to taste
2/3	teaspoon Accent (brings out flavor)

Brown ground beef. Add onion and saute. Add remaining ingredients and heat thoroughly. Serve on hamburger buns.

TACO PLATTER

1	pound ground beef, browned
3/4	cup cooked rice
1	medium onion, diced
1	can stewed tomatoes
1	small can tomato sauce
1	large package Fritos

Brown ground beef. Add cooked rice, onion, stewed tomatoes and tomato sauce. Simmer. Put 3/4 package Fritos on a platter and top with meat and rice mixture. Top with shredded lettuce and grated cheese. Serve with taco sauce. Serves 4 to 5.

PIZZA WITCHES

1-1/2	pounds ground beef
1	pound sharp cheddar cheese, grated
1	medium onion, chopped fine
1	can black olives, drained and chopped fine
1	can tomato soup
1/2	cup salad oil
1/2	teaspoon oregano

Do not leave anything out. Brown ground beef and drain off fat. Mix all ingredients well and let stand overnight to blend. Spoon onto hamburger buns or hard rolls. Do not butter. Broil until cheese bubbles and bread is light brown. (Do not add water to tomato soup.)

TIM'S SPAGHETTI

1-1/2	pounds ground beef
1	small onion, diced
1	small green pepper, diced
1/8	pound mushrooms, sliced
1	can (15 ounce) tomato sauce
1	can (6 ounce) tomato paste
3/4	teaspoon garlic
1/2	teaspoon salt
1/2	teaspoon pepper
1	teaspoon Italian seasoning
1/4	teaspoon celery seasoning (may use fresh celery instead)
1/4 to	
1/2	teaspoon chili powder
	pinch sugar

Brown ground beef. Mix in vegetables and simmer till tender. (Don't overcook vegetables). Add tomato sauce, tomato paste and spices. Mix well. Taste after about 15 minutes. More garlic and Italian seasoning may be added. Let simmer for 1 hour. Serve over spaghetti. Serves 6 to 8.

SAUCY TACO PIZZA

2   pounds lean hamburger
1   medium onion, chopped
1   cup taco sauce
1   (4 ounce) can green chilies, drained and chopped
1/2   cup ripe olives
1   (8 ounce) package refrigerated crescent rolls
        (homemade crust below)
1   medium tomato, diced
1-1/2 cups corn chips, crushed and divided
1   cup cheddar cheese, shredded
1   cup sour cream
1   cup shredded lettuce
1   avocado, peeled and sliced

In skillet, brown ground beef with onion. Drain off liquid. Add taco sauce, green chilies and olives. Pre-heat oven to 375 degrees. Separate crescent rolls into 8 triangles and press into pizza pan to form crust (or use homemade crust). Sprinkle 1 cup of crushed chips evenly over dough. Spread meat mixture evenly over chips, then the sour cream. Cover with shredded cheese then sprinkle with remaining chips. Bake at 375 degrees for 20 to 25 minutes until crust is golden. Serve in wedges and pass the lettuce, tomatoes and avocado.

KRIS'S PIZZA CRUST

2   cups lukewarm water
2   packages yeast
1/2   cup dry milk
6   tablespoons sugar
2   teaspoons salt
1/2   cup oil
6   cups flour

Add and mix in order given. Makes 3-16 inch pizzas.

TOSTADO PIZZA

2   tablespoons yellow cornmeal
2   cups biscuit mix
1/2   cup cold water
1   pound ground beef
3/4   cup water
3   tablespoons canned green chilies, seeded and chopped
1   envelope taco seasoning mix
1   can (15-1/2 ounce) refried beans
1   cup shredded sharp American cheese
1   cup shredded lettuce
1   tomato, chopped
1/2   cup chopped onion

Generously grease a 12 inch pizza pan. Sprinkle with the cornmeal. In a bowl combine biscuit mix and 1/2 cup cold water. Stir with fork till dough follows fork around bowl. Turn out on lightly floured surface. Knead 5 or 6 times. Roll to 14 inches and pat into prepared pizza pan. Crimp edges. Brown meat in skillet and drain off excess fat. Add 3/4 cup water, chilies and taco seasoning mix and bring to boil. Reduce heat and simmer, uncovered, 15 minutes or until thick. Spread beans on dough and top with meat mixture. Bake at 450 degrees for 18 to 20 minutes. Top with cheese and bake about 4 minutes more, till cheese is melted. Cut in 6 wedges and garnish with fresh green chili peppers if desired. Pass around tomato, lettuce and onion. Drizzle with taco sauce if desired. Makes 6 servings.

CHEESEBURGER PIE

1   pound ground beef
1-1/2 cups chopped onion
1/2   teaspoon salt
1/4   teaspoon pepper
1   cup milk
3/4   cup biscuit mix
2   eggs
1-2   tomatoes, sliced
1   cup shredded cheese

Grease a 9 inch pie pan. Brown onion and beef and drain. Stir in salt and pepper and spread in pan. Blend eggs, milk and biscuit mix for 15 seconds in blender. Pour over hamburger mixture and bake at 400 degrees for 25 minutes. Top with tomato slices and cheese. Bake 5 minutes more. Cool 5 minutes before serving.

CHINESE CASSEROLE

Don't stir layer in casserole.

First layer:

| 1 | pound ground meat, browned |

Second layer:

| 1 | cup chopped onion |

Third layer:

1	cup chopped celery
1	can water chestnuts, sliced
1	can cream of mushroom soup

Sprinkle 1 can Chinese fried noodles over top and press in slightly. Cover loosely with foil and bake at 350 degrees for 30 minutes. Serve with soy sauce.

HAMBURGER CORN-PONE PIE

1	pound ground beef
1	can kidney beans
1	large can tomatoes
1	teaspoon Worcestershire sauce
2	teaspoons chili powder
3/4	teaspoon salt
1	onion, chopped
1	package jiffy corn bread mix (or homemade)

Brown meat and onions. Drain. Add seasonings and tomatoes, cover and simmer for 15 minutes. Add beans. Pour meat mixture into casserole and top with cornbread batter. Bake at 425 degrees for 30 minutes.

SUPER NACHOS

1/2	pound hamburger
1/2	pound sausage
1	large onion, chopped
1	large can refried beans
1	can (4 ounce) chopped green chilies
1-1/2	cups shredded Monterey jack cheese
1-1/2	cups cheddar cheese
3/4	cup taco sauce
1	small can black olives, sliced or chopped
1	pint sour cream
1	ripe avocado nacho chips

Crumble hamburger and sausage in fry pan. Add salt to taste and onion. Brown and set aside. Spread refried beans in oblong pan and top with drained meat mixture. Sprinkle chilies over meat and spread cheese evenly over top. Drizzle with taco sauce and bake uncovered, at 400 degrees for 20 minutes. Mix sour cream and mashed avocado together until smooth. Spread over cheese and top with black olives. Serve with chips and dig in.

BEEF PUT-TOGETHER

1	pound ground beef
1/2	onion, chopped
1/2	green pepper, chopped
1	clove garlic, chopped
1/2	cup uncooked rice
1	large can tomatoes, chopped
	dash cayenne pepper
	salt

Brown ground beef, stirring to break into bite-size pieces. Add onion, green pepper, garlic and rice. Cook until onion is slightly transparent. Add tomatoes, cayenne and salt to taste. Simmer covered, 1/2 hour or until rice is tender. Serve with tossed green salad.

SATURDAY NIGHT CASSEROLE

1/2	cup chopped onion
1	pound ground beef
1	(16 ounce) can whole kernel corn
1	(8 ounce) package softened cream cheese
1	(10-1/2 ounce) can cream of mushroom soup
1	(2 ounce) jar chopped pimiento
1	teaspoon salt

Combine onion and ground beef in a 2 quart casserole. Microwave 2-1/2 minutes on high, stir and microwave an additional 2-1/2 minutes. In a separate bowl, combine remaining ingredients and mix well. Add to meat and onion, stirring to blend. Cover and microwave 8 minutes.
Serves 6 to 8.

CHILI CASSEROLE

3	medium potatoes
1	(30 ounce) can chili without beans
3	tablespoons butter
1	small can mushrooms
	Swiss and American cheese

Grease a 13 x 9 x 2 inch pan. Slice potatoes thinly and place in bottom of pan. Melt butter and drizzle over potatoes. In a large saucepan, heat chili and mushrooms. Slice cheese and place over top of potatoes. Pour hot chili over cheesed potatoes and then top with more cheese. Bake at 350 degrees 45 to 55 minutes until potatoes are tender.

CHICKEN ORIENTAL

1	(2-1/2-3 pound) Washington fryer, cut up
1/4	cup butter or margarine
1	(#2) can pineapple chunks
1/4	cup brown sugar
2	tablespoons corn starch
1/2	teaspoon salt
1/3	cup vinegar
1	tablespoon soy sauce
1	tablespoon sesame seeds
1	can (4 ounce) sliced mushrooms
1	small green pepper, thinly sliced
1/2	medium onion, thinly sliced

Brown chicken pieces slowly in butter. Cover and cook for 20 minutes.

Remove lid and cook 20 minutes longer. While chicken is browning, drain syrup from pineapple and measure 1 cup. Heat syrup to boiling and stir in mixture of brown sugar, salt, cornstarch and vinegar. Stir constantly until sauce thickens. Add pineapple chunks and remaining ingredients. Continue to simmer on low heat, stirring occasionally to prevent sticking. Pour sauce over chicken and simmer for 15 minutes. Serve with steamed rice. Makes about 4 servings.

FRUITED CHICKEN

3/4	cup flour
1/4	teaspoon salt
1/4	teaspoon celery salt
1/4	teaspoon garlic salt
1/4	teaspoon nutmeg
1	(3 pound) frying chicken
1/2	cup butter
1	(20 ounce) can pineapple tidbits (drain and reserve)
3	tablespoons flour
1	tablespoon sugar
1/3	cup soy sauce

Shake chicken in paper bag with flour and spices. Brown chicken in the butter and then place in baking dish. Save pineapple juice and place tidbits around chicken in dish. Stir the 3 tablespoons flour and 1 tablespoon sugar into the butter remaining in skillet. Add the pineapple juice and soy sauce and cook till mixture thickens and bubbles. Spoon over chicken, cover and bake in 350 degree oven for 1 hour.

CHICKEN CHOW MEIN

1	small onion, chopped
2	stalks celery, chopped
2	pounds chicken, cooked and diced
1	can cream of mushroom soup
3/4	cup chicken broth
	small can chow mein noodles

Saute onion and celery until tender. Add soup, broth and chicken. Mix well. Add 1 cup noodles to mixture and pour into a buttered casserole dish. Bake for 35 minutes at 350 degrees. Add 1/2 cup noodles and bake an additional 10 minutes.

TURKEY-RICE SPECIAL

A good way to use leftover turkey. Chicken may also be used.

1/2   pound pork sausage
1/2   cup chopped celery
3/4   cup chopped onion
3/4   cup uncooked rice
2   cans chicken noodle soup
3/4   cup water
2   tablespoons chopped pimiento (optional)
1   cup sliced turkey or chicken

Saute sausage, celery and onion until meat is brown. Put into 11 x 7 inch casserole. Add remaining ingredients. Cover casserole with foil and bake at 325 degrees for 45 to 55 minutes. Remove foil and continue baking 10 to 15 minutes more. May wish to garnish top of casserole with 1/2 cup sliced almonds. Serves 6 to 8.

ROAST ORANGE-STUFFED CHICKEN

3   chickens (2-1/2 to 3 pounds each)
1   can (11 ounce) mandarin oranges, drained
1   cup walnuts, chopped
2   cups apples, chopped
2   cups herb-seasoned stuffing mix
1/3   cup orange marmalade
6   slices bacon

Stuff chickens just before roasting. To make stuffing, combine mandarin orange segments, walnuts, apples and stuffing mix. Mix well. Add orange marmalade and toss. Fill each wishbone area with about 1/4 cup stuffing and fasten neck skins to backs. Fill each body cavity with about 2 cups stuffing. Tie drumsticks to tails. Place chickens, breast side up, on rack in shallow roasting pan. Place 2 slices of bacon on top of each chicken. Add no water. Roast at 375 degrees, uncovered, until drumstick meat feels soft, 1-1/4 to 1-3/4 hours. Garnish with parsley, orange slices and cranberries. 12 servings.

CHICKEN CORDON BLEU

4   chicken breasts
4   slices boiled ham
4   slices Swiss cheese
1   package Shake and Bake for chicken
1   can cream of chicken soup
1   can chicken broth

Remove skin and bone from chicken breasts. Pound until thin. Place a slice of ham and a slice of cheese on each chicken breast and roll up as for jelly roll. Use toothpicks to hold together. Roll in shake and bake mix and bake for 20 minutes uncovered, at 400 degrees. Mix together 1/2 can cream of chicken soup and 1/4 cup of chicken broth. Pour over chicken rolls and continue baking 30 minutes longer.

CHICKEN ORE'

Roll a chicken in flour and fry for 20 minutes. Place in baking pan and bake in moderate oven for 20 minutes longer.

Add:

    syrup from 1 can pineapple
1/4   cup brown sugar
2   tablespoons corn starch
1/2   teaspoon salt
1/3   cup vinegar

Heat above ingredients until thick.

Add:

    pineapple chunks
1   tablespoon soy sauce
1   (4 ounce) can mushrooms
1/2   green pepper
1/2   sliced onion

Simmer and pour over chicken. Bake for 10 minutes longer. Very good with sauce served over rice.

FINGER DRUMSTICKS

3	pounds chicken wings or legs
1/2	cup sugar
3	tablespoons cornstarch
1	teaspoon salt
1/2	teaspoon ground ginger
1/4	teaspoon pepper
3/4	cup water
1/3	cup lemon juice
1/4	cup soy sauce

Cut tips off wings and discard. Divide each wing in half by cutting through joint with sharp knife. Place in single layer on broiler pan rack. Bake at 400 degrees, turning once after 30 minutes. Mix sugar, cornstarch, salt, ginger and pepper in small pan. Stir in water, lemon juice and soy sauce. Cook, stirring constantly until it thickens. Boil 3 minutes. Brush sauce over chicken. Continue baking, turning and brushing sauce on several times, about 40 minutes.

CRUNCHY FRIED CHICKEN

1	(2-1/2 to 3-1/2 pound) fryer, cut up flour
1	egg, beaten
2	tablespoons water
1	cup crushed corn flakes
1/2	cup flour
	salt and pepper
	paprika
1/2	cup butter or margarine

Dust chicken with flour. Combine egg and water. Dip chicken in mixture, then into blended crumbs and flour. Sprinkle with salt, pepper and paprika. Cook in hot butter until golden brown on all sides. Lower heat and cook, turning occasionally for 30 to 45 minutes until tender. Yields 4 servings.

JEANNE'S DOWN ON THE FARM CASSEROLE

2	pounds (6 cups) yellow summer squash
1/4	cup chopped onions
1	can condensed cream of chicken soup
1	cup dairy sour cream
1	cup shredded carrots
4	cups herb-seasoned stuffing mix
1/2	cup melted butter
2	cups cooked chicken

Cook squash and onions in boiling salted water 5 minutes. Combine soup and sour cream. Stir in carrots and chicken. Fold in squash and onion. Combine stuffing mix and melted butter. Spread half of stuffing mixture in bottom of 12 x 8 x 2 inch baking dish. Spoon all of vegetable mixture on top. Sprinkle remaining half of stuffing mixture over vegetables. Bake at 350 degrees for 25 to 30 minutes. Serves 6 to 8. This recipe was developed for the Washington State Dairy Women's Association in Cowlitz County.

Microwave Instructions:

Add 1/2 cup water to dressing. Use a 20 ounce package of French style green beans instead of squash. Cook vegetables in 2 quart casserole 8 to 10 minutes. Drain vegetables. Stir soup and sour cream into vegetables. Combine stuffing mix, butter and water. Spread half of mixture in a 12 x 8 x 2 inch baking dish. Spread vegetable mixture over stuffing. Sprinkle remaining stuffing over vegetables. Insert probe. Microwave on roast to 160 degrees or 15 to 20 minutes until heated through. Because of sour cream, dish needs delicate speed setting.

PORK CHOP DISH

4	pork chops
4	cups sliced potatoes
1	can mushroom soup
	milk
2	onions, sliced
	salt and pepper to taste

Brown pork chops and set aside. Put potatoes in bottom of greased casserole. Mix can of mushroom soup with 2/3 can of milk, onions, salt and pepper. Pour this mixture over potatoes and top with the browned chops. Bake at 375 degrees for about 1-1/4 hours.

CELIA'S PORK AND SAUERKRAUT

2	slices bacon, diced
1	large onion, chopped
2-3	clove garlic, minced
3	tablespoons flour
1-1/2	cups water
1	can sauerkraut, drained
3	medium potatoes, sliced thick
3	pork steaks

In large casserole over medium heat, cook bacon until lightly browned. Add onion and garlic and cook till lightly browned. Add flour and cook until flour is browned. Add water and stir constantly until mixture is thickened to a soft gravy, using a little more water if necessary. Add sauerkraut and mix well. Layer potatoes over sauerkraut mixture and top with pork steaks which have been lightly browned. Cover and cook in medium oven (350 degrees) until potatoes and pork are done, about 40 to 45 minutes. Serves 3.

HARVIES SPAGHETTI

4-5	pound pork roast (pork hocks are good too!)
3	cans tomato sauce
3	cans tomato paste
3	onions
2	cloves garlic
1	can mushrooms
1	tablespoon oregano
1	tablespoon chili powder
1	tablespoon sweet basil
1	tablespoon sugar
1	teaspoon rosemary
	salt and pepper

Saute chopped onions and garlic until light brown. Add tomato sauce and paste with 3/4 can water for each can used. Add spices and simmer, covered, for 2 hours. Brown the meat. Add to sauce and simmer until meat is cooked, about 2 hours. Serve with ravioli or mostaccioli.

PORK CHOPS WITH HICKORY DRESSING

5	loin chops (1 inch thick)
1	small onion, chopped
1	clove garlic, minced
1	tablespoon vegetable oil
1-1/2	cups soft bread crumbs
3/4	teaspoon salt
1/4	cup parsley, chopped
1	egg, beaten
3/4	cup hickory flavored catsup
1	(8 ounce) can tomato sauce

Saute onions and garlic in skillet. Combine with bread crumbs, salt, parsley and egg. Mix catsup and tomato sauce together and add 1 cup of it to crumb mixture. In another skillet, brown the pork chops. When brown, lift out and arrange dressing in the bottom of skillet. Place pork chops on top, cover, and bake in oven at 350 degrees for 30 minutes. Uncover and pour on remaining sauce mixture. Bake uncovered 30 minutes longer.

SAUCY TWIST PORK DISH

4	ounces uncooked corkscrew shaped macaroni
1/2	cup onion, finely chopped
1/3	cup green pepper, chopped
1	tablespoon butter
1	can (12 ounce) pork luncheon meat, cubed
1	can (10-1/2 ounce) cream of mushroom soup
1/2	cup catsup
1/3	cup shredded cheddar cheese

Heat oven to 400 degrees. Cook macaroni per directions. Drain. In large skillet, cook and stir onion and green pepper in butter until onion is tender. Stir in macaroni and remaining ingredients. Cover and bake for 30 minutes.

BAKED PORK CHOPS

4-6 loin pork chops. Salt, pepper and flour lightly each chop. Fry until brown. Arrange in layers in a greased baking dish; 3 large potatoes, thinly sliced; and 2 small onions, thinly sliced. Season lightly with salt and pepper. Place chops on top. Mix a can of your favorite soup with an equal amount of water and pour over the pork chops. Bake at 375 degrees, covered, for about 50 minutes or until potatoes are tender. Uncover and brown if desired.

RICE HOT DISH

1	pound pork sausage
6	celery stalks
1	medium onion

Brown till onions and celery are soft.

Add:

2	cups raw rice
2	packages chicken noodle soup mix
6	cups water
1	small can bean sprouts

Mix all together in a very large pan or 2 casserole dishes. Add 1/2 cup slivered almonds on top. Bake 1 hour at 350 degrees. When done, pour 1 can of undiluted mushroom soup over the top and mix in. Stir rice dish a few times while baking. Good for a big group.

BAKED PORK CHOPS

4	pork chops
1/3	cup finely diced celery
2	tablespoons brown sugar
	juice of 1/2 lemon
1/2	teaspoon mustard
1/2	teaspoon salt
1/8	teaspoon pepper
2	(8 ounce) cans tomato sauce
1/2	cup water

Brown chops in fat. Place in shallow greased baking dish. Sprinkle with celery, brown sugar, lemon juice and seasonings. Pour tomato sauce and water over chops. Cover baking dish and bake at 350 degrees for 1-1/4 hours or until chops are tender. Yields 4 servings.

TUNA CASSEROLE

4	cups sliced potatoes
1/2	cup chopped onions
1	large can tuna
1	can mushroom soup
1/2	green pepper (optional)

Boil potatoes until nearly done. Drain. In separate bowl, add enough milk to the mushroom soup to make 2 cups. Add onion, green pepper and tuna. In a buttered casserole, add alternate layers of potatoes and tuna mix ending with tuna on top. Sprinkle with bread crumbs and bake for 20 to 25 minutes at 350 degrees.

QUICKLY BROILED SANDWICH

4	slices bread
1	can tuna (flaked and drained)
1	can cream of chicken soup
4	slices cheese

Combine tuna and undiluted can of soup. Spread evenly over bread. Place under broiler until bubbly. Remove and put a slice of cheese on each piece of bread. Return to broiler until evenly melted and slightly browned. Excellent with a tossed salad.

ETHEL'S CALICO BEANS

Mix together and saute:

1/4	pound bacon (cut fine)
1	cup chopped celery
8-1/2	cups onion, chopped
1	pound link sausage (fried and cut in 1 inch pieces)
2	cans pork and beans (large size)
1	can lima beans
1	can kidney beans
1	can butter beans
1	can garbanzo beans
1	cup catsup
1/4	cup vinegar
1/2	cup molasses
1	cup brown sugar
2	large apples (peeled and chopped fine)
	garlic powder
	salt and pepper to taste

Bake at 375 degrees for 45 minutes or longer. Add small amount of water if needed. Ham, wieners, etc. may be added if desired.

JIFFY BARBECUE HOT DOGS

1/2	cup chopped onions
1/2	cup chopped celery
2	tablespoons butter

Simmer in fry pan till tender.

Stir in:

1	cup catsup
1/3	cup water
1/4	cup brown sugar
3	tablespoons vinegar
1	tablespoon prepared mustard
1	tablespoon Worcestershire sauce
1	package hot dogs

Heat on top of stove or in 350 degree oven for 30 to 45 minutes. P.S. You can also use lunch meat cut in strips in place of the hot dogs.

SEAFOODS

SANDY'S SEAFOOD TIPS

Where possible, use the canned salmon liquid because it contains nutrients. Bones and skin can also be eaten. Bones of canned salmon are soft and can be mashed if desired.

If you don't care for the dark insides of oysters, cut them open and clean them. Rinse well. Cook or fry using your favorite recipe.

I only use the white meat on a tuna. The dark is full of a cod liver like tasting oil and my family prefers only the white meat.

Two easy ways to clean razor clams: (1) Take a knife and cut along the belly of the clam and shell and remove shell, or a better way (2) Pour hot water over clams and let set for a few minutes. The shells will loosen and you can remove them with your hands. Also, using this method loosens the scummy belly liner (as I call it). Rinse clams real good several times to make sure all the sand is out.

Stretch shrimp by splitting lengthwise. Cooks very quickly and is very good stir-fried with vegetables.

Freeze small amounts of leftover fish and shellfish in plastic bags. When you have a variety, thaw and mix to make a seafood sauce for spaghetti or fold into a cream sauce and bake in shells for seafood thermidor.

MARY'S SHRIMP CREOLE

1	pound cooked shrimp
1/2	can tomato paste
2-1/2	teaspoons flour
1/2	cup onions, chopped
3/8	cup salad oil
1/2	green pepper, cut in 1 inch squares
1/2	clove garlic, chopped
	salt and pepper to taste

Preheat fry pan to 360 degrees. Clean shrimp and dry thoroughly. Heat salad oil and flour to form roux. Brown slightly. Add onions and garlic and brown slightly in roux. Lower temperature of pan to 260 degrees and add shrimp. Stir the shrimp in roux until each piece is completely coated and none is left sticking to the pan. Add tomato paste and green pepper. Turn heat up to 300 degrees and stir gently until paste is sticking to the shrimp. Add 1/2 cup hot water, cover and simmer at about 220 degrees for 15 minutes. Then very gently pour in one more cup of hot water, being careful not to add it too fast. Simmer 20 minutes longer or until it has cooked down some. Serve over hot fluffy rice. I have used this recipe for over 30 years to the delight of my family and friends. I have no idea who originated this Creole recipe, but I do thank them and hope you can print this so all Washingtonians can enjoy this wonderful dish!

SHRIMP CREOLE

1-1/2	cups chopped onion
1	cup finely chopped celery
2	medium green peppers, finely chopped
2	cloves garlic, minced
1/4	cup butter
1	can (15 ounce) tomato sauce
1	cup water
2	teaspoons snipped parsley
1	tablespoon salt
1/8	teaspoon cayenne red pepper
2	bay leaves, crushed
14-16	ounces fresh or frozen cleaned raw shrimp
3	cups hot cooked rice

Cook and stir onion, green pepper and garlic in butter until onion is tender. Remove from heat. Stir in tomato sauce, water and seasonings. Simmer, uncovered for 10 minutes. Add water if needed. Stir in shrimp. Cover and cook over medium heat 10 to 20 minutes or until shrimp are pink and tender. Serve over rice. 6 servings.

SHRIMP COCKTAIL

1	can shrimp, drained
4-1/2	tablespoons lemon juice
3/4	cup catsup
1/2	teaspoon A-1 sauce
3/4	cup finely chopped celery
1/2	cup finely chopped sweet pickle
	horseradish to taste
	salt to taste

Mix. Chill several hours.

JAMBALAYA

1/8	pound (1/2 stick) margarine
1/4	pound mushrooms, sliced
1	cup chopped green pepper
1	cup onion slices
2	cups chicken broth
1	can (1 pound) tomatoes, undrained
2	medium cloves garlic, minced
1	teaspoon salt
1/4	teaspoon basil, crushed
1/8	teaspoon pepper
1/8	teaspoon thyme, crushed
1	teaspoon Worcestershire sauce
1-1/2	pounds large raw shrimp, shelled and deveined
1	cup uncooked rice
1	cup cooked chicken, cubed
1	cup cooked ham, cubed

Melt margarine in large heavy saucepan. Add mushrooms, green pepper and onion. Cook gently 5 minutes. Add chicken broth, tomatoes, garlic, salt, basil, pepper, thyme and Worcestershire sauce. Bring to a boil; add shrimp and rice. Cover and cook over low heat 15 minutes, stirring occasionally. Add chicken and ham. Cook until rice is tender and liquid is absorbed. Serve with French rolls. Serves 6.

DEVILED SHRIMP AND EGG CASSEROLE

6	hard boiled eggs, halved
2	tablespoons mayonnaise
1/8	teaspoon dry mustard
1/8	teaspoon pepper
3/4	teaspoon salt
1	cup shrimp
1	cup cooked mushrooms
2	tablespoons butter
1/4	cup flour
1-3/4	cups milk
1	cup grated cheese
1	tablespoon chives or green onions, chopped

Remove egg yolks and mix with mayonnaise, mustard, pepper and 1/4 teaspoon salt. Stuff into egg whites and place in buttered casserole. Cover with shrimp and mushrooms. Melt butter; blend in flour and remaining salt. Gradually add milk. Cook and stir until thickened and smooth. Add cheese and chives and pour over casserole. Bake at 350 degrees for 25 minutes. Yields 6 servings.

SUPER SHRIMP SALAD

3	cups water
1	pound large shrimp
1/4	pound lump crab meat
1/4	cup celery, chopped
1/2	cup green peppers, chopped
2-1/4	tablespoons sweet pickle, chopped
1	shallot, minced
1-1/2	teaspoon fresh parsley, minced
1/2	cup ripe olives, sliced
1/2	cup pimiento-stuffed olives, sliced
1	cup Italian salad dressing
2	tablespoons olive or walnut oil
1-1/2	teaspoons lemon juice
	leaf lettuce
1/2	medium head iceberg lettuce, coarsely shredded
2	medium tomatoes, cut into wedges

Bring water to a boil. Add shrimp and return to boil. Lower heat and simmer 3 to 5 minutes. Drain well and rinse with cold water. Peel and devein shrimp. Combine shrimp and next 11 ingredients in an airtight container. Cover and refrigerate overnight. Line a serving platter with leaf lettuce and top with iceberg lettuce. Spoon on shrimp mixture. Garnish with tomato wedges. Serves 4 to 6.

DELICIOUS SHRIMP JELLO

1	package (3 ounce) lemon or lime jello
1	cup tomato or V-8 juice
3/4	cup diced celery
1	can shrimp, well drained
1/2	cup coarsely broken walnuts

Dissolve jello with 1 cup boiling water. Stir in tomato juice. Cool in refrigerator. Add rest of ingredients and stir well. Place in square pan and refrigerate till set. Top servings with a bit of mayonnaise. Makes 8 medium servings.

SHRIMP POTATO SALAD

6	medium potatoes, cooked and cubed
6	hard cooked eggs, sliced
1	cup shrimp, broken into pieces
1	teaspoon parsley
1-1/2	teaspoons salt
1/2	teaspoon pepper
1	cup chopped celery
1	medium onion, chopped

Combine all ingredients, reserving a few pieces of egg and shrimp.

Dressing:

3	tablespoons milk
3	tablespoons wine or tarragon vinegar
1	cup salad dressing
	paprika

Mix milk and vinegar with salad dressing and beat. Pour over salad and mix well. Garnish with reserved egg, shrimp and paprika. Chill for 2 to 3 hours. Yields 6 to 8 servings.

RICE-SHRIMP SALAD

1	(8 ounce) package chicken rice a roni
2	green onions, diced thin
1/2	medium green pepper, chopped
8	pimiento stuffed olives, sliced
2	(6 ounce) jars marinated artichoke hearts
1/2	pound small shrimp meat
1/4	teaspoon curry powder
1/2	cup mayonnaise

Cook rice as directed; cool. Add onions, olives, green pepper and shrimp. Drain artichokes. Mix juices with curry powder and mayonnaise. Add artichokes to rice mixture. Mix all together lightly. Chill.

SWISS AND CRAB QUICHE

2	cups Jarlsburg swiss cheese
1	nine inch baked pie crust
1	cup fresh crab meat, cartilage removed
2	tablespoons fresh chives or chopped green onions
3	eggs, beaten
1	cup light cream
1	teaspoon grated lemon peel
1/4	teaspoon dry mustard
	pinch ground mace
1/4	cup sliced almonds

Spread half the cheese evenly over bottom of pastry shell. Top with crab meat. Sprinkle with chives or onion and cover with remaining cheese. Combine eggs, cream, lemon peel, dry mustard and mace. Pour evenly over crab meat. Top with sliced almonds. Bake in 400 degree oven for 15 minutes, then reduce heat to 325 degrees and bake for an additional 45 minutes or until set. Remove from oven and let stand for 10 minutes before serving. Makes 6-8 servings.

CRAB STUFFED MUSHROOMS

1	pound crab meat
24	large mushrooms
1	tablespoon flour
1/2	teaspoon salt
1/4	teaspoon lemon pepper
1/4	cup melted butter
1/2	cup light cream
1	tablespoon parsley
1	tablespoon sherry
2	tablespoons Parmesan cheese, grated
	dash paprika

Rinse mushrooms and dry. Remove stems and chop. Blend flour and seasonings into butter. Add cream gradually and cook until thick and smooth, stirring constantly. Add chopped mushroom stems, parsley and sherry. Mix well. Stir in crab meat. Stuff mushroom caps with crab mixture. Sprinkle with cheese and paprika. Place on well greased baking sheet and bake at 350 degrees 15 to 20 minutes. A very delicious and elegant dish!

OPAL'S DEVILED CRAB-RONI CASSEROLE

(All I can say about this dish is it is lickin' good!)

1	can crab meat (or equivalent fresh)
2	cups cooked shellroni
1	teaspoon lemon juice
	bread crumbs

Sprinkle crab flakes with lemon juice.

Make a sauce using:

2	tablespoons flour
2	tablespoons butter
1	teaspoon dry mustard
	few drops Tabasco sauce
1-1/2	cups milk
	dash of celery salt, onion salt and garlic salt

Combine and make like white sauce. Combine crab meat and shellroni. Place in casserole, alternating layers with sauce. Top with crumbs, a dash of paprika and chopped parsley. Bake at 350 degrees until mixture bubbles, then turn on broil until golden brown. Serves 6.

CRAB MEAT CASSEROLE

1	package (9 ounce) spaghetti
1-1/4	cups condensed cream of mushroom soup
3	tablespoons butter
1	cup milk
1/2	pound sharp American cheese, grated
1-1/2	cups crab meat, flaked
1/8	teaspoon pepper
	extra mushrooms may be added if desired

Cook spaghetti in boiling salted water until tender. Drain. Heat soup, stirring till smooth. Add butter and milk. When hot, remove from heat and stir in grated cheese, saving some to sprinkle on top. Combine cheese sauce with spaghetti, crab meat and pepper. Place in greased shallow casserole and sprinkle with remaining cheese. Bake at 400 degrees for 30 minutes. Serves 6.

CRAB BROCCOLI CASSEROLE

1	package frozen broccoli spears
2	cans (16 ounce each) King or Snow crab
1	can cream of celery soup
1	cup heaping, Pepperidge Farm cornbread stuffing mixed with 1/2 cup water
1/3	cup grated sharp cheddar cheese

In shallow casserole (1-1/2 quart) separate and layer partially thawed broccoli. Sprinkle with salt and pepper and half the celery soup. Spread undrained crab meat over soup. Top with stuffing mixture and remaining soup. Sprinkle with cheese. Bake uncovered at 350 degrees for 45 minutes. Serves 4 to 6.

CRAB DELIGHT

1	can cream of mushroom soup
1	envelope Knox gelatin
3	tablespoons cold water

Heat soup. Dissolve gelatin in cold water and add immediately to warm soup.

Blend:

3/4	cup mayonnaise
6	ounces soft cream cheese

Add to soup mixture and blend.

Add:

1	(7 ounce) can crab meat or fresh crab
1	cup finely diced celery
1	small onion, grated
3-4	drops Tabasco Sauce

Rinse mold in cold water and pour mixture into mold. Refrigerate overnight. Turn out of mold and serve with Ritz crackers.

CRAB OR SHRIMP CASSEROLE

1   (6-1/2 ounce) can crab or shrimp meat
1   cup diced celery
1   can cream of mushroom soup
1   (3 ounce) can chow mein noodles
1/2   teaspoon Worcestershire sauce

Combine all ingredients and place in buttered casserole. Bake at 325 degrees about 45 minutes.

RICE SEAFOOD CASSEROLE

1   cup celery, diced
1   medium onion, diced
1   green pepper, diced
2   tablespoons margarine
1   cup rice, cooked

Simmer celery, onion and green pepper in margarine for 5 minutes.

White Sauce:

1   tablespoon Worcestershire sauce
3   tablespoons margarine
1   tablespoon salt
3   tablespoons flour
2   cups milk

Cook together. Add vegetables to white sauce.

Add to sauce:

1   can crab meat
1   can tuna
1   can shrimp
1   (4 ounce) can mushrooms
1   cup mayonnaise

Line bottom of large baking dish with cooked rice. Pour seafood sauce over rice and cover with buttered cracker crumbs. Bake at 350 degrees for 30 to 40 minutes.

WILD RICE AND SEAFOOD CASSEROLE

1-1/4 pounds fresh mushrooms, sliced
1   cup chopped celery
1   green pepper, chopped
       butter
2   pounds fresh shrimp
2   pounds fresh crab
1   onion, chopped
1   jar pimiento, chopped
3   packages white and wild rice mix, cooked
2   cans cream of mushroom soup
1   cup milk

Almond Sauce:

1   cup slivered almonds
1/4   cup sherry
6   cups white sauce

Saute mushrooms, celery and green pepper in butter. Add shrimp, crab, onion, pimiento and rice. Dilute soup with milk. Stir into rice mixture and pour into casserole. Bake at 350 degrees for 45 minutes. Saute almonds in butter; add sherry. Blend with white sauce. Serve casserole with almond sauce. Serves 10 to 12.

TUNA, SHRIMP OR CRAB PIE

1   (6-1/2 ounce) can fish, drained
1   cup shredded cheese
1   (3 ounce) package cream cheese
1/4   cup minced onion
2   cups milk
4   eggs
1   cup biscuit mix
3/4   teaspoon salt
       dash nutmeg

Mix together fish, cheese, cream cheese and minced onion. Put mixture in greased 10 inch pie plate. Combine milk, eggs, biscuit mix, salt and nutmeg. Beat well and pour over fish mixture. Bake at 400 degrees 35 to 40 minutes. Cool 5 minutes and serve.

CRAB AND SHRIMP CASSEROLE

1	cup thinly sliced celery
1/2	cup chopped onion
1/2	teaspoon curry powder
3	tablespoons butter
1	tablespoon lemon juice
1	cup chopped ripe olives
1	can (7-1/2 ounce) crab meat
1	can (4-1/2 ounce) shrimp
1	package (10 ounce) frozen peas
3	cups cooked rice
1/2	cup sour cream
1/2	cup mayonnaise
	narrow strips of cheddar cheese

Cook celery and onions in butter and curry powder until tender. Add lemon juice, olives, crab (drained), shrimp (rinsed and drained) and defrosted peas. Combine with rice, sour cream and mayonnaise. Turn into lightly greased casserole. Top with cheese strips. Bake at 375 degrees about 25 minutes, until cheese melts and mixture is bubbly.

SHRIMP AND TUNA BAKE

2/3	cup regular rice
1	(9 ounce) package frozen cut green beans
1	(10 ounce) can condensed cream of celery soup
1/2	cup milk
	dash cayenne
2	tablespoons canned pimientos, chopped
1/4	teaspoon dried thyme, crushed
1	(6 to 7 ounce) can tuna, drained and broken into chunks
1	(4-1/2 ounce) can shrimp, drained
1	cup canned french fried onions

Cook rice and set aside. Cook beans, drain and set aside. Mix soup, milk, pimiento, thyme and cayenne till smooth. Stir half of the soup mixture into rice, then fold in tuna. Turn into 1-1/2 quart casserole. Spread beans over rice and top with shrimp. Pour remaining soup mixture over all. Bake, covered, at 325 degrees for 25 to 30 minutes. Sprinkle onions on top and bake, uncovered about 5 minutes more. Serves 6. This dish, served with a tossed green salad, makes your meal very colorful, simple and nutritious!

FAR EAST TUNA CASSEROLE

1	medium onion, chopped
4	tablespoons butter
2	(10-1/2 ounce) cans condensed cream of mushroom soup
2	(7 ounce) cans waterpacked tuna, drained and flaked
1	(5 ounce) can water chestnuts, drained and thinly sliced
1	(13 ounce) can pineapple tidbits, drained
2	cups thinly sliced celery
2	(3 ounce) cans chow mein noodles
3	tablespoons soy sauce
1	teaspoon onion salt
1/4	teaspoon hot pepper sauce

Saute onion lightly in 2 tablespoons butter. Add 1/2 cup water and next 6 ingredients. Put in shallow 2 quart baking dish. Melt remaining butter and mix with last 3 ingredients. Spread on mixture and bake at 350 degrees about 45 minutes. Serves 6 to 8.

BIG CATCH SALMON CASSEROLE

1	can cream of celery soup
1/2	cup salad dressing
1/4	cup milk
1/4	cup shredded Parmesan cheese
1	can (1 pound) salmon, drained and flaked
1	(10 ounce) package frozen peas, cooked
1	teaspoon chopped onion
4	ounces (2 cups) noodles, cooked

Combine soup with salad dressing, milk and cheese, blending well. Stir in salmon, peas, noodles and onion. Pour into 1-1/2 quart casserole and bake at 350 degrees for 25 minutes. Serves 6.

SALMON QUICHE

Prepare the crust and refrigerate it ahead of time. Then the filling takes only 10 minutes.

Crust for Salmon Quiche:

1	cup whole wheat flour
2/3	cup sharp cheese, shredded
1/4	cup chopped almonds
1/2	teaspoon salt
1/4	teaspoon paprika
6	tablespoons oil

Combine whole wheat flour, cheese, almonds, salt and paprika in a bowl. Stir in oil. Set aside 1/2 cup of crust. Press remaining mixture into bottom and up sides of a 9 inch pie pan. Bake crust at 400 degrees for 10 minutes. Remove from oven and reduce oven temperature to 325 degrees.

Salmon Quiche Filling:

1	(15-1/2 ounce) can salmon
1	cup sour cream
3	eggs, beaten
1/4	cup mayonnaise
1/2	cup sharp cheddar cheese, shredded
1	tablespoon grated onion
1/4	teaspoon dill weed
3	drops hot pepper sauce

Drain salmon, reserving liquid. If necessary, add enough water to reserved liquid to make 1/2 cup. Flake salmon, removing bones and skin; set aside. In bowl, blend together eggs, sour cream, mayonnaise and reserved salmon liquid. Stir in salmon, 1/2 cup cheese, onions, dill weed and hot sauce. Spoon filling into crust. Sprinkle with reserved crust mixture. Bake at 325 degrees for 45 minutes or till firm in center. Makes 6 servings.

SALMON LOAF

2	cans (16 ounce) salmon (take skin and bones out)
3	eggs
1-1/2	cups liquid (salmon juice and milk)
3	cups bread crumbs
2	tablespoons lemon juice
1/2	onion, chopped
1/2	teaspoon dill weed
1/4	teaspoon salt
1/4	teaspoon pepper

Heat oven to 350 degrees. Grease a 9 x 5 x 3 inch loaf pan. Flake salmon and remove bones and skin. Blend in eggs. Stir in remaining ingredients. Spoon lightly into pan. Bake 45 minutes. Garnish with lemon wedges. Serves 8.

BARBECUED SALMON WITH SPECIAL SAUCE

	whole salmon or steaks
1/4	cup cooking oil
1	cup honey
3/4	cup wine vinegar
1/4	cup Worcestershire sauce
1/4	cup soy sauce
1	teaspoon oregano
1	tablespoon dry mustard
1/2	teaspoon thyme
	garlic and onion salt to taste

Prepare sauce by mixing all ingredients except salmon. Simmer about 10 minutes to blend. Butterfly whole salmon or use steaks. Place on foil over hot charcoal. Baste with sauce frequently while cooking. Additional sauce may be served at the table.

BAKED SALMON WITH DRESSING

5	pound salmon (remove skin)
1	cup crackers
1/4	teaspoon poultry seasoning
1/4	cup melted butter
4	cups bread crumbs
1/3	cup chopped onion
2	teaspoons salt
1/2	cup water
1/4	pound sliced bacon

Mix together in order given except bacon. Slice fish open and fill with dressing. Place bacon slices over top. Bake at 400 degrees for 1 hour.

SALMON NOODLE CASSEROLE

4	tablespoons butter
2	ribs celery, sliced thin
2	green onions, chopped

Melt butter in 4 quart pan. Cook celery and onions until tender.

1/4	cup flour
	salt and pepper
3	cups milk
1	(3 ounce) package cream cheese
1	(8 ounce) package wide noodles
1	(7-3/4 ounce) can salmon

When celery and onions are tender, stir in flour and salt and pepper. Gradually stir in 3 cups milk and cook till slightly thickened. Stir in cream cheese until melted. Remove from heat. Cook noodles per directions. Stir noodles and salmon into sauce. Pour into 13 x 9 inch baking dish. Sprinkle with 1/4 cup dry bread crumbs mixed with 2 tablespoons melted butter. Bake at 350 degrees for 30 to 40 minutes.

SALMON AND RICE BAKE

1	pound can salmon, flaked
1	cup cooked rice
1/4	teaspoon salt or celery salt
2	eggs, beaten
1	tablespoon minced onion
1/2	cup bread crumbs
2	tablespoons green pepper, chopped

Mix and combine above ingredients and form into balls. In the bottom of a casserole dish, place 1 can mushroom soup and 1/2 soup can of water. Mix. Drop the salmon balls in the soup mix and bake at 350 degrees for about 30 minutes.

BAKED SALMON

30 minutes before cooking, season fish with salt, pepper and oregano. Fillet fish. Heat oven 400 to 450 degrees. Melt 1 cube butter. Put fish skin side down. Bake 20 minutes. Baste with juice of one lemon. Cook 10 minutes more, basting from time to time. Sprinkle with salt.

SALMON-RICE PUFFS

1	can (1 pound) salmon
1/2	cup milk
2	eggs, slightly beaten
1	cup cooked rice
1/2	cup green onions, chopped
1/2	cup celery, chopped
4	teaspoons lemon juice
1/2	teaspoon Worcestershire sauce
	salt and pepper to taste

Flake the salmon. Stir in rest of ingredients in order given. Pour into a greased casserole. Bake at 375 degrees for 30 minutes or until firm. Sprinkle top with grated cheese and allow to melt.

SANDY'S SALMON SOUP

2	cups canned salmon
2	tablespoons butter
1/2	cup minced onion
1	cup chopped celery
1	medium can creamed corn
5	slices bacon, cut and fried crisp
2	cups potatoes, cooked and chopped
	salt and pepper to taste

Prepare bacon by cutting into small pieces and then fry till crisp. Add to big pot. Add 2 quarts of milk to pot. Add de-boned salmon pieces, celery, onion, butter, cooked potatoes, canned corn, salt and pepper. Heat. Add 3 tablespoons cornstarch to a little water to thicken soup. Heat and serve.

SMOKEY SALMON SPREAD

1	(15-1/2 ounce) can salmon
2	tablespoons lemon juice
4	teaspoons grated onion
3	teaspoons horseradish
1/2	teaspoon liquid smoke
2	(8 ounce) packages cream cheese, softened
1/2	cup chopped pecans
4	tablespoons snipped parsley

Drain and flake salmon. Combine lemon juice, onion, horseradish and liquid smoke with cream cheese. Add salmon. Blend together well. Shape into a ball or log on wax paper. Wrap and chill several hours. Combine nuts and parsley on wax paper. Roll salmon mold in this. Chill. If desired, just before serving, shape into fish shapes and garnish. Can be frozen if well wrapped in foil. Makes 5 cups spread. Excellent!

ORIENTAL FISH

8	ounce fish fillet
1	square piece heavy foil
1	tablespoon soy sauce
1/3	cup celery, sliced diagonally
2	teaspoons dehydrated onion flakes

Place fish on foil. Top with remaining ingredients. Bake at 375 degrees for 15 to 20 minutes. Makes 1 serving.

HALIBUT FISH STEW

1	can (16 ounce) Italian tomatoes
2	cups water
1	cup celery, diced
1	cup frozen corn niblets
1	onion, chopped
1	clove garlic, crushed
2	teaspoons salt
1/2	teaspoon pepper
1/8	teaspoon basil
1	pound halibut, cut in chunks

Combine all ingredients. Vary amount of fish according to the number to be served. Use 1 pound fish for 4 to 6 people. Simmer until vegetables are tender, about 20 minutes.

NEWPORT RED PEPPER CHOWDER

4	tablespoons butter
2	medium onions, chopped
1/2	pound mushrooms, sliced
1	tablespoon lemon juice
2	large red or green peppers, diced or pimientos
2	cans (14 ounce) chicken broth
1	pound new potatoes, diced
2	tablespoons each cornstarch and water
1-1/2	pounds white fish (cod or turbot)
1	cup sour cream
1/2	cup minced parsley lemon wedges

Melt butter. Add onions, mushrooms, lemon juice and pepper. Cook on medium-high heat, stirring till limp (about 5 minutes). Add broth and potatoes. Bring to boil, cover and simmer gently about 45 minutes (till potatoes are done). Blend together cornstarch and water. Stir into sour cream. Add a little liquid to sour cream and stir into soup. Cut fish in bite-size pieces and add to soup along with parsley. Return to boil for 5 minutes until fish flakes. Do not boil to re-heat.

CURRIED COD FILLETS

2	pounds frozen cod, thawed and cut in 6 pieces
3/4	teaspoon salt
1/4	cup butter
1	tablespoon curry powder
1	cup chopped onion
1	cup chopped, peeled apple
3/4	cup catsup
3/4	cup light cream

Arrange fish in buttered, shallow 2 quart baking dish, Sprinkle with salt. Melt butter in skillet. Add curry, onion and apple. Simmer, stirring, about 5 minutes. Divide on fish. Add catsup and cream to skillet. Stir to mix and pour around fish. Bake at 350 degrees for 30 minutes, or until fish is opaque and flakes easily with fork. Good with sauteed bananas and hot cooked rice. Makes 4 to 6 servings.

BAKED FISH WITH VEGETABLES

3	medium carrots, scraped and thinly sliced
	salt
1	large onion, sliced
2-3	stalks celery, thinly sliced
	pepper
1	pound flounder or other fish fillets
	light cream
	butter
	paprika

Cook carrots in small amount of salted boiling water, until just tender; drain. Arrange onion slices in center of shallow 9 inch square baking dish and top with celery. Sprinkle with salt and pepper. Add carrots, then fish fillets, seasoned on both sides with salt and pepper. Pour cream into dish to cover bottom and partway over vegetables, but do not cover fish. Dot fish with butter and sprinkle generously with paprika. Bake at 425 degrees about 20 minutes. Good with mashed potatoes. Makes 4 servings. Note: if using frozen fish, thaw and drain before cooking.

LONG BEACH, WASHINGTON CLAM CHOWDER

40 to	
60	well-scrubbed clams
1	pound zucchini, thinly sliced
4-6	tablespoons butter
2	large onions, chopped
1	cup lightly packed fresh parsley, chopped (or 1/4 cup flakes)
3	cans (14 ounce each) chicken broth, regular strength
1/2	cup quick-cooking brown rice

Melt 4 to 6 tablespoons butter in a kettle (at least 5 quart size). Add onions and parsley. Cook, stirring until onion is soft. Add 3 cans chicken broth and brown rice. Cover and bring to a boil. Let simmer 10 minutes or until rice is tender. Add 40 to 60 clams (about 10 per person) and zucchini. Cover, bring to boiling and simmer about 5 minutes or until clams open.

Ladle chowder into bowls to serve. Pluck the clams from shells with a fork and discard shell. Eat chowder with a spoon. Salt and pepper to taste.

GEN'S HARSTINE ISLAND OYSTER SOUP

1/4	pound butter
1	quart fresh oysters, chopped
1	teaspoon salt (or to taste)
1/4	teaspoon pepper
1/4	teaspoon thyme
1	quart whole milk
1	can cream of onion soup
1	can cream of celery soup
1	soup can water
1	cup mashed potatoes
1	tall can evaporated milk

Melt butter in large pot. Add oysters and cook over medium heat 5 to 7 minutes or until oysters are well done. Add salt, pepper and thyme and cook 1 minute longer. Mix whole milk, soups and water until smooth. Add to oysters. Bring to just below boiling point (DO NOT BOIL). Add mashed potatoes and stir until smooth. Add evaporated milk and heat again to just below boiling point (again, DO NOT BOIL). Serve with oyster crackers or crusty French bread. Serves 8. This soup is good made ahead and re-heated. It also freezes well.

OYSTER STEW

1	pint oysters with liquid (about 3 dozen)
2	cups half and half
1/4	teaspoon thyme
	dash hot pepper sauce (to taste)
1/2	teaspoon salt
1/4	teaspoon fresh ground pepper
2	slices buttered toast, cut into small cubes
	chopped parsley and paprika for garnish (optional)

Drain liquid from oysters into saucepan. Add half and half, thyme, pepper sauce, salt and pepper. Heat till bubbles form around edge (do not boil). Add oysters and cook over low heat 4 to 5 minutes or until edges of oysters curl. Ladle into bowls. Sprinkle with toast and garnish with parsley and paprika. Serves 4. A favorite dish of the Oystermen of Nahcotta, Washington.

SIDNEY'S BAKED CLAMS

12	fresh clams on the half shell
1	green onion, chopped fine
1	tablespoon fine cracker crumbs
2	tablespoons soft butter
	dash fresh ground pepper
1/2	clove garlic, minced
1	teaspoon finely chopped parsley
1	teaspoon white wine
12	thin squares Jarlsberg cheese

Mix together all ingredients except clams and cheese. Spread mixture on each of the 12 pieces of cheese and place on top of each clam. Bake at 400 degrees 6 to 8 minutes till light brown. Makes 12 appetizers. Delicious!

FRANK'S CLAM PATTIES

1	cup minced clams
1	cup flour (add flour gradually)
1	teaspoon salt
1	teaspoon baking powder
1/2	teaspoon sage
1/4	cup minced onion
1	clove garlic, minced (optional)
2	tablespoons catsup
1	egg, beaten

Mix clams, catsup, onion and garlic to beaten egg. Stir in dry ingredients mixing until well moistened. Thin batter by adding more clams or catsup as preferred. Fry slowly in hot skillet, dropping batter from tablespoon. If clams are plentiful, increase to 2 cups or more per mix.

CLAM FRITTERS

1	(7-1/2 ounce) can minced clams
	milk
1	cup all-purpose flour
2	teaspoons baking powder
1/2	teaspoon salt
1	egg, beaten
	fat for frying fritters

Drain clams and reserve liquid. Add enough milk to liquid to equal 2/3 cup. Stir together flour, baking powder and salt. Combine milk mixture, drained clams and the beaten egg. Stir into dry ingredients just till moistened. Carefully drop by teaspoons in deep hot fat (365 degrees). Fry 6 to 8 fritters at a time until golden, 2 to 3 minutes. Drain on paper toweling. Serve with a seafood sauce or tartar sauce.

FRIED SCALLOPS

Marinate scallops in a mixture of oil, lemon juice, salt and pepper. Let marinate 2 hours. Roll in cracker dust, then in egg and again in the cracker dust. Fry in hot fat till a golden color. Easy and good!

MRS. BOYLE'S LOBSTER COOKING METHOD

Step 1: buy live lobsters on the day they'll be served. Keep chilled in large bowl till cooking time. In large kettle, bring 12 cups water and 1 tablespoon salt to boiling. Hold lobster just behind the eyes; rinse under cold running water. Drop it head first into the boiling water. Add second lobster.

Step 2: return water to boiling. Reduce heat and simmer, uncovered for 20 minutes. Remove lobster with tongs.

Step 3: place lobster on its back on cutting board. Halve the lobster lengthwise with poultry shears, leaving the back intact.

Step 4: with a knife, cut away membrane on the tail to expose meat.

Step 5: remove and discard the black vein that runs the length of the body and all organs in the body cavity near head, except the red coral roe (found only in females) and the liver, which are delicacies.

Step 6: crack open the large claws with a nutcracker; remove from body.

Step 7: use a seafood fork to remove meat; dip in melted butter. Pull off smaller claws; suck out meat. Serves 4 to 6. This recipe really makes it easy for you to be an expert!

SEAFOOD FRYING BATTER

3/4	cup unsifted flour
1	cup cornstarch
3	teaspoons baking powder
1/2	teaspoon salt

Sift above ingredients together. Beat 1 egg with fork.

To the beaten egg add:

1	cup less 2 tablespoons cold water
1/4	cup oil

Beat with fork. Then mix all at once with dry ingredients. Good for any seafood. Also good on onion rings.

BEER BATTER FOR FISH

Select preferred fish fillets and cut in small pieces. Moisten and dredge in salt, pepper and flour. Then dip in the following mixture: 2 eggs; 3 ounces beer; 3 ounces milk. Roll in finely crushed cracker crumbs. Fry in deep fat at 375 degrees until nicely browned, about 1 minute.

SUPER TARTAR SAUCE

1	cup mayonnaise
1-2	tablespoons chopped onions
2	tablespoons chopped dill pickle
1/2	teaspoon mustard
1	tablespoon chopped parsley
	dash of paprika

Combine above ingredients. Very good.

CLAM DIP

2	(3 ounce) packages cream cheese
1	tablespoon salad dressing
1	teaspoon Worcestershire sauce
1	teaspoon lemon juice
1/2	teaspoon salt
1/2	cup minced clams, drained

Blend cream cheese with all ingredients. Thin to desired consistency with clam broth. Chill.

SMOKED SALMON DIP

1	(8 ounce) package cream cheese
1	cup smoked salmon
1	tablespoon parsley
1/4	teaspoon onion salt
1/4	cup (about) milk to thin

Blend all ingredients together, thinning it with milk. Chill and serve. Really easy and delicious!

CRAB DIP

1	(8 ounce) package cream cheese
1	cup crab meat
2	tablespoons minced onion
1-1/2	cups salad dressing
1/2	teaspoon salt
2	tablespoons minced dill pickles

Put cream cheese in a bowl and blend in all ingredients. Mix well. Chill before serving.

PICKLED FISH

Clean and skin fish (especially good with white fish). Cut in small pieces and soak 24 hours in salt brine strong enough to float an egg. Drain and soak in white vinegar for 24 hours. Keep fish refrigerated while soaking in salt water and vinegar. Drain and make brine:

2	cups white vinegar
2-1/2	cups white sugar
1/4	cup mixed spices

Boil for 5 minutes. Let cool and add 4 ounces of white port wine. Put fish, onion and 2 lemon slices in layers in quart jars. Pour brine over all. Do not crowd. Use additional wine to fill jar to top. Let stand in refrigerator for 7 days.

OTHER LANDS

BETTY'S PEROKE

Crust for Peroke:

4	cups flour
1	teaspoon salt
1-1/3	cups shortening
3	teaspoons vinegar added to 1/2 cup water and chilled

Combine ingredients for crust adding chilled water. Roll and line bottom and sides of 9 x 13 inch pan with slightly more than half the dough. Save rest of dough for top.

Filling for Peroke:

2	cups rice, cooked
4	green onions
4	tablespoons butter

Saute 4 green onions in 2 tablespoons butter. Add sauted onions and the other 2 tablespoons butter to rice. May add 1 tablespoon parsley to rice.

4	(1 pound each) cans salmon or 1 fresh salmon
1	large onion, sliced
1	medium rutabaga, grated
1	medium carrot, sliced
2	sticks celery, sliced
1/2	package frozen peas or 1 cup fresh peas
1/2	teaspoon season salt
1/4	cup butter
	pinch pepper
1/8	cup evaporated milk

Melt 1/4 cup butter in frying pan. Saute onion, rutabaga, celery and carrots till slightly tender. Add peas. Drain salmon and remove skin and bones. Layer about 1-1/2 inches of rice in bottom of crust. Next, layer salmon, then on top of this add vegetables. (If fresh salmon is used, season with more salt and pepper). Next, add about 1 inch of rice on top of vegetables. Lastly, put crust on top with dotted holes. Brush with canned milk. Will look nice and brown when done. Bake at 350 degrees for 1 hour. Serve with potato salad, creamed peas or cole slaw. This was hard to write up, as it is an old recipe (Russian Pie) which is handed down by mouth and made in various ways. Like the rice, which can be dry and some vegetables are optional. Very good main dish!

POLLO ESTILO YUCATAN (Mayan chicken)

2	whole chicken breasts, split
2	tablespoons oil
	salt and pepper to taste
1	slice bread, toasted and crumbled
2	cloves garlic or 1/4 teaspoon garlic powder
1/8	teaspoon cinnamon
1/8	teaspoon ground cloves
1/2	cup tomato soup
1	teaspoon vinegar
1/2	cup malaga wine or creme sherry
1	teaspoon sesame seeds, toasted
	(on cookie sheet at 375 degrees, 10 minutes)

In a 10 inch frypan, brown chicken in oil on medium heat. Remove chicken and brown garlic, bread crumbs, cinnamon and cloves. Add tomato soup and continue cooking for 5 minutes. Remove garlic if using cloves. Add chicken to skillet. Cover and cook on low until chicken is tender, about 30 minutes. Serve with sesame seeds as garnish.

CHICKEN CORDON BLEU

2	chicken breasts
4	thin slices ham
2	(1 ounce) triangles Gruyere cheese, sliced
4	tablespoons butter
1/2	teaspoon salt
1/8	teaspoon paprika
1/2	cup dry bread crumbs

Split chicken breasts. Remove skins if desired. Cut meat in one piece from bones. Pull each half breast open in the middle to make a deep pocket. Fold ham around cheese slices, one for each pocket. Melt butter and set aside. Mix bread crumbs, salt and paprika. Roll stuffed chicken in butter then in crumbs. Place single layer in buttered baking dish. Bake at 400 degrees for 40 minutes or until golden.

SWISS CORDON BLEU CUTLETS

7	pork chops (1/2 to 1 inch thick)
7	slices cooked ham
7	slices Gruyere cheese
	flour
	salt and pepper
4	eggs
4	pieces of toast, crumbled or blended in blender
6	tablespoons butter
3	tablespoons oil
	lemon quarters

Make a horizontal cut in the chops up to the bone and place a slice of ham and a slice of Gruyere inside. Roughly sew up the edge with a darning needle and thin string. Dip the chops in flour, shaking off any surplus and then in beaten egg to which salt and ground pepper have been added. Finally coat with bread crumbs. Fry chops on both sides in mixture of hot butter and oil until brown and crisp. Lower the heat and continue frying until the inside meat is cooked and the cheese has melted. Remove string and serve immediately with lemon quarters. Same recipe may be used for veal chops.

HUNGARIAN DELIGHT

2	cups noodles
2	pounds chuck
2	cups tomatoes
1/2	cup diced celery
1	green pepper, chopped
2	tablespoons flour
4	cloves
1	cup diced salt pork
1/2	cup diced onion
2	cups diced carrots
2	tablespoons minced parsley
	salt and pepper

Cut beef in 1-inch cubes. Roll in flour. Combine pork and beef. Cook until brown, stirring constantly. Add sufficient water to prevent sticking. Cover. Cook until meat is tender. Add vegetables, cloves and sufficient water to cover. Season to taste. Simmer until vegetables are tender. Serve with noodles which have been cooked in boiling salted water. 6 servings.

CHICKEN A LA FRANCAISE

2	whole chicken breasts (boned, skinned and cut into strips)
1-1/2	teaspoons salt
1/4	teaspoon pepper
2	tablespoons butter
1	cup diced green onions, with tops
1	can (8 ounce) sliced mushrooms
1/2	cup dry sherry
1	cup fresh or frozen peas
1-1/2	cups chicken broth
3	fresh tomatoes, peeled and cut
2	tablespoons cornstarch
3	cups hot cooked rice

While rice is cooking, season chicken with salt and pepper. Saute in butter until browned. Add onions and mushrooms and continue cooking 2 minutes longer. Stir in sherry, peas and broth. Cover and simmer about 20 minutes. Add tomatoes. Dissolve cornstarch in mushroom liquid and stir into chicken mixture. Cook, stirring often, about 5 minutes longer. Serve over beds of hot fluffy rice. Makes 6 servings.

GEN'S PASOLE

1	tablespoon oil
1	pound lean boneless pork
1	large onion, chopped
2	cloves garlic, minced
2-3	tablespoons chili powder (or to taste)
1	teaspoon salt
2	cups water
1	(4 ounce) can tomato sauce
1	(10 ounce) can red chili sauce or enchilada sauce
1	(15 ounce) can white hominy, drained

Cut pork into 1/2 inch cubes and brown in hot oil. Add onion and garlic and cook 5 minutes. Add chili powder and salt and cook 1 minute longer. Add tomato sauce and water, cover loosely and simmer 30 to 40 minutes or until liquid is reduced by about half. Add red chili sauce or enchilada sauce and hominy. Simmer another 10 to 15 minutes. Serve with refried beans, green salad and hot flour tortillas for a hearty, inexpensive Mexican meal.

SOUR CREAM ENCHILADAS

2	pounds ground beef
1	large onion, chopped
1/2	green pepper, chopped
1/4	teaspoon salt
1/4	teaspoon cumin
1/4	teaspoon coriander
1/2	teaspoon garlic powder
2	drops hot sauce
1/4	cup picante sauce
1	tablespoon Worcestershire sauce
1	teaspoon chili powder
1/2	cup black olives, chopped
2	tablespoons chili sauce
1	package corn tortillas

Brown meat and drain well. Add the remaining ingredients and simmer 15 minutes. Then fry in hot shortening or oil until limp. Drain on paper towels. Put a large spoonful of meat mixture on each tortilla and roll up. Place in 9 x 13 inch dish.

Sour Cream Sauce:

1	stick (1/2 cup) butter
2	tablespoons flour
1-1/2	cups milk
1	(16 ounce) carton sour cream

Mix butter and flour together. Add milk and sour cream. Cook until thick. Pour sauce over enchiladas and sprinkle 1 cup grated cheese over the top. Bake at 350 degrees for 20 minutes.

MARGRET'S COUNTRY BORSCHT

2	pounds pork with bones
2	cans diced beets
1/3	cup dried navy beans
2	medium onions, diced
1/2	head cabbage, shredded
1	quart tomatoes (canned)
1	cup diced carrots
1	cup cooked mashed potatoes
2	cups sour cream

Cover pork (neck bones or shanks are good) with water. Add beets (with juice) and beans. Bring to boil and simmer until beans are tender. Meanwhile, saute onions and cabbage in butter till tender. Add to pork mixture. Stir in tomatoes and carrots (add more water if needed) and simmer until carrots are tender. Stir in mashed potatoes. Carefully stir in 1 cup sour cream. Do not allow to boil after cream is added. Use remaining sour cream to dollop on bowl of soup. This is authentic Ukrainian borscht!

ESAU'S POTAGE

1-1/2	cups lentils (raw or sprouted)
1	cup brown rice, uncooked
1	medium onion, chopped
2	tablespoons olive oil
2	tablespoons brewer's yeast
3	cups water

This recipe may be made with either raw or sprouted lentils. If you are using lentil sprouts, make sure the sprouts are young, 1 to 2 days old with 1/8 inch tails on them. When using raw lentils, you will need to partially cook them for 1/2 hour prior to adding to the rice mixture. Saute chopped onion in 2 tablespoons olive oil until soft. Add rice and cook over medium heat for 10 minutes, stirring frequently to prevent burning. You may need to add some additional oil. Next add 3 cups water to rice mixture and place the top on skillet turning heat down to simmer. Cook 20 to 25 minutes and then add partially cooked lentils or lentil sprouts. Continue to cook for 20 minutes or until rice is done. Stir in 2 tablespoons brewer's yeast prior to serving. Note: this is a good dish to cook in an iron skillet as iron will be naturally added to the food during cooking.

LUCILLE'S GERMAN POTATO SOUP WITH RIVLINGS

3	medium potatoes, cubed
1	medium onion, diced
2	stalks celery, sliced
3	strips bacon
1	teaspoon salt
	pepper
3	cups water
1	cup flour
1	egg
2	cups milk
1/2	can evaporated milk

Cover potatoes, onion and celery with 3 cups water and boil gently until tender. Fry bacon. Crumble and add bacon and 2 tablespoons bacon grease to vegetables. Break egg in the cup of flour and with a fork, stir it till it crumbles and has small chunks. That is the rivlings. Add to vegetable bacon soup. Cook 6 to 10 minutes. The rivlings should be yellow and tender. Add milk and canned milk. Heat, but don't boil. If you like oysters, you can use a 10 ounce jar. Saute them in butter and cut in pieces. Very good!

My favorite soup recipe came from Berlin, Germany. I am the last and only one left of 10 children, so I never knew my Grandmother. She came from Berlin. I was raised on potato soup. We lived on a farm in Montana and times weren't too good. However, we never went hungry. I had potato soup in my restaurant twice a week. People would have two large bowls. The Heinz soup salesman was always trying to get me to sell his soup, but I was an old-fashioned cook. One day he had a bowl of it and said I should put it on the market.

ELLEN'S "RIESKAA" (Finland flatbread)

2	cups buttermilk plus
1/2	cup cream
1	teaspoon soda
3	teaspoons baking powder
1	teaspoon salt
4	tablespoons melted shortening
2-1/2	cups graham flour
2-1/2	cups unbleached white flour

Mix all together in large bowl to be sure all are blended. Press dough down firmly on well greased cookie sheet to about 1/2 inch thickness.

Prick over all of dough area with fork till full of holes. Brush lightly with whole milk so it will brown. Pre-heat oven to 425 degrees. Bake on middle rack of oven for 15 or 20 minutes so it will not burn on bottom. Slide gently off cookie sheet to cool on wire rack. After cooling, place on a cutting board and cut diagonally to diamond shape.

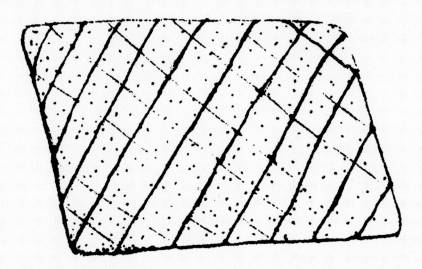

May be served at mealtime with butter or at coffee time when top is well garnished with salmon or tuna spread. This recipe has been handed down in my family for several generations, originating on the Island of Hailuoto, Finland.

LAVINA'S BROWN BREAD

1	quart warm water
2	cakes yeast
1-1/2	cups molasses
2	cups all-bran
2	cups Zoom cereal
2	tablespoons salt
	all-purpose flour

Mix all ingredients and add enough flour to handle dough easily. Let rise until double in size. Knead and shape into loaves. Let rise again for 1 hour. Bake at 350 degrees for 45 to 50 minutes. Makes 3-4 loaves. This is the bread I learned to make from my Finnish grandmother.

FINNISH BISCUITS

1	package dry yeast
2	tablespoons granulated sugar
2/3	cup granulated sugar
1/2	teaspoon salt
10	cardamon seeds
1/4	cup warm water
2	cups lukewarm milk
2	eggs, beaten
1/3	cup soft butter
7	cups sifted flour

Dissolve the yeast in warm water. Add 2 tablespoons sugar to the milk, then add yeast mixture. Stir well. Add 2 cups flour to make a light sponge. Cover and let rise about 1 hour until bubbly. Stir down and add the sugar, salt, eggs, butter and the cardamon seeds, which have been hulled and crushed. Slowly add flour until a soft dough forms. Knead on lightly floured board, then place in greased bowl and allow to rise until doubled, about 1-1/2 hours. Punch down and let raise again for 30 minutes. Divide dough in half. Make cinnamon rolls from one half. Divide the other half into 3 pieces and roll each into a long rope and then braid together. Place in greased pan and let raise 45 minutes. Bake at 375 degrees for 25-30 minutes; until golden brown. Brush top with mixture of 1/4 cup sugar and 1 tablespoon water while warm, then sprinkle with sugar.

CORNISH PASTIES

Pastry:

2	cups flour
2/3	cup shortening
1	teaspoon salt
1/3	cup cold water

Mix as per regular pastry. Roll out thin. I get 2 large pasties to bake on a jelly roll pan.

Filling:

potatoes, peeled and sliced thin
carrots, peeled and sliced thin
onions, peeled and sliced thin
hamburger or sirloin steak chunks
pat of butter

After spreading pastry out on pan, place potatoes, salt and pepper to taste, onions, carrots, etc. Add meat chunks and pat of butter. Fold pastry up over sides and top. Bake at 400 degrees for 1 hour or until vegetables are tender.

BETTY'S BOUREKAKIA

1	pound cream cheese
1	pint ricotta cheese
1	cup grated Parmesan cheese
1-1/2	cups Swiss cheese, grated
3	eggs
1/2	pound (about) melted butter
	salt and pepper to taste (may use lemon pepper)
	fillo dough to wrap

Mix ingredients together in mixing bowl. Easier to do if you let the cheese warm up, especially cream cheese. Using the sheet of fillo dough that one buys, cut the sheets in half. Take one piece (actually half a sheet) of fillo dough and brush with butter. Fold (bring shortest ends together) and brush again with butter. Place a bit of cheese filling on dough, fold edges and roll up. Place on baking sheet (no grease needed) about 1/2 inch apart to allow for expansion. Butter the top of rolls lightly. Bake at about 400 degrees for 10 to 15 minutes. Notes for Bourekakia: use half of above recipe for 1 pound (a box) of fillo dough. Remember, you cut the sheets of fillo dough in half, so the yield from a box of dough is about 60 bits of yummies.

One half of recipe will just be used up for a pound of dough if you do not put lots of filling on each sheet. About a mounded teaspoon is right. Too much filling will cause the crust to burst and you will have cheese all over rather than inside. You need not be fussy about measurements. Add more or less of other kinds of cheese. Too much egg will cause the most change. Have fun with flavors. Add a bit more of dill weed or some lemon juice to filling mixture. You can make them a day ahead and keep in refrigerator. Fillo dough can be bought at Frederick and Nelson. Super good!

DANISH EGG

Take a slice of your favorite bread. Pinch hole from center. Butter both sides. Place in hot frying pan. Break an egg in the center. Break yolk and lift up edges of bread to let part of the egg through. Brown, turn and brown other side. Salt and pepper to taste.

TOMOKO'S FRIED RICE

2	cups uncooked rice
1/2	pound hamburger
1	small to medium onion, chopped
1-2	medium carrots, finely chopped
2	eggs
2	tablespoons milk
2	stalks celery, chopped
	soy sauce

Cook rice. In the meantime, put 1 to 1-1/2 tablespoons oil in a large skillet and saute chopped onions, carrots and celery. When onions are translucent, push all to one side of skillet. Beat eggs with milk. Add a pinch of salt and scramble in other side of skillet. Add beef and cook until lightly browned. Add rice. Cook until rice begins to stick to skillet, stirring constantly. Stir in about 1/4 cup soy sauce or enough to completely coat rice. Serve with more soy sauce available.

MEXICAN SQUASH

2	slices bacon
1	medium onion, chopped
1-2	cloves garlic, minced
1	(4 ounce) can roasted and peeled green chilies, chopped
2	pounds squash (yellow crookneck, pattipan or small zucchini), sliced
1	tomato, peeled and chopped
	salt and pepper to taste

Fry bacon in heavy skillet until lightly browned. Add onion and garlic and cook 5 minutes. Add squash, tomato, salt, pepper and green chilies. Cook until squash is done, about 15 minutes. Serves 6.

LINDA'S RELLENOS

	large egg roll skins
	canned green chilies, whole
1	egg
	flour
	mild cheddar cheese, grated
	pan of melted lard or oil
1	can pork and green chili sauce

Split chilies and take out seeds. Dip in flour and place half of one on an egg roll skin. Squeeze some grated cheese together and put it on top of the chili. Dip the other half chili in flour and put it on top of the cheese. Fold skin over and seal all edges with egg. It is important that there are no holes or splits in the skin. Deep fat fry the relleno, turning it over when slightly browned on one side. Serve with heated pork and green chili sauce.

H.D.'S GREEN CHILI

1	pound lean pork, cut into 1/2 inch cubes
2	tablespoons lard
2	tablespoons flour
1/2	cup chopped onion
1	clove garlic, minced
2	cups coarsely chopped tomatoes
1-1/2	cups chopped green chilies
1/4	teaspoon oregano
1	teaspoon salt (slightly more if using fresh not canned chilies)
2	cups water

Dredge meat in flour. Melt lard in a deep skillet or Dutch oven and brown meat. Add onion and garlic. Cook till onion is soft and yellow. Add remaining ingredients and simmer, covered, about 2 hours. Remove cover and simmer about 5 to 10 minutes to desired consistency. Serve in bowls with tortillas, crackers or chips. Note: 2 cups cooked pinto beans may be added, but true green chili has no beans.

MEXICAN CORN

2	tablespoons butter
1	large onion, chopped
1-2	cloves garlic, minced
1	(4 ounce) can peeled whole green chilies, chopped
2	cans whole kernel corn, drained
1	small jar pimientos, chopped
	salt and pepper to taste

Melt butter in large saucepan. Add onions and garlic and saute about 5 minutes or until onion is limp and clear. Add green chilies and cook 2 minutes more. Add corn, salt and pepper to taste and pimientos. Cook 5 minutes, stirring frequently until corn is thoroughly heated. Serves 6 to 8.

Variation: when green chilies are added, also add 1 large ripe tomato, peeled and chopped. Omit pimientos.

ETHEL'S KIM CHEE

1	large Chinese cabbage **or** Bok Choy
1/2	cup salt
4	cups cold water
1	tablespoon sugar
1	teaspoon green ginger **or** 1/2 teaspoon ground ginger
2	green onions, finely chopped
3	small cloves garlic, finely chopped
1-1/2 to 2	tablespoons dried red chili peppers (remove seeds)

Cut cabbage into 1-1/2 inch lengths. Mix in the salt and add the water to cover (can be weighted down). Soak four hours. Drain cabbage well, it should be limp. Combine cabbage with remaining ingredients. Pack into jars and seal. Refrigerate for 2 days before using. Note: Kim Chee is a Korean recipe, used as a pickle or garnish. This pickle is strong smelling, so seal carefully. Otherwise, the other foods in the refrigerator will pick up the flavor and odor. Any type jar may be used as long as it has a lid. You may wish to use less of the dried peppers, as it is a very spicy recipe.

CROATIAN POVITICA

8	cups flour
1	cup lukewarm milk
1-1/2	cups lukewarm water
2	packages dry yeast (or 2 cakes)
3/4	cup sugar
4	teaspoons salt
2-3	eggs
1/4	pound melted butter

Mix as for any bread dough, adding flour as you knead to make soft dough. Grease large bowl, put in dough and turn over so top of dough is greased. Let rise till double. Knead and let rise again. After dough is light, turn out on large table with a well floured cloth. Roll dough as much as possible and spread with the following cooked filling.

Filling:

1 to 1-1/2	pounds ground walnuts
3	cups milk
1	scant cup sugar
3-4	eggs
1/4	pound butter
1	cup honey

Mix well and bring to boil over medium heat being careful not to scorch. Cool and spread on dough. Roll up as for jelly roll. Coil and put in large pan. Let rise till light. Bake at 350 degrees for at least 1 hour. Dough may be cut into smaller loaves and baked in bread pans. Makes 5 to 6 loaves.

MAIYIM'S VIENNESE BIRTHDAY TORTE

8	ounces finely ground dry pecans (may substitute walnuts)
1	cup sugar
1	tablespoon oil
7	eggs

In small bowl, beat egg whites until stiff, but not dry. In large bowl, beat 6 egg yolks until thick. Slowly add the sugar and oil. Add nuts. Fold in egg whites, stirring as little as possible. Bake in 2 layer pans or 1 sheet pan that have been lined with foil and buttered. Bake at 350 degrees for 1/2 hour. Will loosen from side when done. Test with a fork.

Viennese Torte Icing:

Cream 1/3 stick butter. Add 7th egg yolk and about 3 tablespoons very strong coffee (can be made from instant). You may use rum for part of the coffee. Sift 2/3 box powdered sugar and whip into the butter. This makes a slightly thin and glossy frosting. If you ice this light torte too heavily, it will tend to sink a bit in the middle. If you want more icing, use more liquid and then more sugar.

"MAKEA-LEIPA" (Finnish Sweet bread)

1-1/2	cups hot water
2	tablespoons butter
1	tablespoon white sugar
2	tablespoons brown sugar
1	teaspoon salt
1-1/2	teaspoon cinnamon

Mix above in large bowl and cool until lukewarm. Dissolve 1 package yeast in 1/2 cup warm water for 5 minutes, then add to above.

2	cups whole wheat flour
1	cup rye flour
2	cups unsifted unbleached white flour

Stir in rye and whole wheat flour to above mixture. Beat for 1 minute. Add white flour and blend well. Turn out on well floured board (1/2 pip or more). Knead for 10 minutes. Add more flour if necessary or until the surface of dough is satiny. Place dough in a greased bowl. Brush top with melted butter and cover with slightly damp cloth. Allow to rise in a warm place until nearly double, about 1 hour. Punch dough down and knead lightly. Divide dough in half. Shape each half in a round loop and place on lightly greased cookie sheet. Press dough loops down with hands to nearly 1 inch thick. Cover and allow to rise for about 45 minutes or until nearly doubled. Bake in pre-heated hot oven (400 degrees) for 25 to 30 minutes. Before removing from oven, test with a toothpick. Round cut in wedge shape at serving time. Excellent with coffee or at mealtime.

SCOTCH DATE NUT CAKE

1	cup oatmeal
1	cup flour
1	teaspoon cinnamon
1/2	teaspoon cloves
1-1/2	cups brown sugar
1/2	cup Crisco
2	eggs
1-1/4	cups boiling water
1	cup dates, cut up
1/2	cup nuts chopped

Pour boiling water over oatmeal. Stir and set aside. Sift flour, cinnamon and cloves. Cream brown sugar and Crisco. Blend in 2 unbeaten eggs, one at a time. Beat well. Add dry ingredients and mix well. Stir in dates and nuts. Pour into 12 inch pan. Bake at 350 degrees 40 to 45 minutes.

ULA'S CHRISTMAS RICE GROTT (Swedish family recipe)

3	beaten eggs plus 1/2 to 1 cup milk
1	quart milk
1/2	cup sugar
1/2	cup rice
1/2	teaspoon salt
1/8	teaspoon cardamom (powdered)

Cook all except eggs and cardamom in double boiler until rice is done, then add beaten eggs in 1/2 to 1 cup milk and cardamom to rice mixture and continue to cook until thickened. Cool and serve. The extra 1/2 to 1 cup milk is to keep it a creamy rather than stiff consistency. A nut is added during the serving process, preferably to an unmarried girl. For to find the nut in your dish foretells of a bit of luck or a near marriage.

BROWN PEPPERNUTS (old German cookie)

2	cups sugar
1	cup molasses
1	cup dark Karo
1/2	cup shortening
2	eggs
1/2	cup butter
1	tablespoon cloves
2	tablespoons cardamom
1	teaspoon soda in little hot water
1-1/2	cups walnuts
8-9	cups flour

Cream butter and shortening. Add sugar, Karo and molasses. Add soda in a little hot water. Add cloves and cardamom to mixture. Add flour. Mix and add nuts. Dough should be a little sticky. Let set overnight in refrigerator. Roll like marbles. Bake at 350 degrees about 10 minutes. This is a German cookie you dunk in coffee, gently, upside down. When they start to sink, pick up quickly with a spoon. If too much flour, they will not sink. Can be made ahead to season. Store in tight containers. Made for Christmas.

GERMAN CREAM CHEESE BROWNIES

1	package (4 ounces) Bakers German Sweet Chocolate
5	tablespoons butter
1	(3 ounce) package cream cheese
1	cup sugar
2	eggs
1/2	cup plus
1	tablespoon flour
1-1/2	teaspoons vanilla
1/2	cup chopped nuts
1/2	teaspoon baking powder
1/4	teaspoon almond extract
1/4	teaspoon salt

Melt chocolate. Cream together first four ingredients, including chocolate. Add eggs one at a time; then add flour, vanilla, baking powder, almond extract and salt. Stir in nuts. Put in an 8 x 8 greased and floured pan. Bake at 350 degrees 30 to 35 minutes. Yummy!

SPRINGERLE

4	eggs
1	pound powdered sugar
1	tablespoon lemon rind
1	teaspoon anise seeds
4	cups cake flour
1	teaspoon baking powder
	anise seeds (for later)

Beat eggs until light. Stir in powdered sugar and beat until blended. Add remaining ingredients and mix thoroughly. Chill 1 hour. Roll out to 1/2 inch thick, then roll pictures in using a Springerle rolling pin. Trim out bad pictures and edges. Put on wax paper and air 8 to 10 hours. Cut apart with sharp knife. Place on greased cookie sheets, putting a small pile of anise seeds under each cookie. Bake at 350 degrees 15 to 20 minutes. Makes 4 to 6 dozen cookies.

DANISH DAPPLES

2	cups flour
1	teaspoon baking soda
1/2	teaspoon salt
1	teaspoon cinnamon
1	teaspoon nutmeg
1	cup uncooked oats
3/4	cup shortening
1	cup brown sugar
2	eggs
3/4	cup applesauce
1	cup chopped nuts

Sift flour, baking soda, salt, cinnamon and nutmeg together. Add oats. Beat shortening, brown sugar, eggs and applesauce until light and fluffy. Add dry ingredients. Stir in 1 cup chopped nuts. Drop by spoonfuls onto cookie sheet. Bake at 375 degrees for 12 minutes.

FINNISH VAHTO PUUROA (whipped cranberry pudding)

2	cups water
1/2	cup cranberries
1/2	cup sugar
1/4	cup cream of wheat

Boil water and cranberries gently for 20 minutes. Strain and add sugar. Bring to a boil and add cream of wheat. Cook 15 minutes. Cool slightly, then whip until fluffy and light in color. Serve with half and half and a sprinkling of sugar.

WASSAIL PUNCH

The word "wassail" means to "be well". Wassail punch is a Christmas drink the English have served for many years. At one time it was a custom to sprinkle the punch on apple trees to make them healthier. Wassail is still a popular drink today.

1/2	cup lemon juice concentrate
1	(6 ounce) can frozen orange juice
1	tablespoon allspice
4	sticks cinnamon
1	gallon sweet cider
1	quart water
2	cups sugar

Combine all ingredients and boil for 10 minutes. Pour the punch into a punch bowl. Remove cinnamon sticks.

RUSSIAN TEA

1	quart boiling water
2-3	sticks cinnamon
12	whole cloves
1-3/4 to 2	cups sugar

Boil above ingredients together 15 minutes. Add 4 tea bags, cover and let steam 10 minutes.

Add the following:

> juice of 4 fresh oranges
> juice of 4 fresh lemons

Let set overnight. In morning when ready to serve, add 3 quarts of boiling water. May be stored as needed.

VEGETABLES

GLENN E. EMMONS © 1982

PINWHEEL LASAGNA

2 packages frozen chopped spinach
1 pint ricotta cheese or small curd creamed cottage cheese
1/3 cup grated parmesan cheese
1 package (1 pound) lasagna noodles
1 tablespoon grated parmesan for garnish

Special Tomato Sauce:

3/4 cup chopped onion
1 clove garlic, minced
3 tablespoons olive oil
1 can (28 ounce) stewed tomatoes
1 can (15 ounce) tomato sauce with tomato bits
1 can (6 ounce) tomato paste
1 cup water
1 tablespoon sugar
1-1/2 teaspoons salt
1/2 teaspoon pepper
1-1/2 teaspoons crushed oregano
3/4 teaspoon nutmeg
1 bay leaf

Cook onion and garlic in oil until translucent. Stir in remaining ingredients and simmer, uncovered, about 30 minutes. Remove bay leaf. While sauce is simmering, cook spinach according to package directions. Drain thoroughly and cool. Mix cooled spinach with ricotta cheese and 1/3 cup grated parmesan cheese. Cook the lasagna in boiling salted water until tender. Drain and cover with cold water. Working with 4 to 6 pieces at a time, lay strips of cooked lasagna on a sheet of waxed paper. Spread the spinach and cheese mixture over strips. Roll up each strip like a pin wheel. Stand on ends in a 9 x 13 inch casserole dish. When all are rolled up, pour the tomato sauce over all. Sprinkle 1 tablespoon grated parmesan cheese over the top and bake at 350 degrees, uncovered, for about 45 minutes. Your own sauce may be substituted for the one given. Serves 6 to 8.

MUSHROOM BUSINESS

1/2 to
1 pound mushrooms
 butter
8 slices white bread
1/2 cup chopped onion
1/2 cup chopped celery
1/2 cup chopped green pepper
1/2 cup mayonnaise
3/4 teaspoon salt
1/4 teaspoon pepper
2 eggs
1-1/2 cups milk
1 can cream of mushroom soup
 grated yellow cheese

Don't peel or wash mushrooms, just wipe with a damp cloth. Saute mushrooms in butter. Butter 3 slices of bread and cut in one-inch squares. Place in a casserole dish. Add onion, celery, green pepper, mayonnaise, salt and pepper. Cut 3 more slices buttered bread the same way and add on top. Slightly beat the eggs with milk and pour over top. Refrigerate at least one hour. One hour before serving, spoon one can of undiluted mushroom soup over top. Add 2 more slices buttered bread, diced smaller. Bake at 300 degrees for 60 to 70 minutes or 325 degrees for 50 to 60 minutes. About 10 minutes before done, sprinkle yellow grated cheese on top. Serves 6 to 8. This is a good recipe to replace potatoes when serving a roast or steak.

GREEN BEAN MUSHROOM MEDLEY

Saute one medium onion, chopped, in butter.

Add:

1 can green string beans
1 can (5 ounce) water chestnuts
 salt and pepper
1 small can mushrooms

Combine and heat.

CHEESE & VEGETABLE SHORT CAKE

2	cups flour
4	teaspoons baking powder
4	tablespoons shortening
3/4	cup milk
1/2	teaspoon salt
1	cup grated cheese

Sift together flour, baking powder and salt. Add shortening, mix and blend well with fork. Add cheese and liquid to make soft dough. Turn out on floured board and toss lightly until outside looks smooth. Divide dough into 2 equal parts. Roll out 1/4 inch thick and place each piece in an 8 inch cake tin. Bake in 400 degree oven about 25 minutes. Serve with hot vegetable filling.

Vegetable Filling:

1/4	cup chopped onion
1/2	cup chopped celery
2	tablespoons butter
4	tablespoons flour
1	large can tomatoes
1	cup cooked carrots
1	cup cooked string beans
1/2	teaspoon salt
	pepper

Melt butter and add onion and celery. Cook slowly, until soft. Add flour, then tomatoes. Bring to a boil stirring constantly. Add remaining ingredients. Simmer 12 minutes. Serve with cheese cake.

GREEN BEAN AMANDINE

2	(10 ounce) packages frozen julienne green beans
1-1/2	teaspoons Accent
1/3	cup butter
1/3	cup almonds, blanched and sliced

Cook beans per package instructions, adding Accent along with salt. While beans are cooking, melt butter in skillet. Add almonds and cook until almonds are slightly browned. Toss with hot cooked beans. 8 servings.

VEGETABLE DELIGHT

1	package (10 ounce) frozen French style green beans, partially thawed
6	fresh small yellow crook-neck squash or 6 fresh zucchini or 3 of each, thinly sliced
1/2	green bell pepper, chopped
2	small onions, chopped
4	fresh tomatoes, peeled and quartered
1/2	pound fresh mushrooms, sliced
1/4	cup instant uncooked rice
	salt and pepper

In a 2-1/2 quart casserole, place green beans, squash, rice, green pepper, onions, mushrooms and tomatoes. Salt and pepper and dot with butter. Cover and bake at 350 degrees for 1-1/2 hours. To cook faster (30 minutes) cook rice before adding to vegetables. If desired, just before serving top with grated Parmesan or Romano cheese. Serves 4 to 6.

EGGPLANT CASSEROLE

1	large eggplant, peeled and diced
1/3	cup milk
1	can condensed mushroom soup
1	egg, beaten
1/2	cup chopped onion
3/4	cup Pepperidge Farm herb seasoned stuffing

Cook eggplant in salted boiling water, about 7 minutes. Drain. Mix soup, milk and blend in egg. Add eggplant, onion and stuffing. Toss thoroughly and put into greased casserole or 10 x 6 glass pyrex dish.

Cheese Topping:

1/2	cup Pepperidge Farm stuffing
1	cup sharp cheddar cheese, grated
1/4	cup melted butter

Mix well and put on top of eggplant. Bake at 350 degrees about 20 minutes or until cheese dressing bubbles.

GREEN TOMATO PIE

4	cups thinly sliced green tomatoes
1-1/3	cups white or brown sugar
1/4	teaspoon salt
3	tablespoons cornstarch
1/3	cup lemon juice
	grated rind of 1 lemon
3	tablespoons butter
	pastry for 9 inch pie

Combine sugar, salt, flour and cornstarch. Arrange sliced tomatoes in pastry lined pan. Cover with combined dry ingredients. Sprinkle lemon juice and rind over top and dot with butter. Adjust top crust or pastry strips. Bake at 450 degrees for 15 minutes. Reduce heat to 350 degrees and bake 25 to 30 minutes longer.

FIVE BEAN CASSEROLE

8	strips bacon (cut in small pieces)
1	can (15 ounce) kidney beans, drained
1	can (15 ounce) butter beans, drained
1	can (15 ounce) baby lima, drained
1	can (21 ounce) B & M baked beans
1	can (large) pork and beans
1/2	large onion, diced
1/4	cup vinegar
3/4	cup brown sugar
1	teaspoon dry mustard

Brown bacon. Drain, then add onions, vinegar, brown sugar and mustard. Simmer 15 minutes. Add beans. Bake in a 3 quart casserole at 300 degrees for 3 hours uncovered or 1 hour covered. Cubes of cheddar cheese may be added before serving, about 1 cup.

HOLIDAY CORN CASSEROLE

1	can cream-style corn
2	eggs, beaten
1	cup milk
1	cup cracker crumbs (or more)
1	teaspoon salt
1	teaspoon sugar
2	tablespoons melted butter

Melt butter in baking dish. Add all ingredients, but reserve a few cracker crumbs for the top. Bake at 350 degrees for 5 minutes. Stir reserve crumbs over top and sprinkle with paprika. Continue baking until brown.

CIDER SQUASH

2	medium acorn squash
1/2	cup apple cider
1/4	cup packed brown sugar
1/2	teaspoon salt
1/8	teaspoon ground cinnamon
1/8	teaspoon ground mace

Cut squash in half lengthwise. Remove seeds and membrane. Cut crosswise into 1 inch slices. Spread slices in ungreased 15 x 10 x 1 inch pan. Pour apple cider over slices. Mix remaining ingredients and sprinkle over squash. Cover with aluminum foil and bake at 325 degrees until tender, about 45 minutes to 1 hour.

ASPARAGUS CASSEROLE

1	can cut asparagus
1	cup cracker barrel sharp cheddar cheese, grated
2	hard boiled eggs
1	can cream of mushroom soup
1	package soda cracker crumbs (about 25 crackers)

Put cracker crumbs in the bottom of a 1 quart casserole dish. Use just enough to cover the bottom. Pour in asparagus without liquid. Cover with grated cheese. Slice hard boiled eggs thin and place on top of cheese. Spread mushroom soup over all and add small chunks of butter throughout. Salt and pepper to taste. Bake at 350 degrees for 25 to 30 minutes or until cheese is melted and dish is heated through. Serves 4.

LEEK AND TOMATO QUICHE

3	eggs
1	baked pie crust
3-4	leeks
3	tablespoons butter
2	cups grated Jarlsberg Swiss cheese
	salt and pepper to taste
1/2	teaspoon sweet basil
1-3/4	cups half and half
1	tomato, thinly slice
	fresh Parmesan for sprinkling on top

Wash leeks and slice thinly. Saute leeks in butter. Sprinkle about 1/3 of the Swiss cheese into the baked pie crust. Spread sauteed leeks on top of cheese. Sprinkle remaining cheese over leeks. Beat eggs together with half and half, salt, pepper and basil. Pour egg mixture over the leeks and cheese and cover with a layer of thinly sliced tomatoes. Top with grated Parmesan cheese. Bake in pre-heated 400 degree oven for 15 minutes. Turn the heat down to 325 degrees and continue baking for 30 to 40 minutes longer or until mixture is set. Makes 6-8 servings.

SPINACH BALLS

2	packages (10 ounce each) frozen chopped spinach
2	cups seasoned croutons **or** stuffing mix
2	eggs
1/2	cup butter, melted
1/2	cup grated Parmesan cheese
1/2	teaspoon thyme
1	clove garlic, minced
1	large onion, minced
	salt and pepper to taste

Microwave frozen spinach on high 4 minutes to partially cook. Drain well, squeezing out all juice. If using croutons, crush slightly with rolling pin. Combine with remaining ingredients, mixing well. Cover and chill 2 hours or longer. Shape into 1 inch balls. Place 6 balls in circle on paper plate. Microwave on high 1 to 2 minutes and check for doneness. Size and amount of balls cooked at one time will determine cooking time.

MINTED-GLAZED CARROTS

12	carrots (about)
1/4	cup honey
1/4	cup butter
2	teaspoons chopped mint leaves (fresh or dried)

Cook carrots until tender; drain. Add honey and butter. Cook over low heat until glazed, turning several times. Just before serving, sprinkle with mint leaves.

DELICIOUS AND EASY CABBAGE

	cabbage
	milk
	salt and pepper
1/2	cube butter **or** margarine

Shred the amount of cabbage needed for your family. Place in top of double boiler and add milk to nearly cover. Add butter, salt and pepper to taste. Place over hot water, cover and cook over gently boiling water for about 1 hour, stirring and tasting several times.

BROCCOLI AND CHEESE CASSEROLE

1	(10 ounce) package frozen chopped broccoli
1/2	cup chopped onion
1/2	cup chopped celery
1	can cream of chicken soup
2	cups cooked rice
1	medium jar cheese spread

Cook broccoli as directed on package. Set aside. Saute onion and celery in butter. Mix all ingredients in large bowl. Pour into casserole and bake at 350 degrees for 30 to 35 minutes. Serves 6 to 8. Can be made ahead of time and frozen. Bake 15 minutes longer.

BROCCOLI AU GRATIN

Cook and drain 1 package frozen broccoli. Make white sauce.

White Sauce:

Melt 2 tablespoons butter in a pan over low heat. Blend in 2 tablespoons flour, 1/2 teaspoon salt, 1/8 teaspoon pepper, 1/8 teaspoon Worcestershire and a dash of cayenne pepper. Cook over low heat, stirring until mixture is smooth and bubbly. Stir in 1 cup of milk slowly. Heat to boiling, stirring constantly. Boil and stir one minute. Place vegetable and sauce in alternating layers in 1 quart greased casserole. Top with 1/2 cup soft buttered bread crumbs mixed with 1/2 cup grated sharp cheddar cheese. Sprinkle top with paprika. Bake at 375 degrees until nicely browned, 15 to 20 minutes.

BROCCOLI CASSEROLE

1	package frozen chopped broccoli
1	cup cooked rice
1	cup cheddar cheese, shredded
1	can cream soup

Mix all together. Bake at 350 degrees for 30 to 45 minutes.

ZUCCHINI FRITTATA

1/4	cup minced onion
1-1/2	cups sliced zucchini
1/4	teaspoon basil
1/4	teaspoon salt
3	eggs
1/8	teaspoon pepper
2	tablespoons Parmesan cheese

In skillet, cook onion and zucchini till soft. Add basil and 1/8 teaspoon salt. Beat eggs with remaining salt and pepper. Pour over zucchini and cook 3 minutes. Sprinkle with Parmesan cheese. Broil 3 minutes (be sure to use broiler safe skillet). Serve immediately.

ZUCCHINI PIE

3	cups finely chopped zucchini
1	cup chopped onion
1	teaspoon salt
2	eggs
1	cup dry bread crumbs
	grated cheese

Combine all ingredients except grated cheese. Mix well. Press into greased 9 inch pie pan. Bake at 375 degrees 25 minutes. Last 10 minutes, top with grated cheese.

ZUCCHINI STUFFING CASSEROLE

4	medium zucchini, sliced
1/2	inch thick
3/4	cup shredded carrot
1/2	cup chopped onion
6	tablespoons butter (or less, depending on taste)
2-1/4	cups herbed stuffing cubes (reserve 3/4 cup)
1	can condensed cream of chicken soup
1/2	cup dairy sour cream

Cook zucchini in a little salted boiling water until just tender. Drain. In saucepan, cook onion and carrot in 4 tablespoons butter until tender. Remove from heat, stir in stuffing cubes, soup and sour cream. Gently stir in zucchini and turn into 1-1/2 quart casserole. Melt remaining 2 tablespoons butter, add remaining 3/4 cup stuffing cubes, toss gently and top casserole. Bake at 350 degrees for 30 to 40 minutes. Serves 10.

SAUTEED ZUCCHINI

1	medium onion, sliced
2	medium tomatoes, sliced
1	small zucchini, quartered and diced
10	mushrooms, sliced
2	tablespoons butter
2	tablespoons lemon juice
2	tablespoons white wine
	lemon pepper
	salt

Lightly saute the onion in butter and lemon juice. Add wine and remaining ingredients, except tomatoes, and cook until slightly tender. Add tomatoes at the last minute and heat through. Serve while zucchini is still slightly crisp.

DELUXE HASH BROWN POTATOES

1	large (2 pounds) package frozen hash brown potatoes
1	can cream of potato soup
1	can cream of celery soup
	chopped green onion and green pepper to taste
1	small (1 cup) carton sour cream
	salt and pepper to taste
	parsley and paprika to taste

Combine all ingredients and bake at 325 degrees for 45 minutes. Serves 4 to 6.

CHEESE POTATO BAKE

2	tablespoons butter
1/2	cup onions, diced
6	medium potatoes, boiled and sliced
1-1/2	teaspoons salt
	pepper to taste
3/4	cup cheese, shredded
2	eggs, beaten
1	cup sour cream

Saute onion in butter. Mix with potatoes, seasonings and cheese. Beat eggs and sour cream together and pour over potato mixture. Bake at 375 degrees for 45 minutes. Serves 6.

DELICIOUS FRIED SPUDS

3	medium potatoes, peeled
2	cloves garlic
	onion
	cooking oil
	salt and pepper

In fry pan or on griddle put enough oil to cook potatoes. Grate the potatoes. As you grate the potatoes, also grate some onion and the cloves of garlic. Mix together and place on griddle. Salt and pepper. Brown well, turn and brown the other side.

SLIP "N" GO DOWN

6	medium potatoes
6-8	slices bacon, cut in 1/2 inch pieces
1	tablespoon vinegar
1	tablespoon sugar
6-8	green onions or 1 medium onion, chopped
4-6	cups shredded lettuce (romaine, escarole or bibb)

Boil potatoes till done. Mash like regular mashed potatoes until free from lumps. Add salt and pepper. Fry bacon. Cool fat and add vinegar and sugar. Mix lettuce and onion in bacon fat to wilt. Pour and mix into hot potatoes. Doesn't sound good, but is delicious and economical.

SOUPS AND SALADS

HEARTY BEEF CHOWDER

1-3/4	cups hot water
1	package (5-1/2 ounce) hash browns with onions
2	tablespoons onion, chopped
1/4	cup butter
1	tablespoon flour
4	cups milk
1	can (12 ounce) whole kernel corn with sweet peppers
1	package (3-1/3 ounce) dried beef, cut in small pieces
1/2	teaspoon salt
1/2	teaspoon lemon pepper
1/4	teaspoon celery salt

Pour water on potatoes and let stand for 10 minutes. Cook onion in butter in 3 quart saucepan until lightly brown. Stir in flour. Cook and stir 1 minute. Stir in milk gradually. Drain potatoes and rinse. Add potatoes, corn (with liquid) dried beef, salt, lemon pepper and celery salt. Stir well and bring to a boil. Simmer uncovered until beef and vegetables are hot, 2 to 3 minutes.

BEAN AND VEGETABLE SOUP

4	cups cold water
3/4	cup navy beans
1	tablespoon beef bouillon granules
1/2	teaspoon sugar
1/2	teaspoon thyme, crushed
1	small bay leaf
1	(14 ounce) can tomatoes, cut up
1/2	cup chopped onion
1/4	cup sliced carrot
1/4	cup chopped celery
1/2	cup tiny shell macaroni (cooked)
1	(8 ounce) can peas
1	(8 ounce) can corn

Place water and beans in a large kettle. Bring to a boil and simmer 2 minutes. Remove from heat, cover and let stand 1 hour. Add bouillon, sugar, thyme, bay leaf, 1/4 teaspoon salt and dash of pepper. Bring to a boil, cover and simmer 1 hour. Add tomatoes, onion, carrot and celery. Cover and simmer 20 minutes. Add shell macaroni and cook 10 minutes. Remove bay leaf. Stir in slightly drained peas and corn and serve.

VEGETABLE CHOWDER

1	small onion, diced
2	tablespoons butter
2	cups carrots, shredded
2	cups potatoes, shredded
1	cup zucchini, diced
1	bouillon cube
1-1/2	teaspoons salt
3	cups milk
1	can cream soup
1	cup shredded American cheese
	pepper to taste

Saute onion in butter. Add vegetables and bouillon cube and cook until tender in small amount of water. Add milk, soup and pepper and heat to almost boiling. Stir in cheese and serve. Serves 4 to 6.

BETSY'S FAVORITE VEGETABLE-HAM SOUP

1	large can whole tomatoes
1	zucchini, sliced
1/2	cup green beans
1	onion, sliced
2	stalks celery, chopped
2	carrots, chopped
2	bouillon cubes
1	pint water
2	teaspoons Italian seasoning
1/4	cup macaroni
1	cup leftover ham, diced

Place all in pressure cooker. Bring to boil and cook 12 minutes. Cool under cold water. Serve with crackers. May be cooked conventionally.

LOW CALORIE VEGETABLE SOUP (30 PER CUP)

1	(46 ounce) can tomato juice
3	cups water
6	beef bouillon cubes
1	large onion, chopped
4	carrots, chopped
4	large celery stalks, chopped
1/2	head cabbage, chopped
1	bay leaf
	salt and pepper to taste

Mix tomato juice, water, bouillon cubes, bay leaf, salt and pepper. Add chopped vegetables and simmer for 1 hour.

BEEF BORSCHT

2	pounds beef for stew
4	cups water
2-1/2	teaspoons salt
1/2	teaspoon pepper
1	bay leaf
2	cups sliced celery
1	large onion
2	cloves garlic, chopped
1	tablespoon vinegar
2	teaspoons sugar
1/4	teaspoon thyme
1/2	medium cabbage, sliced
1	jar (16 ounce) crinkle cut beets
2	tablespoons flour
	dairy sour cream

Cut beef for stew into 1 inch pieces and place in large pot. Add water, salt, pepper and bay leaf. Cover tightly and simmer 1-1/2 hours. Remove bay leaf.

Add cabbage, celery, onion, garlic, vinegar, sugar and thyme. Cover and simmer 15 minutes or until meat and cabbage are tender. Drain beets. Save liquid and combine with flour to blend. Stir into soup and cook, stirring constantly to thicken slightly. Add beets and simmer 5 minutes. Serve sour cream to top individual servings of soup. Makes 8 servings 1-1/2 cups each.

SPLIT PEA SOUP

1	pound dried split peas (green or yellow)
1	quart ham bone broth
1	quart water (use 2 quarts water if you don't have a bone for broth)
2	stalks celery, diced (leaves and stalks together)
1	medium onion, chopped
1	large carrot, diced
	bits of leftover ham, diced

Wash peas. Put in kettle with the 2 quarts of cooking liquid and bring to a boil. Add celery, onion and carrots. Cover and simmer 2 hours, stirring occasionally. Soup is done when peas are thick and mushy. Add a little more water to make soup of desired consistency and bits of croutons at serving time. Store leftovers in the refrigerator. Soup will get thicker, so add a little water when reheating. Makes about 8 generous servings.

COUNTRY STYLE PEA SOUP

2	cups split peas
8	cups hot water
1-2	pounds ham bones or hocks
1	garlic clove, finely chopped
1	medium onion, grated
1	stalk celery and tops, chopped
1	tablespoon salt
1/2	teaspoon pepper

Combine all ingredients. Heat to boiling, reduce heat and simmer 1 hour and 15 minutes or until peas are very soft. Put through coarse strainer. Reheat and serve. 8 servings.

HOT SPINACH SALAD

In wok: cut up 4 to 5 slices of bacon in small pieces. Fry until crisp. Remove bacon bits leaving in the grease.

Add to bacon grease:

1	tablespoon honey
1	teaspoon celery seed
1/4	cup lemon juice
1/2	cup wine vinegar

Mix in:

	fresh cut-up spinach, as much as you want
2	cups fresh cut-up mushrooms reserved bacon bits

Serve hot immediately.

MARINATED VEGETABLE SALAD

1	large head cauliflower
1	bunch broccoli
6	large carrots, sliced
1	medium onion, sliced
6	ripe olives, sliced
4	ounces grated Parmesan cheese Creamy Italian salad dressing

Wash and cut cauliflower and broccoli in bite-size pieces. Cook carrots partially and drain. Mix all the ingredients together and add enough dressing to coat vegetables. Marinate overnight.

PARSNIP SALAD

2	cups grated parsnip
1	cup diced celery
1/4	cup sliced green onions (or regular ones)
1/2	cup sliced stuffed green olives

Combine vegetables and mix with dressing made of mayonnaise thinned with catsup and a small amount of cream.

CORNED BEEF SALAD

2	small packages lemon jello
2	cups boiling water
2	cups mayonnaise

Mix and cool.

Add to cooled mixture:

2	cups chopped celery
4	tablespoons chopped green onion
6	hard boiled eggs, diced
1	can corned beef

I cool corned beef in refrigerator and then dice. May use 1 egg as garnish. Can put in a mold. Very good!

MAKE AHEAD SPINACH DINNER SALAD

1	(11 ounce) can mandarin oranges
1-1/2	cups mayonnaise
2	teaspoons curry
1/4	teaspoon ground coriander
4	ounces fresh spinach (4 cups torn)
8	hard cooked eggs
1	(10 ounce) package frozen peas
1/2	cup chopped mild onions (or green onions)
1	medium cucumber, cut lengthwise and sliced
1	(8 ounce) can water chestnuts
1-1/2	cups chopped chicken

Blend together mayonnaise, curry, coriander and syrup from oranges. Set aside. Save some eggs and oranges for garnish. Put torn spinach in 13 x 9 x 2 inch pan. Layer all ingredients (except mayonnaise mixture) ending with egg layer. Spread mayonnaise mixture on top and garnish with egg and orange slices. Cover and refrigerate for several hours or overnight. Makes a complete meal. Serve with favorite rolls.

MARY'S HOT POTATO SALAD

1	cup Miracle Whip (do not use mayonnaise)
3/4	cup milk
8	slices bacon, cut in 1 inch pieces
1/2	onion, chopped
6	potatoes

Cook potatoes till tender. Remove from water and cool for 1/2 hour. While potatoes are cooling, make dressing. Add milk slowly to Miracle Whip, mixing till smooth after each addition. Set aside. Fry bacon till almost crisp. Remove all but about 2 tablespoons bacon grease. Add onions and cook slightly. Add Miracle Whip to bacon and onions and bring to boil. Simmer uncovered at least 10 minutes. While dressing is cooking, peel and slice warm potatoes. Pour hot dressing over warm potatoes. Mix thoroughly. (Potatoes may be kept in warming oven and dressing may be simmered longer if desired, but do not combine dressing with potatoes till just before serving).

SWEET POTATO SALAD

2	cans sweet potatoes (4 good-sized if raw and cooked)
4	finely cut green onions, plus tender green tops
1-1/2	cups finely chopped celery
4	mashed or finely cut hard boiled eggs (put through a coarse sieve is best)
1/2	cup mayonnaise
1/2	cup Durkee's dressing
1/2	teaspoon salt

Mash potatoes, add eggs, combine other ingredients. Improves with standing.

POTATO SALAD

Mix together:

2	cups cooked potatoes, cubed
1	cup celery, finely diced
1/2	cup onion, diced
2	tablespoons parsley (dried)
1/4	cup black olives
3/4	cup salad dressing
2	tablespoons lemon juice
1-1/2	teaspoon salt
1/8	teaspoon turmeric (for coloring)

Mix all together and chill.

SAUERKRAUT SALAD

Rinse and drain 1 quart of sauerkraut.

Add:

1	green pepper, diced
1	onion, diced
1	cup celery, diced
1	cup carrot, grated
	pimiento for coloring

Sauce:

1	cup sugar
2/3	cup vinegar
1/2	cup salad oil
1/3	cup water

Pour sauce over all ingredients. Mix and refrigerate for at least 3 days before serving. Stir at least once a day.

V-8 ASPIC DEVILED EGG SALAD

4	deviled eggs, cut lengthwise
2	envelopes Knox gelatin
1/2	cup V-8 juice (cold)
3	cups V-8 juice (very hot)
1	cup celery, diced small
	lettuce leaves or salad greens

Soften gelatin in cold V-8 juice. Stir until thoroughly dissolved. Add to hot juice, stir to mix and then cool. Add diced celery. In a square dish or pan, approximately 8 x 8 x 2, place deviled egg halves cut side down about two inches apart. Pour cooled gelatin around eggs, but do not cover completely. Chill until firm. Cut into squares so each square has an egg. Keep refrigerated until ready to use. Place a lettuce leaf or greens on a salad plate and then a gelatin square on top. Add a teaspoon of mayonnaise to each salad and garnish with a small strip of green pepper.

BEAN SALAD

1	can green beans
1	can kidney beans
1	can wax beans
1/2	cup chopped green pepper
1/4	cup chopped onion

Drain all beans well.

Add sauce:

2/3	cup vinegar
3/4	cup sugar
1/3	cup salad oil
1	teaspoon salt
1	teaspoon pepper

Toss well and let stand overnight in the refrigerator. Really yummy!

PIMIENTO FRUIT SALAD

Mix 2 (16 ounce) cans crushed pineapple and 2 (5 ounce) jars pimiento cheese spread. Fold in 1/2 bag miniature marshmallows, 2 cups cream (whipped and sweetened) and 1 cup mayonnaise. Chill.

FROSTED STRAWBERRY SALAD

1	(6 ounce) package strawberry gelatin
2	cups boiling water
1	cup cold water
1	(20 ounce) can crushed pineapple (reserve juice)
1	(10 ounce) package frozen strawberries, thawed
2	bananas, peeled and sliced
1	cup miniature marshmallows
2	tablespoons all-purpose flour
1/2	cup sugar
1/8	teaspoon salt
2	teaspoons butter
1	(1-1/2 ounce) package whipped topping mix (or equivalent homemade)
1/2	cup chopped pecans
1/2	cup plus 1 tablespoon shredded coconut, divided

Dissolve gelatin in boiling water. Stir in cold water. Add drained pineapple, strawberries, bananas and marshmallows. Pour mixture into a 9 inch square pan. Chill until firm. Combine flour, sugar and salt in a small saucepan. Add reserved pineapple juice and butter. Cook over medium heat until mixture reaches a boil and thickens. Remove from heat. Let cool completely. Prepare whipped topping mix per directions. Fold in cooled juice mixture, pecans and 1/2 cup coconut. Spread mixture over chilled gelatin. Top with remaining coconut. Makes 9 servings.

JELLO SALAD

3	tablespoons vinegar
1/2	cup sugar
1	(small) can crushed pineapple
1	cup celery, diced small
1	cup sweet pickles, chopped fine
1	small package lemon jello
1	small package lime jello
1	small jar pimientos, cut up fine
3-1/2	cups boiling water

Dissolve the jello, add remaining ingredients and place in refrigerator to set. Put into an oblong 12 x 8 inch pyrex dish.

7-UP SALAD

Dissolve 2 small packages lemon jello into 2 cups boiling water and pour into 9x13 inch dish. Stir in 2 cups 7-Up (chilled). Add 1 (20 ounce) can crushed pineapple (drain and save juice). Add 1 cup small marshmallows and 2 sliced bananas and let set in refrigerator till firm. Then add topping.

Topping:

1/2	cup sugar
2	tablespoons flour
1	egg, beaten
1	cup pineapple juice (add water to make full cup)

Mix ingredients together. Cook until thick as pie filling. Remove from stove, add 2 tablespoons butter and let cool. Then add 1 cup Cool Whip (or whipped cream) and blend in gently. Spread over the top of firm jello and sprinkle with grated cheese.

APRICOT CHEESE SALAD

1	(29 ounce) can apricots
1	(29 ounce) can crushed pineapple
1	(6 ounce) package orange jello
2	cups water
2	cups miniature marshmallows

Drain fruits and reserve 1 cup of mixed juice. Add the rest of juice to the water, bring to a boil and dissolve the jello in it. Mix in the marshmallows and chopped fruits. Pour into 9 x 12 inch pan and chill to set.

Topping:

1/2	cup sugar
2	tablespoons flour
1	egg
1	cup reserved juice
2	tablespoons butter

Mix together in saucepan. Bring to boil, stirring constantly to thicken. Cool. Fold in 1 cup cream (whipped) and spread over jello. Top with 1 cup shredded cheddar cheese.

CRANBERRY SALAD

1	package cranberries
1	cup sugar
1	pint whipping cream
3/4	pound mini-marshmallows
1	cup crushed pineapple, drained
1/2 to	
1	cup walnuts, chopped
1	cup celery (chopped quite fine)

Clean, wash and grind the cranberries. Add the sugar, mix well and set aside for 2 hours. In a large bowl, whip the cream. Mix in the marshmallows and set aside in the refrigerator for 2 hours. After the 2 hours are up, fold everything into the whipped cream. Let stand overnight in the refrigerator. Will keep for several days.

24 HOUR SALAD

1	pound marshmallows (small)
1	cup nuts
1	pound grapes (Tokay) red
1	(#2-1/2) can crushed pineapple
1	pint whipping cream
2	eggs
1	lemon

Beat eggs. Add juice of 1 lemon and 1/2 cup pineapple juice. Cook until thick. Let cool. When cold, mix with all ingredients, add whipping cream and set for 24 hours.

LIME JELLO SALAD

2	packages (3 ounce) lime jello

Add 1 cup boiling water and mix. Add 1 cup cold water and set aside until it jells a little. Whip 1 can of evaporated milk and add to jello. Add 1 cup drained crushed pineapple, 1 cup cottage cheese, 1 cup small marshmallows and 1 cup mayonnaise. If desired, add some cut up maraschino cherries and cut up walnuts. Yummy!

ICE CREAM & JELLO SALAD

Take a 3 ounce package of lime jello and mix with 1 cup boiling water. Stir and dissolve. Pour over 1 quart vanilla ice cream. Drain a small can of crushed pineapple and add to jello. Stir and let jell up. Makes a quick and delicious salad.

FRUIT SALAD

1	(3 ounce) package lemon jello
10	large marshmallows
1	small package cream cheese
1	cup hot water
1	cup cold water
1/2	pint whipping cream
1	can fruit cocktail, drained

Dissolve jello in hot water. Cut up marshmallows and add with cream cheese. Whip until smooth then add 1 cup cold water. Let stand until it starts to set. Whip cream and fold into above mixture. Add fruit cocktail and allow to set. Delicious!

ORANGE ANGEL

1/2	pint sour cream
1/2	cup flake coconut
1	(8-1/2 ounce) can crushed pineapple (drained)
1	(11 ounce) can mandarin oranges (drained)
1	cup miniature marshmallows

Mix all ingredients in large bowl; refrigerate one hour.

BEST EVER 24 HOUR SALAD

1/2	pound marshmallows
1	(#2) can crushed pineapple
1/2	cup walnuts, chopped
1/4	cup maraschino cherries, chopped

Dressing:

	juice of 1 lemon
2	tablespoons sugar
1/4	cup fresh cream
1	egg, beaten
1	cup whipping cream

Cut first 4 ingredients into small pieces. Boil lemon juice, sugar, cream and

beaten egg until thick like mayonnaise. Cool, then add 1 cup whipped cream. Pour over pineapple mixture and let stand overnight. This is an old recipe my family loves. Make for Christmas or Easter.

MANDARIN MOLD WITH FRUITED CREAM

2	packages (3 ounce each) lemon flavored gelatin
1	cup hot water
1	cup cold water
2	tablespoons lemon juice
1	large can (12 ounce) frozen orange juice, undiluted
2	cans (11 ounce each) mandarin oranges, drained
1	banana
1	small can (8 ounce) crushed pineapple, well drained
1	cup mayonnaise
1	cup (1/2 pint) whipping cream
	salad greens

Dissolve gelatin in the hot water. Stir in cold water, lemon juice, orange juice and the oranges. Turn into a 1-1/2 quart mold and chill until firm. For dressing, mash the banana and mix with drained pineapple and mayonnaise. Whip cream and fold in. Unmold salad on salad greens and pass the dressing separately. Makes about 8 servings.

ROQUEFORT SALAD DRESSING

1	pint mayonnaise
1/2	teaspoon garlic powder
1	teaspoon onion salt
1-1/2	cups sour cream
3	tablespoons wine vinegar
1	pound bleu or Roquefort cheese

Beat with mixer after each addition. Makes gobs.

PEARL'S SALAD DRESSING

Blend:

1 cup water and tops from two bunches of green onions Add:

1/3	cup soy powder (heaping)
1	teaspoon paprika
1	teaspoon salt
1/4	cup brewer's yeast (more if desired)

Blend and add enough oil to fill the container, with enough room for 1/3 cup lemon juice. Let set for 10 minutes.

FRENCH DRESSING

1	can tomato soup
1	cup salad oil mixed with 1/2 teaspoon salt
3/4	cup vinegar mixed with 1-1/2 teaspoons paprika
1/2	cup sugar mixed with 1/4 teaspoon garlic powder

Mix all ingredients in a quart jar and shake. Store in refrigerator. Easy to make and so good!

BOILED SALAD DRESSING

2	eggs, beaten
2	tablespoons flour
1/2 to	
3/4	cup sugar
1	tablespoon butter
1	teaspoon prepared mustard
1	teaspoon salt
1/2	cup vinegar
1	cup boiling water

Put eggs and all other ingredients in double boiler. Cook until thick.

HERBED CROUTONS

1/4	cup grated Parmesan cheese
2	tablespoons oregano
2	tablespoons garlic powder
1	tablespoon basil
1/2	teaspoon salt
1/2	teaspoon fresh ground pepper
4-5	cups dry bread cubes
3	tablespoons oil

In small bowl, mix cheese, oregano, garlic powder, basil, salt and pepper. Set aside. In large bowl, toss bread cubes with oil, then toss with cheese-herb mixture until well mixed. Spread on ungreased cookie sheet. Bake in 225 degree oven 1 hour or until crisp and light golden, stirring occasionally so all sides are toasted. Cool. Makes 4 to 5 cups. Store in plastic bags secured with tie. Will keep about 1 month.

KITCHEN SINK

"HOW TO COOK A HUSBAND"

A good many husbands are entirely spoiled by mismanagement in cooking and so are not tender and good. Some women keep them constantly in hot water, others freeze them, others put them in a stew, others roast them and others keep them constantly in a pickle. It cannot be supposed that any husband would be good and tender managed in this way, but they are really delicious when properly treated.

In selecting your husband, you should not be guided by the silvery appearance, as in buying mackerel, nor by the golden tint as if you wanted salmon. BE SURE AND SELECT HIM YOURSELF, as tastes differ. Do not go to the market for him, as those brought to the door are always best. It is far better to have none, than not to learn how to cook them properly. It does not make so much difference what you cook him in, as how you cook him.

See that the linen in which he is wrapped is white and nicely mended, with the required number of strings and buttons. Don't keep him in the kettle by force, as he will stay there himself if proper care is taken. If he splutters or fizzes, do not be anxious. Some husbands do this. Add a little sugar in the form of what the confectioners call "Kisses", but no vinegar or pepper on any account.

A little spice improves them, but it must be used with judgement. Do not try him with anything sharp to see if he is becoming tender. Stir him gently the while, lest he become flat and tasteless. If thus treated, you will find him very digestable, agreeing nicely with you and he will keep as long as you want.

Taken from: The Fairbanks Cookbook of Tested Recipes

Compiled by: Ladies of the Presbyterian Church Fairbanks, Alaska 1909

JEAN'S KITCHEN A LA QUEEN

Take four walls, add a floor that's been waxed.
Sprinkle lightly with small boy tracks.

Add:
Cupboard and pans
A refrigerator, a sink
A stove and a percolator,
A table to rest your elbows on.
A kettle that sings,
And a telephone.

Set a corner aside for a rocking chair, that you and a yellow cat can share.

Place an old stone jar on a window sill, for daisies or bittersweet to fill.

Arrange antiques on shelves, in nooks. Leave room for dishes and recipe book. Season with essence of new baked bread.

Add hungry youngsters, keep well fed. Mix cookies and milk as the need arises, have hot dogs handy for club day crisis.

Sift and discard unessential chores. Put worries to soak while you step out of doors.

As a final touch, for a perfect blend, garnish your kitchen with loving friends.

OLD RECIPE

4	pounds teasing
2	dozen kisses
1	cup moonlight
3	pints squeezings

Place in a dimly lit room. Mix teasing with a little squeezing. Pour in the moonlight and slowly add the kisses. Now beat it before the old man gets home!

Anonymous

IN TERMS OF CUPS AND SPOONS

If it calls for a pinch
Don't use a dash,
Instead of dinner,
You'll end up with hash.

ALZORA'S HOMEMADE SOAP

With folks watching cholesterol and calories, most of us throw away a lot of fat. Yet soap is more and more expensive to buy! So, you may care to use your scrap fats, or your children may like to make soap for a school project.

1. Strain all fat scraps into clean containers as you accumulate them. When you have about 7 pounds of fat, you are ready to make soap. (You need 6 pounds CLEAN CLEAN fat per can of lye).

2. Go to a junk store and find an old granite iron pail or slop jar. Sickroom supply places often have them too. (DO NOT USE ALUMINUM KETTLES FOR LYE!)

3. Melt the fat you have and strain it (for the second time) into a kettle. It is a good idea to do your fat-cooking outside, as the globules mix with steam and grease your kitchen walls. I use an extension cord and a hot plate, outside.

4. Fill the kettle you put the strained fat into, with water. You need about twice as much water as you have fat. Boil the mixture for 5 minutes.

5. Set the kettle in a cold place and let the fat form a disc on top. Lift off the disc of fat. Rinse out the kettle.

6. Put the disc of fat into the clean kettle with double its bulk in clean water. Boil it again for 5 minutes, just as you did before. You must get the salt and other impurities out! In the second boiling, add a few drops of oil of cloves (the druggist sells it).

7. Again, chill the fat mixture, lifting off the solid disc of clean fat.

8. Into that big granite iron pail, put 3 pints of cold water. You NEED a big pail because it boils up when you add lye. Remember that lye is very poisonous, so make plans for small children, pets or anyone who might get hurt!

9. CAREFULLY pour into the big granite iron pail, one 13 ounce can of LYE. Stir with a long wooden spoon or a clean stick of kindling. Guard it until the lye mixture is cool.

10. Stir in 1 cup of borax.

11. Melt the clean fat disc again, this time without water. Pour it into the lye mixture, stirring with wooden spoon or clean stick of kindling. When it is like thick cream, it is ready to pour.

12. When you were saving up that strained fat, you were also cutting the tops off your milk cartons and washing them clean, in warm soapsuds and then turning them upside down to dry thoroughly. Get out some of these clean, dry milk cartons. (You can use a wooden soap mold and cheesecloth linings as Grandma did, but Grandma did not have milk cartons, poor dear!)

13. Pour the soap into the clean dry milk carton or cartons.

14. Cover the soap with an old clean bath towel and let it stand to 2 days in a warm (but not hot) place.

15. Peel off the milk cartons, and slice off your bars of soap with a very sharp knife or wire cheese-cutter.

16. Wrap the soap if it seems apt to absorb moisture from the air. Depends on your climate.

17. When you get good at it, your soap will make acceptable gifts, if you tie them up prettily. Some washing machines do not seem to do well on homemade soap, but others do. If you experiment carefully, on a small scale, you will know whether your machine will run well on homemade soap. This is chiefly meant for hand soap, not for laundry soap, however.

KITCHEN AND HOUSEHOLD HINTS

To remove blood from clothes, cover the area with meat tenderizer. Apply enough water to make a paste. Wait 15 to 20 minutes and sponge with cold water. If necessary, soak in enzyme pre-soak for 30 minutes before washing.

To brighten and put sizing back into curtains, add 1 cup of Epsom salts to 1 gallon of warm water for final rinse. I add 2 cups Epsom salts to warm rinse cycle on gentle. Even the ruffles will not need ironing.

Greasy gravy?? Simply add a small amount of baking soda to gravy. Start with 1/4 teaspoon and add a little more if needed.

Place a piece of white chalk in the jewelry box to keep costume jewelry from tarnishing.

To remove sticky residue after removing labels or price tags, (not from clothes), rub a little peanut butter and wipe clean. Also works on tar and bandaid adhesive.

Use a glycerine soaked cloth and wipe sides and shelves of refrigerator. Future spills will wipe up easier. After freezer has been defrosted and cleaned, spray with Pam or any other spray. Next time you defrost the ice will fall off easier.

Moisten a clean cloth with Formby's Lemon Oil furniture treatment. Wipe both sides of shower doors. This leaves them very clean and water does not stay on the door after a shower. Smells good too.

Bottom of electric skillet gummy? Place the pan in a large plastic bag containing a cloth that has been saturated in ammonia. Close the bag tightly, leaving the handle and electrical parts outside. In a few hours remove pan from the bag. Wipe with a paper towel before washing.

To make new tennis shoes last longer, spray heavy with starch.

Should a foot or arm need to be soaked in warm or cold water, consider a foam ice chest. The chest will retain the temperature of the water for a longer time than a metal basin.

To cool down "hot spicy" foods, add a little cocoa.

Use a drinking straw to hold up a leaning houseplant. You can also fill the straw with plant food to feed the plant.

To keep shower heads clean and free flowing without having to take them apart, pour full-strength vinegar into a plastic bag and fasten the bag tightly over the shower head so that the vinegar covers the head. Secure the bag with a rubber band and let the shower head soak overnight. The result will be free-flowing water.

In winter weather, the lock on your car door may freeze and leave you unable to insert your key. Carry a squeeze bottle of rubbing alcohol. One or two squirts, and the lock will unfreeze.

If a cracked dish is boiled for 45 minutes in sweet milk, the crack will be so welded together that it will hardly be visible, and it will be so strong it will withstand the same usage as before.

Peanut butter rubbed into the hair will take out chewing gum. Mayonnaise rubbed into the hair will eliminate dryness and result in a beautiful shine. A half-cup of bran mixed with a tablespoon of baking soda makes a fine dry shampoo for dirty hair, and a teaspoon of sugar dissolved into a cup of warm water will give you a great setting lotion.

Having trouble separating egg whites and yolks? Try breaking them into a small funnel. The whites go through, the yolks don't.

Coffee drinkers — if inflation has caused you to sacrifice your favorite higher quality ground coffee for a less expensive brand, try this: Buy your favorite and an equal size can that is less expensive. Then mix them thoroughly in a large sealable container. The higher quality flavor will dominate, you won't taste the difference and you will save money.

Boric acid eyewash powder makes excellent roach poison. Sprinkle wherever roaches crawl, and it will destroy roaches (not waterbugs). Powder will not harm children or pets, and will last for one year. Starts slow, but in a month, roaches will all be gone.

If your perfume is getting low in the bottle, try dropping in a few small glass beads. They will keep the liquid level high, eliminate air space and thereby reduce evaporation of your perfume.

Food storage-size plastic bags are great for filing papers. They hold standard letters beautifully, and you can always see what's inside.

Your linen closet can be the tidiest in town if you always stack sheets and towels with the thickest folds forward with all the edges concealed in back.

If you have installed ceiling tiles and have any left over, use them as bulletin boards; they're soft enough to take pins easily and can be decorated and painted to match the room. This is a good project for a group of cub scouts, camp fire girls, brownies or any group that needs a project. You can buy damaged ones from lumber yards very cheaply.

After the freezer has been defrosted, spray it with alcohol or vegetable oil spray (such as Pam). The next time you defrost, it will be less work.

For a sparkling white porcelain sink, place paper towels across the bottom of the sink and saturate with household bleach. Let it set for half an hour or so.

Sprinkle cream of tartar on a damp cloth to clean porcelain surfaces. This method also removes rust.

Rub stainless steel sinks with lighter fluid if rust marks appear.

If the screw attaching an appliance to wall or ceiling has stripped the plaster and is no longer holding firm, saturate a cotton ball with Elmer's glue. Gently push the entire cotton ball into the hole. Allow to dry at least 24 hours and reinsert the screw gently with a screw driver.

No bread crumbs? Use finely crushed corn flakes, wheat flakes or any other unsweetened cereal instead.

No shortening? Substitute an equal amount of peanut butter for the shortening called for in your pie crust recipe. You may use the crunchy or the smooth peanut butter. Mix with other ingredients in your recipe and roll out as you would any pie crust.

When whipping cream ahead of time, it will not separate if you add a touch of dissolved unflavored gelatin (1/4 teaspoon per cup of cream).

For the lightest pancakes ever, replace liquid in pancakes and waffles with club soda. Use up all the batter, do not store as it will go flat.

Brush the unbaked bottom crust of your pie with well-beaten egg whites before filling. This keeps berries and other fruits from making pie bottoms mushy.

Submerging a lemon in hot water for 15 minutes before squeezing it will yield almost twice the amount of juice.

Keep yolks centered in eggs by stirring the water while cooking hard-boiled eggs. (Especially good for deviled eggs.)

To prevent mold, store cheese in a tightly covered container with some sugar cubes.

Cottage cheese will remain fresher longer if stored upside down in your refrigerator.

Brush a little oil on the grater before you start grating and the cheese will wash off the grater easily.

Warm the knife when cutting cheese, and you will find the cheese cuts as easily as butter.

A dull knife works much better than a sharp one for slicing cheese.

APPLE CANDLE HOLDER: Needed; apples and candles. Choose apples that are flat on bottom — make hole in stem end with apple corer or knife to fit candle — make hole smaller at bottom and candle will stay straighter.

If you have used too much salt in cooking foods, add a raw potato to it. This will absorb much of the salt.

If cake or bread browns too quickly before it is done, place a pan of warm water on a rack above it.

Sprinkle bananas lightly with sugar to keep them from darkening when slicing on top of a pie, for cake fillings or puddings.

To prevent lemons from drying out, place them in cold water and then into the refrigerator. Change the water at least once a week.

When frying donuts, place a few cloves or a few drops of vinegar into the fat.

Cauliflower will remain white if a little milk is added while cooking.

A strip of bacon placed in the bottom of a pan will keep meat loaf from sticking.

To prevent gummy noodles, rice, macaroni and spaghetti, add 2 teaspoons of cooking oil to the water before cooking.

Place a heel of bread on top of cabbage before putting the lid on the pot and cooking it; there will be no odor. The bread has no effect on the cabbage and should be removed after cooking. Also good for broccoli and brussels sprouts.

A few drops of vinegar in the water when poaching eggs will keep the eggs from running all over the pan.

When cooking vegetables, cover those that grow underground, such as onions and potatoes and leave uncovered all vegetables that grow above the ground.

For mashed potatoes, cook the potatoes with their skins on, then peel them and mash with a little hot milk. The texture is different, but the vitamin value is increased.

When soup is too salty add slices of raw potatoes and boil for a few minutes or add a couple of pinches of brown sugar. This will overcome the salty taste but will not sweeten it.

Poke loaves of bread with a fork after shaping into loaves to remove air and then let rise and bake.

Marinate liver in lemon juice for 30 minutes before cooking.

To prevent soggy French toast, use frozen bread. Keep the bread in the freezer until the last minute and then cook as usual.

Boil carrots with the skin on. When done, place them in cool water and the skins will slip off.

A little vanilla poured on a piece of cotton and placed in the refrigerator will eliminate odors.

After using a beater of any kind, rinse immediately under cold water. Give it a few quick shakes and set aside to dry.

To make copper shine like new, clean with salt and vinegar.

To make cleaning up grease easier, first wipe down with Kleenex. This will absorb most of the grease.

When cutting quilt blocks, make a pattern out of an ink blotter or felt. When placed on the material, it will not slide as paper does.

To clean small intricate designs on silver pieces, use mascara brush.

Put a small amount of cologne in the water when sprinkling clothes. This leaves a nice odor in drawers and closets.

Use a little vinegar to rinse silk stockings. This will increase their elasticity.

Keep a wet sponge handy when ironing. Works well to dampen dried hot spots.

Do not starch linens that are to be stored. They will rot in time.

To mend a leaky vase, melt some paraffin and pour a thick layer into the bottom. Allow to harden.

To remove pitch from hands or clothes, rub well with peanut butter and then wash.

If shirts are wrinkled due to leaving in the dryer too long, wet a hand towel and place in the dryer with shirts. Run dryer on hot for 5 minutes. Take out immediately and hang on hangers. No ironing is needed.

To avoid breaking nut meats, place nuts in a moderate oven until warm. If the shells are then cracked, the nuts will come out whole and the skins can be loosened easily.

When hot cloths are needed to relieve pain, heat them in a steamer instead of wringing them out of hot water.

DRAWING SALVE

4	ounces pure lard
4	ounces bee's wax
2	ounces resin
1/2	fluid ounce carbolic acid

Dissolve first three ingredients. Remove from fire and add carbolic acid. Stir until it thickens.

WEIGHT LOSING FORMULA

3	tablespoons light corn syrup
10	ounces evaporated milk
10	ounces Wesson oil
8	ounces water

Beat with electric beater. Drink 5 ounces between meals or as a snack anytime or before bed.

PLANT FERTILIZER

1	teaspoon epsom salts
1	teaspoon salt peter
1	teaspoon baking powder
1/3	teaspoon ammonia

Mix into 1 gallon of water. Use once a month in place of regular water.

WALL CLEANER

1	cup ammonia
1/2	cup vinegar
1/4	cup baking soda
1	gallon warm water

Apply with sponge. Will not dull paint or streak.

BEEF-OLIVE SPAGHETTI SAUCE

1-1/2	pounds lean ground beef
1	large onion, chopped
1/2	green pepper, chopped
1	large garlic clove, minced
1	carrot, shredded
1/2	pound fresh mushrooms, cut up
2	tablespoons chopped parsley
1	can (28 ounce) stewed tomatoes
1	can (15 ounce) tomato sauce
1	can (6 ounce) tomato paste
1/2	cup dry red wine
2	tablespoons spaghetti sauce seasoning (dry or from a jar)
1/2	teaspoon sugar
1/2	teaspoon salt
1/8	teaspoon pepper
1	can (2-1/4 ounce) sliced ripe olives
1	pound hot cooked vermicelli

Brown ground beef in a large skillet. Reduce heat. Add onion, green pepper and garlic stirring occasionally until soft. Stir in carrot, mushrooms, parsley, tomatoes, tomato sauce, tomato paste, wine, spaghetti seasoning, sugar, salt and pepper. Simmer covered for 1-1/2 hours. Add olives and cook uncovered 30 minutes longer or until sauce is thick. Serve over hot cooked vermicelli and topped with Parmesan cheese. Serves 4 to 6.

SPAGHETTI SAUCE (very good!)

1	clove garlic, chopped fine **or** 1 onion
1/4	cup olive or salad oil
1	can (#2) tomatoes
1	(6 ounce) can tomato paste
2	cups water
1	teaspoon salt
1/8	teaspoon cayenne pepper **or** 2 small dried red peppers
1	pound ground beef
2	tablespoons chopped or dried parsley
1/4	cup chopped celery tops

Cook garlic or onion in 2 tablespoons oil for 5 minutes. Add tomatoes, tomato paste, water and seasonings. Simmer while meat is cooking. In remaining oil, cook meat until redness is gone. Combine meat and sauce and simmer for 2 hours. Add parsley and celery tops and simmer 1 hour more. Serve on cooked spaghetti with grated Parmesan cheese.

STEAK SAUCE FOR BARBECUING

1	cup soy sauce
3	tablespoons white sugar
5	tablespoons brown sugar
2	tablespoons vinegar
2	tablespoons ginger

Mix all ingredients and let sauce marinate on steak for 1 hour or longer. Keep turning and pricking steak so sauce gets through. Very good on 1-1/4 inch sirloin steak.

RAISIN SAUCE

Blend together in saucepan:

| 2 | tablespoons butter, melted |
| 2 | tablespoons flour |

Remove from heat and blend in slowly:

| 2 | cups apple cider |
| 1/2 | cup seedless raisins |

Cook until mixture boils, stirring constantly, then boil 1 minute. Remove from heat. Serve hot. Good over ham. Makes 2 cups.

MAIYIM'S "HOT SAUCE FOR WILLIE"

Loved by a dear friend Will, a hearty aficionado of the spicier things in life, especially Mexican food.

2	(29 ounce) cans tomato sauce
2	(28 ounce) cans whole tomatoes
2	(12 ounce) cans tomato paste
	(or equivalent fresh, cooked till saucy)
12	ounces diced green chilies
1	(3-1/2 ounce) can jalapenos (or more to taste. Use seeds if HOT sauce is desired)
1	large onion, or more, chopped
1	green pepper, chopped
3	cloves garlic, chopped
1	teaspoon cumin seeds

Combine all ingredients in large heavy pot and cook for at least 1/2 hour. Season to taste with salt, cayenne pepper and more garlic and cumin if you like. Ladle into hot canning jars and seal or into freezer containers and freeze. A jar will keep in the refrigerator for about 2 weeks.

CHOCOLATE SUNDAE SAUCE

1	(3 ounce) package chocolate pudding
1-1/2	cups water
1/2	cup sugar
1/2	square unsweetened chocolate
1	tablespoon butter

Combine all but butter in saucepan. Cook and stir until mixture boils. Remove from heat. Add butter and stir. Serve warm or cool. Makes about 2 cups.

BEST AND EASIEST CHEESE SAUCE

1/2	cup milk
1/2	cup mayonnaise
1/4	teaspoon dry mustard
1	cup shredded cheese
	hot pepper sauce to taste
	salt and pepper to taste

Mix milk, mayonnaise, mustard and cheese in saucepan. Heat, stirring until smooth. Stir in seasonings.

ADDIE'S TERIYAKI SAUCE

1/2	cup soy sauce
2-3	tablespoons brown sugar
1-2	cloves garlic, crushed
	piece of fresh ginger, crushed or grated

Combine all ingredients. Marinate meat in sauce at least 1 hour (overnight is better). Broil meat over charcoal or cook as desired. We use New Zealand rib-eye steak (cut thin) or chuck roast. Good on nice buns or as main dish with rice.

SWEET AND SOUR SAUCE

1	cup brown sugar
1	cup vinegar
1	cup soy sauce (if Kikkoman use 3/4 cup)
	fresh ginger

MOCK CHEESE FONDUE (apple juice)

2	cans (10-3/4 ounce) condensed cheddar cheese soup
2	cloves garlic, minced
4	egg yolks, beaten
1/2	cup apple juice or cider dippers

In earthenware fondue pot, heat soup and garlic over low heat to just before boiling. Remove from heat. Stir half of hot soup into egg yolks. Blend into remaining soup. Stir in cider and heat through, stirring constantly. Transfer pot to source of heat at table. Adjust heat when necessary to keep fondue warm. Swir dippers in fondue. Serves 4.

Dippers:

cut up cooked wieners
cooked mini meat balls
dill pickle chunks
cut up french bread
cauliflower
whatever

BETTE'S LIVER CREAM CHEESE PATE

Aspic:

1	envelope unflavored gelatin
1	cup water
2	beef bouillon cubes
1	tablespoon lemon juice
3	pitted ripe olives, sliced

Ham Mix:

2	(4-1/2 ounce) cans deviled ham
1/4	cup prepared sweet mustard relish

Cheese Mix:

2	(8 ounce) packages cream cheese
1/2	cup cultured sour cream
1	tablespoon grated onion

Liver Mix:

2	(4-1/2 ounce) cans liver pate
1/4	cup mayonnaise
2	tablespoons chopped parsley

Put water, bouillon cubes and gelatin in small saucepan over medium heat. Stir constantly until gelatin dissolves. Measure 1/4 cup into a 6 cup mold. Add lemon juice. Place mold in a bowl of ice water. When aspic begins to thicken, arrange olives in it. Make ham, cheese and liver mixes, adding 1/4 cup of aspic to each. Place half of the cheese mixture on top of the first aspic. Let harden in a bowl of ice water. Add ham mixture on top of cheese mix and let harden. Then add remaining half of cheese mix, let harden and lastly add the liver mixture. Refrigerate. Un-mold like a gelatin salad. Serve with various crackers.

Comment: this recipe is a lot of screwing around, but will be the hit of your party—believe me!

TEX-MEX DIP

2	cans (large size) Jalapeno's bean dip
1	(16 ounce) carton sour cream
1	package taco seasoning mix
2	ripe avocados
	lemon juice
	garlic to taste
2	small cans ripe olives, chopped or sliced
1	bunch chopped green onions
1	cup (or more) diced tomatoes
1-1/2 to 2	cups shredded cheddar cheese

Mix the taco seasoning with the sour cream the night before or at least several hours ahead. On a large serving dish, spread the bean dip evenly as a base. Layer the sour cream taco dip on it. Mash the avocados with lemon juice and sprinkle with garlic. Spread on top of the taco dip layer. Sprinkle on in layers the chopped onions, olives and tomatoes. Finish off with the cheese and refrigerate until serving. May be made several hours ahead of time. Serve with tortilla chips. Feeds several people.

PARTY DIP

1/2	cup sweet pickles, chopped
1/2	cup stuffed green olives, chopped
1	small onion, chopped
1/4	cup catsup
1	small green pepper, chopped
1	clove garlic, chopped
1	(8 ounce) package cream cheese
1	tablespoon cream
1/2	cup mayonnaise or salad dressing

Combine pickles, green olives, onion, green pepper and garlic. Drain off all the juice. Blend cream cheese with cream. Add mayonnaise and catsup. Blend with rotary beater. Add chopped ingredients and blend well. Chill.

GUACAMOLE DIP

3-4	avocados, mashed
1	tomato, chopped
1	small onion, chopped
1/4	green pepper, chopped
	garlic salt
	salt
	picante sauce (available in grocery store)

Mix first 4 ingredients. Sprinkle garlic salt and salt to cover top. Add picante sauce to taste. Mix thoroughly.

FRESH HORSERADISH

1	cup horseradish root, cut in 1/2 inch pieces
3/4	cup white vinegar
1-2	tablespoons sugar
1/4	teaspoon salt

Put all ingredients in blender and process at grind until finely grated. Put into jars and seal. Keep in refrigerator.

CURRIED CASHEW SANDWICH SPREAD

1	pound cheddar cheese, grated
3/4	pound raw cashews (to roast: place in dry pan in 250 degree oven for about 20 minutes. Stir often until brown.)
3-4	celery sticks, finely chopped
4	green onions, finely chopped
1/2	bunch parsley, chopped
1-1/2	teaspoons curry powder
	dill weed and garlic to taste

Tofu mayonnaise may be used. Mix all ingredients together. This is delicious on crackers, toast or whole grain bread with tomatoes and sprouts on top.

STUFFED BUNS

Grind the following:

1	can spam
5	hard boiled eggs
	few sprigs parsley
1	onion
1	clove garlic
1	green pepper
1	can pimientos, drained
1	pound medium or sharp cheddar cheese

Add:

1	cup catsup
1	can chopped olives, drained
	salt and pepper

Cut the end off 1-1/2 dozen French rolls and remove the insides. Fill each roll with filling and put end back on. Wrap in foil and place in refrigerator until ready to use. To serve, place rolls on cookie sheet and heat in 325 degree oven for 20 to 30 minutes.

OLIVE CHEESE PUFFS

3/4	cup flour
1/4	cup butter
5	ounces Old English cheese spread
	small stuffed olives (about 36)

Mix flour, butter and cheese spread. Drain olives on paper towels. Put dough in hand and shape around olive. Bake at 400 degrees for 10 minutes.

RIPE OLIVE CHEESE BALL

1	(8 ounce) package cream cheese
1-1/2	cups grated cheddar cheese
1	(5 ounce) jar smoke-flavored cheese spread
1	teaspoon Worcestershire sauce
1/2	teaspoon dry mustard
1/2	teaspoon salt
1	(7 ounce) can ripe olives, chopped

Soften cheeses. Blend with Worcestershire sauce, mustard and salt until smooth. Mix in olives. Shape into balls and chill. Can be rolled in parsley, nuts or ripe olives.

SAUSAGE BALLS

3	cups biscuit mix
1/2	cup water
12	ounces sharp cheese, grated
12	ounces Jimmy Dean sausage (Hot)
7 to	
10	drops Tabasco

Mix all ingredients together. Roll into small balls. Bake at 400 degrees for 10 minutes. Freeze until party time. Bake at 350 degrees 5 to 8 minutes. Serve hot.

CHEESE BALLS

2	(8 ounce) packages Philadelphia Cream Cheese
1	(5 ounce) jar Kraft Roka Bleu Cheese
1	(5 ounce) jar Old English Sharp Cheese
3-4	drops Tobasco Sauce
	pinch of garlic or onion salt

Place all ingredients in a large bowl. Let stand till mixture has softened and can be mixed well with a fork. Refrigerate for thirty minutes. Form two balls. Roll each ball in finely chopped walnuts. Wrap in saran wrap and keep refrigerated. May also be frozen. Makes 2.

TURKEY DRESSING

Bake the turkey the day before. Boil 2 cups chopped celery and save the water. Saute 2 or 3 onions. Use 2 bags of dressing mix, seasoned; 1 teaspoon baking powder; 1 egg; 2 or 3 teaspoons Season-all (found on spice rack in store). Use broth from celery and some of the turkey broth to moisten the bread. Add 2 cups cubed turkey. Mix together real well and bake in a well greased dish for at least 1 hour at 350 degrees.

SHAKE AND BAKE COATING

2	cups dry bread crumbs, rolled fine
1/4	cup flour
3	tablespoons paprika
4	teaspoons salt
1/4	cup shortening
2	teaspoons sugar
2	teaspoons onion powder
2	teaspoons oregano
1	teaspoon cayenne powder
1/2	teaspoon garlic powder

Mix all dry ingredients well. Cut in shortening till mixture is crumbly. Store in a tightly covered container. Makes about 3 cups. When ready to use, dip chicken or chops in milk and then coat with mix. Arrange on a shallow pan and bake at normal time and temperature.

SHAKE AND BAKE

4	cups dry bread crumbs (use blender and chop till a fine crumbly texture)
1/2	cup salad oil
1	tablespoon salt
1	tablespoon paprika
1	tablespoon celery salt
1	teaspoon freshly ground black pepper

In a large bowl, mix all ingredients together with a fork. Store in a container with a tight fitting lid, preferably in the refrigerator. Use to coat chicken, fish or chops. Bake at 375 degrees for 30 to 45 minutes depending on the thickness. Moisten the meat or fish with a little water before coating.

FRIED RICE CAKES

Combine ingredients, cover and chill 1 hour.

2	eggs, beaten
2	cups cold rice
4	slices bacon, fried crisp and crumbled
1/3	cup chopped green pepper
1/4	cup grated Parmesan cheese
1/2	cup finely cut green onions
	salt and pepper to taste

Form into patties and fry 5 minutes on each side. Very good!

FRIED RICE

2	cups long grain rice
4	cups water
1	teaspoon shortening
1/2	teaspoon salt
	onion tops
	Spam
	soy sauce
1	can bean sprouts

While rice is steaming, cut onion tops and Spam into small pieces. Place in frying pan and brown. Add rice, a little at a time, then soy sauce and then bean sprouts. Heat through.

SEASONED POPCORN

3	tablespoons oil
1/2	cup popping corn
	seasoning mix

Heat oil in large skillet or saucepan with tight-fitting lid until corn kernel dropped in oil sizzles and pops. Add corn, cover and cook over low heat, shaking pan often. When popping stops, turn corn into large bowl. Toss with desired Seasoning Mix. Makes about 2 quarts. Serve at once or cool and pack in plastic bags or air-tight containers. Will keep 1 to 2 months. May be re-heated in shallow pan in pre-heated 400 degree oven about 5 minutes or until hot.

Seasoning Mix:

Chili Mix: stir together 1 teaspoon chili powder, 1 teaspoon onion salt and 1/2 teaspoon salt.

Dill Mix: stir together 1 teaspoon dill weed and 3/4 teaspoon salt.

Italian Mix: stir together 1/4 cup grated Parmesan cheese, 3/4 teaspoon oregano and 1/2 teaspoon salt.

CUKE RELISH

10	cups cukes
4	cups ground onions
5	teaspoons salt
6	cups sugar
1	tablespoon mustard (optional)
2	cups vinegar
2	teaspoons celery seed
1/2	teaspoon black pepper
1	tablespoon tumeric
1	tablespoon nutmeg
1/2	teaspoon red pepper

Combine cukes and onions and sprinkle with salt. Let stand overnight. Drain, wash with cold water and drain again. Heat vinegar. Mix remaining ingredients and add to vinegar. Add cukes and onions. Bring to a boil and simmer 30 minutes. Put in jars and seal.

SWEET PICKLED BEETS

Cook beets until tender. Let cool enough to slice. Make a syrup by boiling together:

2	cups vinegar
2	cups water
1	cup sugar
6-8	whole cloves

Pack the beets into jars. Lemon slices may be added, 4 slices per jar. Cover beets with syrup and seal.

SOCIETY CHIPS (canned sweet pickles)

20   dill sized cucumbers

Pour boiling water over cucumbers for 4 mornings in a row. On the 5th morning, drain and slice.

Syrup:

1   quart cider vinegar
8   cups sugar
2   tablespoons salt
3   tablespoons pickling spices

Bring syrup to a boil and pour over cucumber slices. Repeat this process next 2 mornings; draining off syrup, re-heating and pouring back over cucumbers. On next morning (8th morning of process), drain off syrup and place cucumbers in canning jars. Heat syrup and pour into jars over cucumbers. Screw on caps and process jars 20 minutes in hot water bath. Remove jars and place on towel to cool. After cool, check to be sure jars have proper seal.

PICKLED EGGS

Hard boil 12 eggs. Peel and puncture eggs with tines of fork. Place in a quart jar.

Bring to a boil:

1   cup vinegar
3/4   cup sugar
1   teaspoon mustard seed
2   teaspoons tumeric
1   teaspoon celery seed
1/4   teaspoon cayenne
1   cup water

Pour over eggs and cover. Let set 3 days before eating.

MOM'S DILL PICKLES

Bring to a boil:

3   quarts water
1   quart vinegar
1   cup pickling salt

Place dill and garlic cloves in bottom of jars. Pack with cucumbers. After packing, add more dill and cover with hot brine. Seal.

OPAL'S EASY CRANBERRY JELLY

This jelly is delicious to eat as well as to give as a surprise gift. To make 6 half-pints, mix 3-1/2 cups cranberry juice cocktail with one 2-1/4 ounce package powdered fruit pectin in large kettle. Begin to cook and stir until boiling. At that point, immediately stir in 4 cups sugar. Bring the mixture to a full rolling boil and boil hard for 2 minutes, stirring constantly. Next, remove the mixture from heat and stir in 1/4 cup lemon juice. Skim off the foam as the jelly begins to cool, pour into hot jars and seal. A quarter inch of melted paraffin poured on top makes an excellent seal. That's all there is to it!

CRANBERRY NUT JELLY

4   cups cranberries
2   cups water
2   cups sugar
1/8   teaspoon salt
1/2   cup broken nuts
1   teaspoon grated orange rind

Boil berries and water in covered pan until berries are soft. Press through a sieve. Add sugar to pulp and boil for 3 minutes. Add rest of ingredients, mix well and fill small glasses. Chill until firm. Seal with melted paraffin.

BEET JELLY

6   large beets, peeled and sliced

Cook until tender, drain and save juice. Should have about 1 quart.

1   package sure-jell
1   teaspoon almond extract
6   cups sugar
1/4   cup lemon juice

After adding pectin, extract and lemon juice, bring to a boil. Add sugar and boil 3 minutes on a good rolling boil. Seal. Makes 6-1/2 pints, so use a big kettle.

FROZEN RHUBARB JAM

5   cups rhubarb, cut fine
3   cups sugar

Stir together and let set overnight to drain juice. Cook about 20 minutes and add one 3 ounce package strawberry jello. Heat until jello is dissolved. When cold, pack into jars and freeze.

KAHLUA

4   cups sugar
4   cups water
1   vanilla bean
2   ounces instant coffee
1   fifth brandy

Mix sugar and 3 cups water. Bring to a boil and boil for 5 minutes. In a small pan, boil 1 cup water and remove from heat. Add coffee, stir, then add to sugar mixture. Heat to almost boiling. Put in large bowl and add brandy. Pour into 3 bottles. (It is very important that you use dark colored bottles.) Break the vanilla bean into pieces and put equal amounts into the 3 bottles. Let stand for at least two weeks.

KAHLUA

4   cups sugar
4   cups water
13   teaspoons instant coffee

Boil uncovered for 45 minutes. Let mixture cool. When cooled, add and mix 1 quart vodka (cheapest is fine) and 5 teaspoons pure vanilla extract. Pour into dark bottle (1/2 gallon wine bottle). Store in dark place for 2 months. Can be used in cakes, frostings, coffee, milk, etc.

HOT BUTTERED RUM MIX

1   pound soft butter
1   pound brown sugar
1   pound powdered sugar
1   teaspoon cinnamon
1   teaspoon nutmeg
       pinch of all-spice
1   quart very soft vanilla ice cream

Cream together butter and brown sugar. Add powdered sugar, spices and ice cream. Blend. Freeze in pint or half pint containers. For each drink, put 1 tablespoon mix in cup, add boiling water and rum. Top with a sprinkle of nutmeg. Real good!

LINDA'S HOT BUTTERED RUM

1   pound real butter
1   pound dark brown sugar
1   pound cube sugar
1   quart vanilla ice cream

Melt butter. Blend in brown sugar and mix well. Add cube sugar. Use potato masher to mash the sugar. It has to be mashed thoroughly until it is creamy and smooth. Add ice cream and stir some more. When it is all mixed well remove from heat. Cool awhile then pour into a container. While heating the heat can be lowered until on simmer. To make a drink in a large cup, put 1 jigger rum, 3 heaping teaspoonfuls batter, add boiling water to fill cup and stir. Store in refrigerator or freeze.

EGG NOG

(makes 1-1/2 quarts)

1	package vanilla instant pudding
6	cups milk
1/3	cup sugar
2	egg yolks (save the whites)
1	teaspoon vanilla

Beat; set aside. Beat 2 egg whites until stiff peaks form. Carefully fold the beaten eggs into pudding mixture. Chill. Top with nutmeg.

DAIRY BERRY

1/2	cup cranberry juice concentrate (frozen and thawed)
1	cup milk
1/2	cup vanilla ice cream

Blend until just combined. Makes 2 cups.

HAWAIIAN MILK SHAKE

2	cups canned crushed pineapple
2	cups milk
2	cups vanilla ice cream
1	teaspoon lemon or lime juice

Blend or beat all ingredients until smooth. Makes 1-1/2 quarts.

SWEETENED CONDENSED MILK (microwave)

1/2	cup cold water
1-1/2	cups non-fat dry milk powder
3/4	cup sugar

Measure water into 2 cup glass measure. Gradually stir in milk powder until smooth. Microwave 3/4 to 1 minute or until milk is steaming hot. Stir in sugar until dissolved. Allow to cool before using. Use as a substitute in recipes calling for 1 can (14 ounce) sweetened condensed milk.

DESSERTS AND APPLES

DENNIS SMITH

Cakes

Pies

Cookies

Misc

Ice Cream and Sherbet

Apples

RHUBARB CAKE

1/2	cup Crisco
1-1/2	cups sugar
1/2	teaspoon salt
1	egg
1	cup sour milk or buttermilk
1	teaspoon baking soda
2	cups + 1 tablespoon flour
3	cups cut rhubarb
1/4	cup red sugar sprinkles (Cake-Mate)

Cream shortening, add sugar and salt. Add egg and mix. Dissolve soda in sour milk and add alternately with flour. When mixed, add rhubarb and sugar sprinkles. Mix well. Put into 9 x 13 inch greased and floured glass cake pan. Add topping and bake at 360 degrees for 35 to 40 minutes.

Topping

Mix together:

1/3	cup sugar
1	teaspoon cinnamon
1/3	cup cut nutmeats

BROWNIE CAKE

Bring to boil:

1	cup water
2	sticks margarine
4	tablespoons cocoa

In large bowl put:

2	cups flour
2	cups sugar
1	teaspoon soda
1/4	teaspoon salt

Pour hot mixture over dry ingredients and mix lightly. Add 2 eggs and beat.

Add:

| 1/2 | cup buttermilk |
| 1 | teaspoon vanilla |

Mix well. Pour into greased 10-1/2 x 15-1/2 x 1 inch jelly roll pan. Bake at 350 degrees for 30 to 35 minutes. While baking make frosting.

Icing:

Bring to boil:

1	stick margarine
5	tablespoons buttermilk
4	teaspoons cocoa

Remove from heat.

Add:

1	box powdered sugar
1	teaspoon vanilla
1/2	cup nuts

Mix well and pour over cake while both are hot.

MILE-A-MINUTE CAKE

1-3/4	cups flour
2	teaspoons baking powder
1	teaspoon salt
1/2	teaspoon cinnamon
1/2	teaspoon nutmeg
1/3	cup shortening
1-1/3	cups brown sugar
2	eggs
1/2	cup milk
1/2	pound dates, stoned and chopped
1/2	cup nuts, chopped

Sift the flour. Measure and sift again with baking powder, salt and spices. Mix in order given, dates and nuts last. Beat all together 5 minutes. Bake in 9 inch square pan at 350 degrees for 50 to 60 minutes.

CARROT CAKE

3	eggs
2	cups sugar
1-1/2	cups salad oil
3	cups flour
2	teaspoons soda
1/4	teaspoon salt
1	teaspoon cinnamon
1/4	teaspoon nutmeg
1	teaspoon vanilla
1	cup chopped nuts
1	can (#2) crushed pineapple (including liquid)
2	cups grated raw carrots
1	cup raisins (optional)

Beat eggs. Add sugar then oil and beat well. Sift dry ingredients and add to mixture. Add vanilla, pineapple, carrots, nuts and raisins. Pour into greased and floured tube or loaf pan 9 x 13 inches. Bake at 350 degrees. About 1 hour for the tube cake or 40 to 45 minutes for the loaf cake. Let cool and frost.

Cream Cheese Frosting:

1	(3 ounce) package cream cheese, softened
1/4	cup margarine, softened
2	teaspoons vanilla
1/2	box powdered sugar

MAIYIM'S MANDARIN CHOCOLATE CAKE

2	squares un-sweetened chocolate, melted and cooled
1	cup butter
2-1/2	cups (1 pound) packed brown sugar (must be brown)
2-1/2	cups sifted cake flour
1	teaspoon baking soda
2	teaspoons vanilla.
4	eggs, slightly beaten
1/2	cup concentrated orange juice
1/2	cup milk

Cream butter; gradually add sugar and cream till light and fluffy, about 10 minutes. Beat in vanilla, then eggs. Stir in chocolate. Alternately add flour and soda mixture, orange juice and milk, beating till smooth after each addition. Pour batter into three 8 inch pans lined with buttered paper or wax paper. Or use 2 layer pans and make 6 to 8 cupcakes. Do not fill pans over 2/3 full! Bake at 350 degrees for 30 to 35 minutes until done. Do not overbake. Cool in pans 10 minutes, then turn onto rack. Frost and fill with the following frosting.

Super Luscious Chocolate Frosting

(Use with oranges for mandarin cake. Make with milk for a super chocolate frosting.)

1	small can mandarin oranges
4	squares un-sweetened chocolate
1/2	cup butter
4-1/2	cups sifted icing sugar
1/3	cup liquid from oranges (a tablespoon or 2 of orange liqueur is great!)
1	egg or 2 egg whites
2	teaspoons vanilla

Melt chocolate and butter together. Add rest of ingredients gradually and beat to spreading consistency. Frost bottom layer and fill with mandarin oranges. Frost top layer and sides and decorate with orange slices. Note: this recipe works well for a cherry chocolate cake, using cherries in the filling and their juice and/or kirschwasser in the frosting.

HUNTER'S CAKE

2	cups raisins
4	tablespoons shortening
2	teaspoons salt
1	teaspoon cloves
1/2	teaspoon nutmeg
2-1/2	cups water

Boil above ingredients for 5 minutes. Set aside to cool.

Add:

3	cups flour
2	teaspoons soda
1	cup walnuts

Bake at 350 degrees for 30 minutes. If desired, 1/2 cup chocolate chips and 1 apple (diced) can be added to first set of ingredients.

ANGEL FOOD CAKE

1	cup sifted cake flour
1-1/2	cups sugar
1-1/4	cups egg whites
1/4	teaspoon salt
1-1/4	teaspoons cream of tartar
1	teaspoon vanilla
1/4	teaspoon almond extract

Sift and measure flour. Beat egg whites until stiff (not dry), but stand in peaks. Add salt and cream of tartar. Add sugar and flavorings. By hand, fold in flour. Bake in tube pan at 375 degrees for 30 minutes. Invert tin and let cake hang to cool.

MAYONNAISE CAKE

1	cup sugar
1	cup mayonnaise
2	cups flour
3	tablespoons cocoa
1	teaspoon vanilla
1/8	teaspoon salt
1	teaspoon soda
1	cup chopped dates
1	cup boiling water

Pour water over dates and soda. Let set until cool. Cream mayonnaise and sugar. Add date mixture, then rest of ingredients. Bake at 375 degrees for 25 minutes.

COOKIE SHEET CAKE

1	cup margarine
1	cup water
3	tablespoons cocoa
2	cups sugar
2	cups flour
1/2	teaspoon salt
2	eggs
1	teaspoon soda

In medium saucepan, heat margarine, water and cocoa to boiling. Mix sugar, flour and salt. Pour and stir into boiling ingredients. Add eggs and soda. Mix well. Pour into greased and floured jelly roll pan. Bake at 350 degrees 15 to 20 minutes.

WACKEY CAKE

Heat oven to 350 degrees. Sift together in bowl (or 8 x 8 x 2 inch ungreased pan):

1-1/2	cups flour, sifted
1/2	teaspoon salt
3	tablespoons cocoa
1	teaspoon baking soda
1	cup sugar

Now put the ingredients into the pan which you are going to bake this in and make 3 holes in ingredients. In the first hole, put 1 teaspoon vinegar; in the second, 1 teaspoon vanilla; in the third, 5 tablespoons salad oil. Now over the whole thing, pour 1 cup water and mix up well with a fork. Bake 25 to 30 minutes or until done.

CHERRY CHEESE CAKE

1	(8 ounce) package cream cheese
1	can Eagle brand sweetened condensed milk
1	(16 ounce) carton sour cream
4	tablespoons fresh lemon juice
1	envelope Knox unflavored gelatin

Mix sour cream and lemon juice and set aside. In another bowl, add condensed milk and cream cheese a little at a time, whipping until creamy. Dissolve gelatin in 1/4 cup boiling water. Add water and gelatin mixture to cream cheese mixture. Add this to sour cream mixture and blend well. Pour into two graham cracker crusts and top with cherry pie filling in the center of the cake. Cover and refrigerate to chill.

LEMON CHEESE CAKE

Dissolve two 3 ounce packages lemon jello in 2-1/2 cups boiling water. Let congeal. Meanwhile, cream 1 (8 ounce) package cream cheese with 3/4 cup sugar and 3 tablespoons lemon juice. When jello has set, whip. Add to cream cheese mixture. Whip 1 large can evaporated milk and fold into the above mixture. Crush 40 vanilla wafers. Mix with 1 tablespoon sugar, 4 tablespoons melted butter and a dash of vanilla. Place half the crumb mixture in bottom of a 13 x 9 inch pan. Pour in gelatin mixture and sprinkle with remaining crumbs. Chill till set.

BLUEBERRY STREUSEL COFFEE CAKE

2	cups flour
2	teaspoons baking powder
1/2	teaspoon salt
1/4	cup butter or margarine
3/4	cup sugar
1	large egg
1/2	cup milk
2-1/2	cups fresh blueberries, rinsed and drained (or frozen unsweetened)

Stir together flour, baking powder and salt. Cream butter and sugar together in large mixing bowl until light and fluffy. Beat in egg. Add flour mixture and milk, stirring just until dry ingredients are moistened. Fold in blueberries. Turn batter into greased bundt or angel food cake pan. Sprinkle with streusel topping.

Topping:

1/2	cup firmly packed light brown sugar
3	tablespoons flour
2	teaspoons cinnamon
3	tablespoons butter
1/2	cup finely chopped pecans or walnuts

Stir together brown sugar, flour and cinnamon in medium bowl. With pastry blender, cut in butter until particles are fine, then mix in nuts. Bake cake in pre-heated 375 degree oven until tester inserted in center comes out clean, 55 to 60 minutes. If topping begins to get very brown, cover loosely with foil. Cool 5 minutes. Run knife around edges to loosen, remove from pan and cut into wedges.

FRUIT COCKTAIL CAKE

1	cup sugar
1	cup flour
1	teaspoon soda
1/2	teaspoon salt
1/2	teaspoon cinnamon
1	egg
1	(16 ounce) can fruit cocktail (drain and reserve 1/2 cup juice)
1/3	cup brown sugar
1/3	cup nuts
1/8	stick butter or oleo

Mix sugar, flour, soda, salt and cinnamon. Add egg, fruit cocktail and 1/2 cup juice. Mix and pour into 9 x 9 inch greased pan. Crumble brown sugar, nuts and butter over top. Bake at 350 degrees for 40 minutes.

SAUERKRAUT SURPRISE CAKE

1/2	cup butter
1-1/2	cups sugar
3	eggs
1	teaspoon vanilla
2	cups sifted all-purpose flour
1	teaspoon baking powder
1	teaspoon baking soda
1/2	teaspoon salt
1/2	cup cocoa powder
1	cup water
1	(8 ounce) can sauerkraut (drained, rinsed and finely snipped)

In a large mixing bowl, cream butter and sugar till light. Beat in eggs one at a time. Add vanilla. Sift together flour, baking powder, soda, salt and cocoa powder. Add to creamed mixture alternately with water, beating after each addition. Stir in sauerkraut. Turn into greased and floured 13 x 9 x 2 inch pan. Bake at 350 degrees for 35 to 40 minutes. Cool in pan. Frost with Sour Cream Chocolate Frosting.

SOUR CREAM CHOCOLATE FROSTING

Melt one 6 ounce package semi-sweet chocolate pieces and 4 tablespoons butter over low heat. Remove from heat and blend in 1/2 cup dairy sour cream, 1 teaspoon vanilla and 1/4 teaspoon salt. Gradually add confectioner's sugar (2-1/2 - 2-3/4 cups) to make of spreading consistency. Beat well.

ORANGE CAKE

1-1/4   cups sugar
1   orange
1/2   cup shortening
2   eggs, well beaten
1/2   teaspoon salt
1   teaspoon baking soda
1/2   teaspoon baking powder
1   cup pitted dates or raisins
2   cups flour
1   cup sour milk

Combine 1/4 cup sugar and juice from orange. Stir until sugar is dissolved. Cream 1 cup sugar with shortening. Add eggs. Sift flour. Measure and sift with baking powder, baking soda and salt. Add alternately with milk to first mixture. Add dates or raisins which have been ground with orange rind. Mix until well blended. Pour into well oiled loaf pan. Bake at 375 degrees about 45 minutes. Pour orange juice and sugar over cake before removing from pan. I like to use an angel food pan — the cake cooks better in the middle.

BLUEBERRY BRUNCH CAKE

1   cup flour (unsifted)
1/3   cup sugar
1-1/2   teaspoons baking powder
1/2   teaspoon salt
1   egg, slightly beaten
1/2   cup milk
1/3   cup salad oil
1   tablespoon lemon juice
1   cup blueberries nut topping

Combine flour, sugar, baking powder and salt. Sift into mixing bowl. Make a well in the center of the flour mixture and put in the egg, milk, salad oil and lemon juice. Stir until mixture is evenly blended. Pour into well greased 8 inch square pan. Scatter blueberries evenly over top of cake batter. Sprinkle nut topping over berries. Bake at 375 degrees until cake tester inserted in center comes out clean.

PUMPKIN CAKE

3   cups flour
1-1/2   teaspoons salt
1/2   teaspoon baking powder
1   teaspoon soda
1   teaspoon nutmeg
1   teaspoon cinnamon
1   teaspoon allspice
1   cup shortening
2-3/4   cups sugar
3   eggs
1   teaspoon vanilla
1   can (1 pound) pumpkin
1   cup nuts glaze

Line the bottom of a 10 inch tube pan with waxed paper. Sift together flour, salt, baking powder, soda and spices. Cream shortening, gradually add sugar, creaming until light. Add eggs one at a time, beating well after each addition. Stir in vanilla. Add dry ingredients to creamed mixture alternately with pumpkin, beating after each addition. Stir in nuts. Pour into pan and bake at 350 degrees for 1-1/2 hours. Add glaze.

Glaze:

1/2   cup confectioner's sugar
1   teaspoon water

Mix until smooth. Brush on cake while warm.

CHOCOLATE PUDDING CAKE

1-1/2	cups flour
1	cup sugar
3	tablespoons cocoa
3	teaspoons baking powder
3/4	teaspoon salt
3/4	cup milk
1-1/2	tablespoons melted butter
2	teaspoons vanilla
3/4	cup chopped walnuts (optional)
1/2	cup brown sugar
1/4	cup sugar
3	tablespoons cocoa
1-3/4	cups boiling water

Sift together flour, 1 cup sugar, 3 tablespoons cocoa, baking powder and salt. Add milk, butter and vanilla and beat well. Stir in walnuts. Spread batter into greased 13 x 9 x 2 inch pan. Combine brown sugar, 1/4 cup sugar and 3 tablespoons cocoa. Sprinkle over batter. Pour 1-3/4 cups boiling water over all. Bake at 350 degrees for 40 minutes. Top with whipped cream or ice cream. Serve warm or cool. Makes 12 servings.

PRUNE OR CHOPPED APPLE CAKE

Cream together:

1	cup oil
1-1/2	cups sugar
1	cup buttermilk

Sift together:

2	cups flour
1	teaspoon salt
1/2	teaspoon cinnamon
1/4	teaspoon nutmeg
1/4	teaspoon allspice
1	tablespoon soda

To the first creamed mixture, add 3 lightly beaten eggs and 1 teaspoon vanilla. Mix all together and add 1 cup cooked dried prunes (cut up) or 1 cup chopped apples. Bake at 350 degrees about 50 minutes. Let cool a little and spoon over the top the following:

1	cup sugar
1/2	cup buttermilk
1/2	teaspoon soda

Cook in large pan. Boil for about 5 minutes, stirring often. Spoon over the cake while hot.

WASHINGTON CHIFFON PIE OR CAKE

2	egg whites
1/2	cup sugar

* * *

2-1/4	cups sifted cake flour
1	cup sugar
3	teaspoons baking powder
1	teaspoon salt
1/3	cup salad oil
1	cup milk
1-1/2	teaspoons vanilla
2	egg yolks

Beat egg whites till foamy. Gradually beat in 1/2 cup sugar, Continue beating until very stiff and glossy. Sift remaining ingredients into another bowl. Add salad oil, half the milk and vanilla. Beat 1 minute at medium speed on mixer or 150 strokes by hand, scraping sides and bottom of bowl constantly. Add remaining milk and egg yolks. Beat one minute longer, scraping bowl. Gently fold in egg-white mixture with down-up and over motion, turning the bowl. Bake in 2 paper lined 9 x 1-1/2 inch round pans at 350 degrees for about 25 minutes or until done. Cool. Fill between cooled layers with one cup strawberry or raspberry jam mixed with 1/2 cup whipped cream. Sift confectioner's sugar lightly over the top.

ICE CREAM CUPCAKES

1-1/2	cups flour
1	tablespoon baking powder
1	teaspoon salt
1	egg
2	tablespoons melted butter
2	cups vanilla ice cream, softened

Beat until smooth. Spoon into 12 buttered muffin cups. Bake at 425 degrees for 20 to 25 minutes.

CARAMEL FROSTING

Melt 1/2 cup butter over low heat. Blend in 3/4 cup brown sugar. Boil 2 minutes, stirring constantly. Stir in 3 tablespoons milk and cook till boiling. Cool to lukewarm. Add 2 cups powdered sugar and 1 teaspoon vanilla.

PUMPKIN-ORANGE CHIFFON PIE

1/2	cup sugar
1	tablespoon (1 envelope) Knox unflavored gelatin
1/2	teaspoon ginger
1/2	teaspoon nutmeg
1/2	teaspoon cinnamon
1/2	cup milk
3	egg yolks

* * *

1-1/4	cups pumpkin
1/4	cup orange juice
1	teaspoon grated orange peel

* * *

3	egg whites
1/2 to	
1	cup sugar
	whipped cream
	orange peel (for garnish)

Mix first 5 ingredients together in a saucepan. Stir in milk and egg yolks. Cook over medium heat until bubbly. Remove from heat and add next 3 ingredients. Place in the refrigerator till partially set (about 3 hours). Whip egg whites with sugar till stiff and fold into pumpkin mixture. Pour into a baked pie shell. Decorate with whipped cream and garnish with grated orange peel. Very Good!

PUMPKIN PIE

1-1/2	cups cooked pumpkin
1	cup rich milk
1	cup sugar
1/4	teaspoon salt
1/4	teaspoon nutmeg
1/4	teaspoon cinnamon
2	eggs, slightly beaten
1	tablespoon butter

Combine ingredients. Mix thoroughly. Pour into pastry lined pie pan. Bake in hot oven (425 degrees) about 25 minutes or until an inserted knife comes out clean. Serve with whipped cream. If desired, 1/2 cup raisins may be added to pumpkin filling.

PUMPKIN IMPOSSIBLE PIE

4	eggs
3/4	cup sugar
1/2	cup biscuit mix
1/2	teaspoon vanilla
1/2	cup butter or margarine
1	can (13 ounce) evaporated milk
1	can (16 ounce) pumpkin
1/2	teaspoon ginger
1/2	teaspoon nutmeg
	dash salt
3/4	teaspoon cinnamon

Mix all ingredients in blender for 3 minutes. Pour into 9 inch pie pan and sprinkle with nutmeg. Bake at 425 degrees until knife comes out clean. Cover after 30 minutes if too brown.

BETTY'S GORGEOUS PUMPKIN PIE

1	unbaked 9 inch pastry shell
1-3/4	cups canned pumpkin
1	tablespoon butter
3/4	cup light brown sugar
1	tablespoon flour
2	eggs
1	tall can evaporated milk
1	teaspoon cinnamon
1/2	teaspoon ginger
1/8	teaspoon mace
1/2	teaspoon salt
2	tablespoons boiling water
	whipped cream

You will enjoy every minute of this labor of love! Use your favorite pie crust. Heat pumpkin in saucepan for 10 minutes, stirring frequently until pumpkin is somewhat dry. Remove from heat. Stir in butter. Combine brown sugar and flour. Add to pumpkin. Beat eggs and add with milk to pumpkin. Blend spices, salt and water. Add to pumpkin. Stir until well mixed. Pour into pastry lined pie pan. Bake at 450 degrees for 15 minutes. Reduce heat to 300 degrees and bake about 45 minutes longer. Cool. Garnish with whipped cream and grated cheddar cheese.

CUSTARD PIE

2	cups milk, scalded
5	tablespoons sugar
1/4	teaspoon nutmeg
3	eggs
1/2	teaspoon salt
1/2	teaspoon vanilla flavoring

Beat eggs until yolks and whites are blended. Add sugar, salt, nutmeg and flavoring. Mix thoroughly. Add milk slowly, stirring constantly. Pour into pastry-lined pie pan. Bake in hot oven (425 degrees) about 25 minutes or until an inserted knife comes out clean.

OLD FASHIONED CUSTARD PIE

Crust:

1-1/2	cups sifted flour
1/2	teaspoon salt
1/4	cup ice water
1/2	cup shortening

Blend shortening into flour and salt. Add ice water and mix until it forms a ball. Pour onto sheet and roll out 1 inch larger than pie pan. Transfer to pie pan, turn under edge and flute.

Filling:

4	eggs
2-1/2	cups milk or milk mixed with cream
1	teaspoon nutmeg
3/4	cup sugar
1/8	teaspoon salt
1	teaspoon vanilla

Mix well. Pour into unbaked pie shell and bake in moderate oven (350 degrees) 35 to 40 minutes or till knife inserted half way between center and edge comes out clean.

KENTUCKY PECAN PIE

1	cup white corn syrup
1	cup dark brown sugar
1/3	teaspoon salt
1/3	cup melted butter
1	teaspoon vanilla
3	whole eggs, slightly beaten
1	heaping cup shelled whole pecans

Combine syrup, sugar, salt, butter and vanilla. Mix well. Add beaten eggs and pour into unbaked 9 inch pie shell. Sprinkle pecans on top. Bake in pre-heated 350 degree oven for about 45 minutes.

STRAWBERRY GLAZE PIE

9	inch pie shell, baked
1-1/2	quarts strawberries
1	cup sugar
3	tablespoons cornstarch
1/2	cup water
1	tablespoon butter
1	cup heavy cream, whipped
2	tablespoons confectioner's sugar vanilla

Hull and wash berries in cold water; drain. Crush (with potato masher) enough berries to make 1 cup. Combine sugar and cornstarch. Add crushed berries and water. Cook over medium heat, stirring constantly until mixture comes to boil. Continue cooking and stirring over low heat 2 minutes. The mixture will be thickened and translucent. Remove from heat and stir in butter. Cool. Place whole berries in pie shell, reserving a few choice ones for garnish. Pour cooked mixture over berries and chill for at least 2 hours. Serve topped with whipped cream, sugar and vanilla added. Garnish with remaining berries.

CHOCOLATE CREAM PIE

1	cup sugar
1/2	teaspoon salt
1	tablespoon flour
2-1/2	tablespoons corn starch
1	tall can evaporated milk (1-2/3 cups)
1	cup water
2	eggs, beaten
2	squares unsweetened chocolate
2	tablespoons butter
1	teaspoon vanilla extract
1	baked 9 inch pie shell
	whipped cream
	shredded chocolate

Chocolate lovers dream! In heavy saucepan, combine sugar, salt, flour, corn starch, milk, water and chocolate. Bring to boil and cook 3 minutes or until mixture thickens, stirring constantly. Remove from heat. Stir about half of hot mixture into beaten eggs, then combine with balance of mixture in saucepan. Cook 1 minute longer over low heat, stirring. Remove from heat and stir in butter and vanilla. Pour into pie crust and chill. Top with whipped cream and sprinkled shredded chocolate.

GLAZED FRESH STRAWBERRY PIE

1	baked 9 inch pastry shell
3	pints strawberries
1	cup sugar
3-1/2	tablespoons cornstarch
1/2	cup water
	few drops red food coloring
	whipped cream

Mash 1 pint of strawberries. Mix sugar and cornstarch in a 3 quart saucepan. Stir in water and mashed berries. Cook over medium heat stirring constantly, until mixture comes to a boil and boils 2 minutes. Remove from heat. Stir in food coloring. Cool. Fold remaining 2 pints of berries into cooled mixture. Pile into pastry shell. Chill. Serve with whipped cream. Makes one 9 inch pie.

BIG PAN RHUBARB PIE (makes 12 servings)

2-3/4	cups sugar, divided
1/4	cup flour
3/4	teaspoon salt
1	cup whipping cream
6	eggs, separated
5	cups rhubarb, cut up
	shortbread crust
2	teaspoons vanilla

Combine 2 cups sugar, flour and salt. Gradually stir in cream. Beat egg yolks until very light. Blend into sugar mixture. Add rhubarb. Spoon over warm shortbread crust. Bake at 350 degrees for 60 minutes. Beat egg whites until they form soft peaks. Add remaining 3/4 cup sugar, along with 1/4 teaspoon cream of tartar, gradually, beating until stiff and sugar is dissolved. Stir in vanilla. Spread over rhubarb layer, starting at edges and working towards center. Carefully seal meringue to outer edges of pan. Continue baking for 15 minutes or until golden.

Shortbread Crust:

1	cup butter
2	tablespoons sugar
2	cups flour

Combine; mix until crumbly. Press into bottom of 9 x 13 inch pan. Bake at 350 degrees for 10 minutes.

PUMPKIN EGGNOG PIE

Crust:

1	cup graham cracker crumbs (8 double crackers)
1/2	cup pecans, finely chopped
3	tablespoons powdered sugar
6	tablespoons melted butter

Combine and press into 9 inch pie pan. Bake at 375 degrees for 6 to 8 minutes. Cool.

Filling:

1	envelope unflavored gelatin
1/2	cup brown sugar
1/2	teaspoon salt
1/2	teaspoon cinnamon
1/4	teaspoon ginger
	dash ground nutmeg
1	cup eggnog
3	slightly beaten egg yolks
1	cup canned pumpkin (or yellow squash — makes a lighter pie)
3	egg whites
1/2	cup powdered sugar

Combine first 6 ingredients. Stir in eggnog, yolks and pumpkin. Cook over medium heat until thick. Stir frequently. Chill until partially set. Beat egg whites until stiff. Gradually add sugar and beat to form peaks. Fold into pumpkin mixture and pour into pie crust. Chill until ready to serve. Serve with whipped cream.

PEANUT BUTTER PIE

1	cup corn syrup
1	cup sugar
3	eggs, slightly beaten
1/3	cup peanut butter
1	teaspoon vanilla
1	uncooked pie shell

Mix first 5 ingredients thoroughly. Pour into pie shell. Bake at 400 degrees for 15 minutes. Reduce heat to 350 degrees and bake 30 to 35 minutes or until set. Let cool and cover with meringue.

STRAWBERRY PIE

1	(8 ounce) package cream cheese
1	cup powdered sugar
1/2	pint whipping cream
1	teaspoon vanilla
1	(9 inch) baked pie crust

Cream together cream cheese and powdered sugar. Whip cream and add 1 teaspoon vanilla. Fold into creamed mixture. Pour into pie crust. Thaw 1 package strawberries. Bring to boil and thicken with 1 tablespoon cornstarch. Cool. Put on top of pie and refrigerate.

RAISIN PIE

1-1/2	cups raisins
1/4	cup lemon juice
3	tablespoons flour
1	cup sugar
1	cup boiling water
1	tablespoon butter few grains salt

Combine sugar, flour and salt. Add boiling water slowly, stirring constantly. Cook over hot water until thick and clear. Add raisins, lemon juice and butter. Mix thoroughly. Pour into pastry lined tin. Cover with top crust. Bake in hot oven (425 degrees) about 25 minutes.

PIE CRUST SUPREME

1-1/2	cups sifted all-purpose flour
1/2	teaspoon salt
1/4	teaspoon baking powder
1/2	cup lard (I always use lard)
2	tablespoons butter
2	tablespoons beaten egg
3	tablespoons ice water
1/2	teaspoon vinegar

Combine first 5 ingredients and blend with pastry blender. Add liquid ingredients, a little at a time, until all flour is moistened. (You probably will not need all of the liquid.) Divide in half and roll on a floured pastry cloth or between sheets of floured wax paper. Line a 9 inch pie pan. Yields pastry for a 2-crust 9 inch pie.

BEST EVER PIE CRUST

1   pound butter
1   (8 ounce) package cream cheese
4-1/2 cups flour

In mixing bowl, cream butter and cream cheese. Add flour and mix until smooth. For single pie shell, roll out and bake at 350 degrees for 12 to 15 minutes. Never gets tough no matter how many times you roll out.

MRS. LEAHY'S PIE CRUST

1-3/4 cups shortening
4   cups flour
1   tablespoon sugar
2   teaspoons salt
1   tablespoon vinegar (regular)
1   beaten egg
1/2   cup cold water

Cut shortening into dry ingredients. Beat vinegar, egg and cold water and add to above. May be frozen. Makes 4 single crusts or 2 large pies. Will keep in refrigerator for a week.

SANDY'S PIE CRUST

3   cups flour
1-1/2 cups shortening
1   teaspoon salt
1   egg
1   tablespoon vinegar

Mix egg and vinegar together and add water to make 3/4 cup total. Mix all ingredients together. Will make two — 9 inch pies or three to four — 9 inch pies if rolled extra thin.

PIE CRUST FOR OPEN FACED PIES

1/2   cup sunflower seeds, ground fine
1/2   cup sesame seeds, ground fine
1   cup whole oats, ground fine
1   cup crown wheatgerm
1   teaspoon kelp powder
1/2   cup date sugar

Mix this in a large bowl. Whip with a fork, 4 tablespoons of oil and 4 tablespoons of water. Add to first mixture and work in with finger tips. Roll out between two sheets of wax paper. Bake to golden brown or eat raw. Makes 3 pie shells.

JANE'S GRANDMA'S SHORTBREAD COOKIES

1   pound butter
1   cup confectioner's sugar
4   cups flour
1   teaspoon vanilla

No liquid required. Cut butter (not melted) into sugar and flour. Add vanilla and gradually knead a little at a time. It will become creamy in texture. Make into small balls and flatten in palm. Bake at 300 degrees 15 to 20 minutes or until edges are slightly browned. This is a 1940 recipe I acquired from my grandmother.

FRUIT COOKIES

1   cup flour
1   cup sugar
1   cup dates
3   cups large pecan pieces
4   ounces red candied cherries
4   ounces green candied cherries
1   slice green pineapple
1   slice red pineapple

Sift flour and sugar. Add the fruit and nuts. Stir well. Add 3 egg whites that have been stiffly beaten. Drop on a cookie sheet using a teaspoon. Bake 12 to 15 minutes in moderate oven. P.S. The longer you keep these cookies the better they taste.

EVELYN'S GINGERSNAPS

2	cups all-purpose flour
1	teaspoon ginger
2	teaspoons baking soda
1	teaspoon cinnamon
1/2	teaspoon salt
3/4	cup shortening
1	cup sugar
1	egg
1/4	cup molasses (black)

Measure the dry ingredients into a sifter. Cream shortening, sugar, egg and molasses until a smooth texture. Sift in the dry ingredients and blend well with a large heavy spoon. Form balls about the size of a walnut by rolling in palm of hands. Roll each ball in granulated sugar, so it is lightly covered all over. Bake at 350 degrees 12 to 15 minutes or until light brown. Cookies will spread out during baking to about 2 inches in size. Cookies are very soft and break easily when removing from oven, so care should be taken in handling them. These cookies are so very good eaten while still warm with a nice glass of cold milk. They won a blue ribbon at the Cowlitz County Fair, Longview, Washington.

CASHEW COOKIES

Cream together:

1	cup brown sugar
1/2	cup oil
1	tablespoon lecithin

Then add and mix:

1	cup coconut
2	cups quick raw oats
1/2	cup whole wheat flour
1	cup cashew nuts, ground
2	tablespoons soy flour
1/2	tablespoon salt

Mix in 1/2 cup water. Stir well and drop by teaspoon on a greased pan. Bake in 350 degree oven for 20 to 25 minutes.

CARROT BARS

1	cup water
1	cup raisins
3/4	cup honey
1/3	cup shortening
1-1/2	cups grated carrots
1	teaspoon cinnamon
1	teaspoon nutmeg
1	teaspoon soda
2	cups whole wheat flour
1/2	teaspoon salt

Cook raisins and water until raisins are soft. Cream honey and shortening. Add grated carrots and stir. Add dry ingredients. Add raisins and water. 1/2 cup nuts may be added if desired. Spread evenly into 9 x 12 greased pan. Bake at 350 degrees for 25 to 30 minutes. Cool. Frost with icing.

Icing:

1	cup powdered sugar
1/2	cup dry milk
1/2	teaspoon vanilla
	enough milk to make thin consistency

Makes about 24 bars.

SUGAR COOKIES

1	cup butter
1	cup oil
1	cup sugar
1	cup powdered sugar
2	eggs
	vanilla to suit
4	cups flour
1	teaspoon salt
1	teaspoon soda
1	teaspoon cream of tartar

Combine oil, butter, sugar, eggs and vanilla. Beat together and add dry ingredients. Refrigerate dough at least 2 hours and then make into balls. Press with bottom of glass, dipped in sugar. Bake at 350 degrees for 7-10 minutes or until lightly browned. They melt in your mouth!

HONEY SPICE COOKIES

5	cups whole wheat flour
1	teaspoon salt
1	teaspoon baking powder
1/2	teaspoon soda
1	teaspoon cinnamon
1	teaspoon ginger
1/2	teaspoon cloves
1/2	teaspoon nutmeg
1	cup shortening
2	eggs
2	cups honey
1	teaspoon vanilla
1	cup milk

Sift dry ingredients together. Combine eggs, honey, shortening and vanilla. Beat well. Add milk alternately with dry ingredients. Chill dough. Roll out and cut with round cutter or form into balls and flatten with bottom of glass. Bake on slightly greased cookie sheet at 375 degrees 8 to 10 minutes if rolled or about 12 minutes if flattened.

WALNUT-OATMEAL CHEWS

1	cup shortening
1	cup sugar
1	cup packed brown sugar
1	teaspoon vanilla
2	eggs
1-1/2	cups sifted flour
1	teaspoon baking powder
1/2	teaspoon soda
1/2	teaspoon salt
2	cups uncooked rolled oats
1	cup chopped walnuts

Cream shortening, sugars and vanilla. Add eggs, beat well. Sift dry ingredients and add to creamed mixture. Stir in oats and walnuts. Blend thoroughly. Drop dough by teaspoonfuls on greased baking sheet. Press flat with a fork. Bake at 375 degrees for 10 to 12 minutes. Makes 6 dozen.

CHOCOLATE CHIP COOKIES

1	package dark brown sugar
1-2/3	cups white sugar
1-1/4	cups oil
1-1/2	cups Crisco
3	teaspoons vanilla
6	eggs
6	cups flour
3	teaspoons soda
3	teaspoons salt
1	(12 ounce) package chocolate chips
	nuts (optional)

In a large bowl, add ingredients in order given. Drop by teaspoonful on greased cookie sheet. Bake at 325 degrees for about 10 minutes. This makes about 10 dozen cookies. Don't think that's a lot because as good as these are, you won't have them around long.

CHOCOLATE CHIP COOKIES

2/3	cup shortening
2/3	cup butter
1	cup sugar
1	cup brown sugar
2	eggs
2	teaspoons vanilla

Blend:

3	cups flour (add 1/2 cup more for softer cookies)
1	teaspoon soda
1	teaspoon salt

Add:

1	cup nuts
2	cups chocolate chips

Bake at 325 degrees for 10 minutes.

EASY TO MAKE COOKIES

Mix together:

2	cups sugar
4	tablespoons cocoa
1/4	cup margarine
1/2	cup milk
	pinch of salt

Bring this mixture to a boil and remove from stove. Set pan in hot water and add to the mixture:

3	cups dry quick cooking oats
1/4	cup peanut butter
1	teaspoon vanilla

Stir in mixture thoroughly. Drop by spoonfuls on waxed paper and let stand till cold.

EVELYN'S POTATO CHIP COOKIES

2	cups butter
1	cup sugar
2	teaspoons vanilla
3-1/2	cups flour
1-1/3	cups crushed potato chips

Cream butter, sugar and vanilla till blended. Stir in flour and crushed potato chips. Roll small spoonfuls to size of walnut. Top each mound of dough with half a red or green candied cherry. Bake at 350 degrees for 10 to 12 minutes. Cookies do not get brown, so don't bake till they are or you will have bricks! The recipe calls for butter and butter is one of the things about this recipe that makes them so good. I have tried using shortening in the past and they tasted like shortening!!! So, I tried using margarine instead. They got hard as rocks after a couple of days. Now I stick with the butter and they melt in your mouth. When I put the cherry half on, before baking, I just lightly press them on the cookie. I don't flatten the cookie completely, but just sorta press it down a little. You know what I mean — don't you? Also, I found that if I buy the cheap potato chips in the box, one bag usually equals 1-1/3 cups crushed potato chips. I just poke a hole in the corner of the bag and crush them by rolling my rolling pin over the bag several times. No mess to clean up! No, you don't need salt in this recipe and I didn't forget that. There is enough salt on the potato chips to do the job.

FILLED COOKIES

1	cup granulated sugar
1	cup brown sugar
1	cup shortening
2	eggs
1/4	cup buttermilk
1	teaspoon vanilla
3-1/2	cups all-purpose flour
1	teaspoon baking powder
1	teaspoon baking soda
1	teaspoon nutmeg
1	teaspoon salt

Fillings:

strawberry jam
orange marmalade
prepared mincemeat
dates
crushed pineapple

In large bowl cream sugars and shortening. Add eggs, buttermilk and vanilla. Beat well. Stir together flour, baking powder, baking soda, nutmeg and salt. Stir into creamed mixture. Cover and chill. Roll dough to 1/3 inch thick and cut with cookie cutter into 1-1/2 inch rounds. Place 1 teaspoon of jam or desired filling on each of half the rounds. Top with remaining rounds and seal edges with fork. With knife, cut criss-cross slits in tops of cookies. Bake at 350 degrees for 10 to 15 minutes.

CANT BELIEVE ITS A COOKIE

1	cup sugar
1	cup peanut butter
1	egg
1/2	cup chocolate chips

Blend sugar, peanut butter and egg well with mixer. Stir in chocolate chips. Roll into balls and flatten with fork on un-greased cookie sheet. Bake at 350 degrees for about 12 minutes or until lightly browned. Makes about one dozen. Tastes like peanut butter cups.

HAWAIIAN COCONUT COOKIES

1/2	cup shortening
1/2	cup granulated sugar
1/2	cup brown sugar
1	egg, beaten
1	teaspoon vanilla
1	cup sifted all-purpose flour
1	teaspoon baking powder
1	teaspoon soda
1/2	teaspoon salt
1	cup quick rolled oats
1	cup Angel Flake coconut

Cream shortening and sugars. Add beaten egg and vanilla. Sift dry ingredients and add to creamed mixture until well blended. Stir in rolled oats and coconut. Shape dough into small balls and flatten with a fork. Place on greased cookie sheet and bake at 350 degrees for 12 to 15 minutes. Makes 3 dozen.

MOLASSES SUGAR COOKIES

3/4	cup shortening
1	cup sugar
1/4	cup molasses
1	egg
2	cups sifted flour
2	teaspoons baking soda
1	teaspoon cinnamon
1/2	teaspoon cloves
1/2	teaspoon ginger
1/2	teaspoon salt

Cream together shortening and sugar. Add molasses and egg. Beat well. Sift together flour, soda, cinnamon, cloves, ginger and salt. Add to first mixture. Mix well and chill. Form into 1 inch balls. Roll in granulated sugar and place on greased cookie sheets (not too close together). Bake at 375 degrees for 8 to 10 minutes.

ORANGE BALLS

2-1/2	cups crushed vanilla wafers or graham crackers
1	(6 ounce) can frozen orange juice
3	cups powdered sugar
1	cube margarine

Combine ingredients well. Form into small balls and roll in coconut. These freeze well.

FILLED OATMEAL COOKIES

3/4	cup shortening
3/4	cup margarine
2	cups brown sugar
1	cup white sugar
2	eggs
1/2	cup water
2	teaspoons vanilla
2-1/2	cups flour
2	teaspoons salt
1	teaspoon soda
4	cups oats

Combine shortening, margarine, brown sugar, white sugar, eggs, water and vanilla. Mix well. Add dry ingredients and mix well. Bake at 350 degrees till done, 12 to 15 minutes.

Filling:

1	tablespoon flour
1	tablespoon sugar
2/3	cup milk
1	egg
1/2	cup margarine
1/4	cup sugar
1/2	teaspoon vanilla

Combine flour, sugar, milk and egg. Mix and stir over medium heat until mixture boils and is thick. Cool. Beat in 1/2 cup margarine till fluffy. Gradually add 1/4 cup sugar and vanilla. Beat well. Cover and store in refrigerator. Put 2 cookies together with filling and store in refrigerator. These will become very soft.

OATMEAL CRISPIES

1	cup shortening (half butter or margarine, best)
1	cup brown sugar
1	cup granulated sugar

Cream together above ingredients.

Add:

2	eggs
1	teaspoon vanilla

Beat well.

Add:

3	cups quick cooking rolled oats
1/2	cup chopped walnuts
1/2	cup raisins (chopped dates or chocolate chips may be used)

Shape into rolls, wrap in wax paper and chill overnight. Slice 1/4 inch thick and bake on un-greased cookie sheet at 350 degrees for 10 minutes or until brown.

NO BAKE FUDGIES

Combine in saucepan:

2	cups sugar
1	cup evaporated milk
1/2	cup butter

Bring to a boil. Boil 5 minutes, stirring constantly. Remove from heat. Add 1 package (6 ounce) semi-sweet chocolate morsels. Mix and stir until chocolate is melted.

Add:

3/4	cup sifted flour
1	cup graham cracker crumbs
3/4	cup chopped nuts
1	teaspoon vanilla

Mix well. Spread in well greased 11-1/2 x 7-1/2 x 1-1/2 inch pan. If desired, top pieces with walnuts. Cool and cut into squares.

OATMEAL COOKIES

Cream together:

1	cup butter or margarine
1	cup sugar
1/2	cup brown sugar

Add:

1	egg, beaten
1-1/2	cups flour
1	teaspoon soda
1	teaspoon cinnamon

Add:

1-1/2	cups quick oatmeal
3/4	cup nuts
1	teaspoon vanilla

Chill for 1 hour. Roll into balls and flatten with glass bottom dipped in sugar. Bake at 325 degrees for 10 minutes.

JAM DIAGONALS

1/2	cup butter
1/4	cup granulated sugar
1	teaspoon vanilla
1/8	teaspoon salt
1-1/4	cups flour
1/4	cup jam
3/4	cup confectioner's sugar
4	teaspoons lemon juice

With mixer, cream butter, sugar, vanilla and salt until fluffy. Blend in flour. Divide dough into thirds. Roll each section with hand to form 9 inch rope. Place 3 inches apart on lightly buttered cookie sheet. Make 1/2 inch depression down the length of roll (wooden spoon handle works). Ropes will flatten slightly. Fill depression with jam (apricot or raspberry are good). Bake at 350 degrees 12 to 15 minutes. Cool on cookie sheet. Blend powdered sugar and lemon juice and drizzle over jam. When glaze sets, slice diagonally into 1 inch bars. Makes 24.

BUTTERMILK CINNAMON BARS

1/2   cup butter
1-1/4   cups sugar
3/4   cup brown sugar
2   cups flour

Mix like pastry. Use 2 cups of butter mixture (reserve the rest) and combine with 1/2 cup flaked coconut and 1/2 cup chopped nuts. Press into buttered 9 x 13 inch pan to form crust.

Combine:

1   egg, beaten
1/2   teaspoon salt
1   teaspoon cinnamon
1   teaspoon baking powder
1   cup buttermilk
1   teaspoon vanilla

Mix with reserved butter mixture and pour over crust. Bake at 350 degrees for 45 minutes. Thin powdered sugar with milk and pour over to glaze.

GRAHAM CRACKER NO BAKE BARS

Fit graham crackers snugly in the bottom of a 9 x 13 inch baking pan.

Stir together in saucepan:

1/2   cup margarine
1/2   cup milk
1   egg
1   cup sugar

Cook, stirring and boil for 1 minute. Remove from heat.

Add:

1   cup graham cracker crumbs
1   cup coconut
3/4   cup broken walnut pieces

Spread this over graham crackers. Cover with another layer of crackers. Set in refrigerator till top layer of crackers is soft. Cut in desired portions. May be frosted before cutting.

DISAPPEARING MARSHMALLOW BROWNIES

1/2   cup (1/2 of a 6 ounce package) butterscotch pieces
1/4   cup butter
3/4   cup all purpose flour
1/3   cup firmly packed brown sugar
1   teaspoon baking powder
1/4   teaspoon salt
1/2   teaspoon vanilla
1   egg
1   cup miniature marshmallows
1   cup (6 ounce package) semi-sweet chocolate pieces
1/4   cup chopped nuts

Melt in 3 quart saucepan over medium heat, the butterscotch pieces and butter, stirring constantly. Remove from heat and cool to lukewarm. Add ingredients to butterscotch mixture in saucepan. Mix well. Fold marshmallows, chocolate pieces and nuts into butterscotch batter. Spread into greased pan. Bake at 350 degrees for 20 to 25 minutes. Center will be soft, but becomes firm upon cooling.

Icing:

1-1/2   cups powdered sugar
1/2   teaspoon vanilla

Enough milk to make icing of spreading consistency. Enjoy!

RUM BALLS

2-1/2   cups crushed vanilla wafers or graham cracker crumbs
1   cup powdered sugar
3   tablespoons cocoa
1   cup finely cut walnuts

Mix well. Add 3 tablespoons light corn syrup and 1/2 cup rum, bourbon, brandy or cognac. Mix well and form into balls. Roll in powdered sugar. Store in tightly covered container in refrigerator.

PECAN TASSIES

1	(3 ounce) package cream cheese
1/2	cup butter
1	cup flour
1	egg
3/4	cup brown sugar
1	tablespoon soft butter
1	teaspoon vanilla
	dash salt
1	cup pecans, cut up

Mix soft cream cheese and 1/2 cup butter thoroughly. Add flour and mix well. Chill; shape into 1 inch balls. Place in ungreased muffin tins and press in bottom and sides. Place half of nuts into cups. Combine egg, sugar, 1 tablespoon butter, vanilla and salt. Pour over nuts. Top with remaining nuts. Bake at 325 degrees for 25 minutes.

PUMPKIN ROLL

| 3 | eggs, beaten on high speed for 5 minutes |
| 1 | cup sugar |

Gradually add 2/3 cup pumpkin.

Sift together and fold in:

3/4	cup flour
1	teaspoon baking powder
2	teaspoons cinnamon
1	teaspoon ginger
1/2	teaspoon nutmeg
1/2	teaspoon salt

Mix well. Flour and grease a 15 x 10 x 1 inch jelly roll pan. Spread dough and sprinkle with 1/2 cup chopped nuts. Bake at 375 degrees for 15 minutes. Let roll cool for 5 minutes then roll it up in a towel that has been dusted with powdered sugar. Let cool.

Filling:

1	cup powdered sugar
1	(8 ounce) package cream cheese, softened
4	tablespoons butter
1/2	teaspoon vanilla

Beat until smooth. Unroll cake, spread filling on and re-roll. Freeze. Let thaw a few minutes before serving.

4 LAYER PUDDING DESSERT

First layer:

2	cups flour
1	cup melted butter
1	cup chopped pecans

Mix and pat into 9 x 13 inch pan. Bake for 15 minutes. Cool.

Second layer:

2	(8 ounce) packages cream cheese
2	cups powdered sugar
2	cups whipped cream

Beat till smooth and spread on first layer.

Third layer:

2	packages instant vanilla pudding
2	packages instant chocolate pudding (or use 4 packages butterscotch pudding)
6	cups milk

Beat till thick and pour over the first two layers.

Fourth layer: frost with whipped cream and sprinkle with slivered almonds. Very delicious!

MAIYIM'S MAPLE CUSTARD

This recipe is so quick, so easy, well-loved, but little known. Nutritious and a bargain when eggs are plentiful.

3   eggs
1/2   cup maple syrup
2   cups milk
        dash salt if desired

In one baking casserole, beat eggs with syrup and salt. Add milk and blend. Place in pan of hot water and bake in oven at 350 degrees for 40 to 50 minutes or until knife inserted halfway between side and center comes out clean. Note: when dinner's a little "short" and you've got the oven on, you can mix this up in 2 minutes and bake while the family's dining, to finish that dinner off right.

CRANBERRY CRUNCH

1   cup uncooked rolled oats
1/2   cup all-purpose flour
1   cup brown sugar
1/2   cup butter
1   pound fresh cranberries or 1 can cranberry sauce (jellied or whole)

Mix oats, flour and brown sugar. Cut in butter until crumbly. Place half of this mixture in an 8 x 8 inch greased baking dish. Cover with cranberry sauce (if fresh or whole, clean and drain; if jellied, crush with a fork). Top with balance of crumb mixture. Bake at 350 degrees for 45 minutes. Serve hot in squares topped with scoops of vanilla ice cream. Makes 6 to 8 servings. This recipe we acquired while living at Long Beach, Washington, where cranberries are harvested each year.

POPPY SEED DESSERT

1   cup flour
1/2   cup butter
1/2   cup chopped nuts

Mix together and pat into 9 x 9 inch cake pan. Bake at 350 degrees for 15 minutes. Cool.

Mix:

1   cup Cool Whip (or whipped cream)
1   (8 ounce) package cream cheese
1   cup powdered sugar

Spread over crust.

Heat:

2-1/2 cups milk
2   (3 ounce) packages vanilla pudding
2   teaspoons poppy seeds
1   teaspoon vanilla

Cool till thick. Cool and spread over last mixture. Spread over this, Cool Whip and sprinkle over top with coconut. Refrigerate. This can be doubled and made in 9 x 13 inch pan.

OATMEAL-RHUBARB CRUMBLE

Crust:

1   cup flour
1/2   teaspoon salt
1/2   cup sugar
1   cup rolled oats
3/4   cup melted butter

Filling:

3   cups rhubarb
3/4   cup sugar
1   tablespoon flour
1/2   teaspoon cinnamon
1-1/2 tablespoons water

Make crust and press into 8 inch square baking dish. Save about 1/2 cup to sprinkle on top of filling. Combine ingredients for filling and pour into crust. Sprinkle top with remaining crust mixture. Bake at 350 degrees for 45 minutes. Serve hot or cold.

BLUEBERRY TORTE

Part 1:

20	graham crackers
1/2	cup sugar
1/2	cup melted butter

Roll crackers fine and mix in sugar and butter. Line 8 x 12 inch pan including side with this mixture. Let set.

Part 2:

2	eggs
1	(8 ounce) package cream cheese
1/2	cup sugar
1/2	teaspoon vanilla

Cream this well. Pour into crust. Bake at 375 degrees for 20 minutes. Then cool. Add 1 large can blueberry or cherry pie filling on top of the cream cheese. May put whipping cream on top before serving.

PEACH COBBLER (apple, cherry, apricot)

4	cups (7 or 8) fresh peaches, sliced and pared
1	tablespoon lemon juice
1/2	cup granulated sugar
1/3	teaspoon nutmeg
2	tablespoons melted butter
1	cup sifted flour
1-1/2	teaspoons baking powder
1	tablespoon sugar
1/2	teaspoon salt
1/4	cup shortening
1	egg, beaten
1/4	cup milk

Combine first 5 ingredients in the bottom of a shallow baking pan (12 x 7 x 2). Sift together flour, baking powder, 1 tablespoon sugar and salt. Work in shortening until consistency of corn meal. Combine egg and milk and stir in with fork. Spread dough thinly over top of peaches. Bake at 350 degrees for 40 to 60 minutes or until fruit is tender.

FRESH PEACH COBBLER

1-1/2	cups thinly sliced fresh peaches
1/4	cup water
1/2	cup sugar
1	egg
1	tablespoon shortening
1	tablespoon milk
1/2	cup flour
1/2	teaspoon baking powder
1/4	teaspoon salt

Start heating your oven to 375 degrees. Grease 10 x 6 x 2 inch baking dish. In saucepan, combine peaches, water, and 1/2 cup sugar. Bring to a boil stirring all the time. Set aside, but keep hot. Meanwhile, with spoon, beat egg, 1/2 cup sugar and shortening until fluffy. Add milk and stir in flour, baking powder and salt. Spread batter in baking dish. Pour hot peaches over batter. Bake 25 to 30 minutes or until tender. Serve warm with whipped cream if desired, or just plain cream. Makes 4 to 6 servings. Real quick & easy and so good!

PRUNE WHIP

1	envelope Knox gelatin
1/4	cup cold water
3/4	cup hot prune juice
1/2	cup sugar
1/4	teaspoon salt
1	cup cooked prune pulp
2	tablespoons lemon juice
2	egg whites, stiffly beaten
1/2	cup nuts, chopped

Soften gelatin in cold water. Dissolve thoroughly in hot prune juice with sugar and salt, stirring well. Add prune pulp and lemon juice. Chill until consistency of unbeaten egg white. Fold in beaten egg whites. Turn into mold and chill until firm. Unmold or spoon into sherbet glasses. Sprinkle with chopped nuts and whipped cream. Note: If you prefer pie, turn prune mixture into baked pastry shell or graham cracker crust and chill thoroughly. Just before serving, top with whipped cream and garnish with finely chopped nuts.

PUMPKIN PIE SQUARES

1	cup sifted flour
1/2	cup quick cooking oats
1/2	cup brown sugar, firmly packed
1/2	cup butter and margarine
1	can pumpkin (1 pound 13 ounce can)
1	(13-1/2 ounce) can evaporated milk
3	eggs
1-1/2	cups sugar
1	teaspoon salt
2	teaspoons cinnamon
1	teaspoon ginger
1/2	teaspoon cloves

Combine flour, rolled oats, 1/2 cup brown sugar, 1/2 cup butter in mixing bowl. Mix until crumbly using electric mixer on low speed. Press into an ungreased 13 x 9 x 2 inch pan. Bake at 350 degrees for 15 minutes. Combine pumpkin, evaporated milk, eggs, sugar and spices in bowl and beat well. Pour into crust. Bake at 350 degrees for 20 minutes.

Topping:

Combine 1/2 cup pecans, 1/2 cup brown sugar and 2 tablespoons butter. Sprinkle over pumpkin filling and return to oven for 15 to 20 minutes or until set. Cool and cut in pan. Makes about 2 dozen squares.

FROZEN FRESH RASPBERRY YOGURT

4	cups raspberries
2	cups sugar
4	teaspoons lemon juice
4	teaspoons vanilla
3	eggs, separated
1/4	teaspoon salt
1/4	teaspoon cream of tartar
1/4	cup sugar (additional)
2	quarts unflavored yogurt

Combine fruit and 2 cups sugar in saucepan and bring to boil, stirring, over high heat. Reduce heat to medium and cook until fruit softens. Remove from heat, stir in lemon juice and vanilla. Lightly beat egg yolks and stir in 1/2 cup of hot mixture. Then stir egg yolk mixture back into fruit mixture and cool. In large mixing bowl, combine egg whites, salt and cream of tartar. Beat to soft peaks then gradually add 1/4 cup sugar and continue beating until stiff. Put yogurt into 5 quart bowl and stir to smooth.

Fold in fruit mixture and then egg whites. Transfer to one gallon ice cream freezer and freeze following machine directions. Makes one gallon.

FARM STYLE CARAMEL CORN

4	cups popped corn
1	cup brown sugar
1/2	cup butter
1/2	cup honey
1/2	teaspoon baking soda

Melt butter. Add honey and brown sugar. Boil 1 to 2 minutes. Remove from heat and stir in 1/2 teaspoon baking soda. Pour over popcorn. Salt to taste.

BAKED CARAMEL CORN

1	cup butter
2	cups brown sugar, firmly packed
1/2	cup corn syrup (light or dark)
1	teaspoon salt
1/2	teaspoon soda
1	teaspoon vanilla
6	quarts of popped corn

Bring first 4 ingredients to a boil, stirring on low heat. Boil for 4 minutes then remove from heat. Stir in baking soda and vanilla. Pour over the popcorn and stir up till well coated. Bake in 250 degree oven for 1 hour, stirring up every 15 minutes.

MAIYIM'S AMARETTO BITTERSWEET CHOCOLATE MOUSSE

Cook over low heat until dissolved:

1/2	cup sugar
4	tablespoons Amaretto almond liqueur

Melt in it:

1/4	pound un-sweetened chocolate

When melted, stir in 3 egg yolks and mix well. Add 2 to 3 tablespoons cream, to mix into the consistency of heavy cream. Cool and then fold into the chocolate, 3 stiffly beaten egg whites. Then fold this combination into 2 cups of cream, whipped. Chill in dessert glasses for at least 2 hours before serving. Heavenly!

BANANAS FOSTER

2	tablespoons butter
4	small bananas, cut into halves lengthwise
2	tablespoons brown sugar
	dash cinnamon
1	tablespoon banana liqueur
1/2	cup rum
	ice cream

Melt butter and saute bananas until golden. Sprinkle with brown sugar and cinnamon. Remove bananas to a serving dish and pour pan juices over them. Heat banana liquor and rum. Pour over fruit and set aflame. Serve blazing with ice cream. Makes 4 servings.

BANANA SPLITS

3	sticks butter
2	eggs
2	cups graham cracker crumbs
2	cups brown sugar
4	bananas
1	can (20 ounce) crushed pineapple, drained
	whipping cream
	nuts, chopped
	cherries

Melt 1 stick of butter and mix with crumbs. Spread in 9 x 13 inch pan. Beat eggs, remaining butter and brown sugar together for at least 15 minutes. Spread over crumbs. Cover with sliced bananas then spread pineapple over top. Whip cream and spread evenly over all. Sprinkle top with nuts and cherries. Refrigerate overnight.

FANTASTIC FUDGE (microwave)

4	cups sugar
1	(14 ounce) can evaporated milk
1	cup butter
1	(12 ounce) package semi-sweet chocolate pieces
1	(7 ounce) jar marshmallow creme
1	teaspoon vanilla
1	cup chopped nuts

Combine sugar, milk and butter in a 4 quart bowl. Cook on high 20 to 24 minutes or till mixture reaches soft ball stage. Stir often while mixture is cooking and watch carefully to avoid boiling over. Mix in chocolate and marshmallow creme. Stir till well blended. Add vanilla and nuts. Pour into 9 inch square dish.

DIVINITY (microwave)

3	cups sugar
1/2	cup light corn syrup
2/3	cup water
1/4	teaspoon salt
2	egg whites
1/4	teaspoon vanilla
1	cup chopped nuts

In a 3 quart bowl, microwave sugar and water on high 12 to 13 minutes until it spins a fine thread. Add salt to egg whites and beat on high speed till stiff. Slowly pour syrup mixture in a thin stream into the egg whites, beating constantly until mixture loses its shine and thickens. Stir in vanilla and nuts. Drop by spoonfuls onto wax paper. Makes about 30 pieces.

PEANUT BRITTLE (microwave)

1	cup sugar
1/2	cup white corn syrup
1	cup roasted peanuts
1	teaspoon butter
1	teaspoon vanilla
1	teaspoon soda

Stir together sugar and syrup in a 1-1/2 quart casserole. Microwave on high for 4 minutes. Stir in peanuts. Microwave 3 to 5 minutes (up to 6 minutes) until light brown. Add butter and vanilla, stirring to blend well. Microwave on high 1 to 2 minutes. Syrup will be very hot and the peanuts lightly browned. Add baking soda and stir gently until cooking is completed and a nice golden brittle can be poured onto a greased metal cookie sheet. Cool about 15 minutes. Break into small pieces and store in an airtight container. Note: if using raw peanuts, add the peanuts and 1/8 teaspoon salt before the first cooking step. Stir slowly and gently after the soda... too fast and it gets tough, too slow and it gets striped. If poured on a cookie sheet, it can be flexed to remove the candy. Makes one pound.

PEANUT BRITTLE (microwave)

In a 1-1/2 quart casserole, combine 1 cup sugar and 1/2 cup white corn syrup. Microwave on high 4 minutes. Stir in 1 cup roasted, salted peanuts. Microwave on high for 3 to 5 minutes or until light brown. Add 1 teaspoon butter and 1 teaspoon vanilla. Blend well and microwave on high 1 to 2 minutes longer. Peanuts will be lightly browned and the syrup foamy. Pour mixture onto lightly greased cookie sheet and let cool. Break into pieces. Makes about 1 pound.

CREAMY PEANUT BUTTER FUDGE (microwave)

2	cups sugar
2/3	cup milk
1	cup crunchy peanut butter
1	(9 ounce) jar marshmallow creme
1	teaspoon vanilla

Microwave sugar and milk to soft ball stage. Add peanut butter and marshmallow creme, stirring till well blended. Add vanilla. Stir and pour into well buttered 9 inch square pan. Note: cooks very well in microwave in a 4 quart casserole.

PEANUT BUTTER CHOCOLATES

Mix together:

2	cups peanut butter
2	cubes butter
1-1/2	boxes powdered sugar

In double boiler over low heat, melt

1	package (12 ounce) chocolate chips
1/2	sheet parafin

Roll peanut butter mixture in balls (thumb size). Put a toothpick in the center of each ball and dip into chocolate and wax mixture. Put immediately on wax paper to cool. Can be frozen.

DONNA'S CARAMELS

2-1/2	cups white sugar
1	pound dark brown sugar
1	pint dark Karo syrup
1	pound margarine **or** 3 squares butter
1	quart half and half **or** whipping cream
1	teaspoon vanilla

Put everything together, except half the cream and cook to soft ball stage. Add other half of cream. Have on high heat when pouring in cream. Pour slowly and stir constantly while adding. Turn down heat and cook to hard ball stage. Pour over 1-1/2 pounds of nuts. I use whipping cream and real butter for this recipe.

SPICED WALNUTS

3	cups walnut meats
1	cup white sugar
6	tablespoons milk
2	teaspoons cinnamon
1/2	teaspoon vanilla

Combine milk, sugar and cinnamon. Cook to soft ball stage. Remove from heat and add walnuts and vanilla. Stir until you can stir no more. Put on wax paper. Separate.

PEANUT BRITTLE CANDY

1	cup sugar
1	cup white Karo syrup
3/4	teaspoon salt
1	tablespoon butter

Always use a stainless steel frypan, nothing else. Put all together in stainless steel frypan. Cook until sugar is dissolved or boiling. Add 1/2 package raw peanuts. Boil on high until it gets light tan. Keep stirring all the time with a wooden spoon. Now take off heat and add 1 teaspoon soda. Stir up good and pour onto an ungreased cookie sheet.

GOLDEN WALNUT SPECIAL

Combine in saucepan:

1	cup light brown sugar, firmly packed
1/2	cup granulated sugar
1	tablespoon instant coffee
1/4	teaspoon cinnamon
1/2	cup dairy sour cream

Cook, without stirring, over medium heat until soft ball stage. Remove from heat and stir in 1 teaspoon vanilla and 3 cups walnuts. Spread thinly on buttered cookie sheet. Separate into bite-size pieces. This makes a nice gift done up in a pretty dish.

BOSTON CREAM CANDY

6	cups sugar
3	cups rich cream
2	cups white Karo syrup

Boil in large kettle stirring constantly until it reaches 240 degrees on candy thermometer. Beat until it begins to harden, then add:

2	teaspoons vanilla
1/2	pound walnuts, cut fine
1/2	pound Brazil nuts, cut fine
1	small jar maraschino cherries, drained and cut fine

Blend thoroughly and pour into lightly buttered pan. Cut while still warm and store in tightly covered containers in cool place. Makes 5 pounds.

VANILLA ICE CREAM (Custard Base)

2-1/2	cups sugar
6	tablespoons flour
1/2	teaspoon salt
5	cups milk (scalded)
6	eggs
4	cups heavy cream
4-1/2	teaspoons vanilla

For extra-rich ice cream, use all cream and omit milk.

Combine sugar, flour and salt in sauce pan. Slowly stir in hot milk. Cook over low heat for about 10 minutes, stirring constantly until mixture is thickened. Mix small amount of hot mixture into beaten eggs. Add to hot mixture and cook 1 minute longer. Chill in refrigerator. Add cream and vanilla. Pour into gallon freezer and freeze as usual.

COUNTRY VANILLA ICE CREAM

4	eggs
2-1/4	cups sugar
5	cups milk
4-1/2	teaspoons vanilla
1/2	teaspoon salt

Add sugar gradually to beaten eggs. Continue beating until mixture is very stiff. Add remaining ingredients and mix thoroughly. Pour into gallon freezer and freeze according to directions.

Variation with Fresh or Frozen Fruit:

Substitute 4 cups puree sweetened fresh or three 12 ounce packages frozen fruit, thawed and mashed, for 4 cups milk. Reduce sugar to 1-3/4 cups. Use 1 teaspoon vanilla and 1-1/2 teaspoons almond flavoring if desired.

CRANBERRY ICE CREAM

4	cups cranberry sauce
1/3	cup fresh orange juice
1/3	cup fresh lemon juice
1/8	teaspoon salt
3	cups heavy cream, lightly whipped

Combine cranberry sauce, orange juice, lemon juice, salt and slightly whipped heavy cream. Churn and freeze.

PINK PEPPERMINT ICE CREAM

2	cups evaporated milk
1	pound peppermint candy
2	cups heavy cream
1/4	teaspoon salt

Pour undiluted evaporated milk over the peppermint candy. Let stand 6 to 8 hours in the refrigerator. Pour mixture through a cheesecloth to strain out undissolved particles of candy. Whip heavy cream with salt until stiff and fold into peppermint mixture. Churn and freeze.

PUMPKIN ICE CREAM

1	cup cooked fresh pumpkin (about 1 small pumpkin or 1 pound) or canned pumpkin
6	egg yolks
1	cup granulated sugar
1/4	teaspoon salt
1/2	teaspoon ground cinnamon
1/2	teaspoon ground nutmeg
1/2	teaspoon ground ginger
4	cups heavy cream

Peel, seed, and cut pumpkin into small pieces. Cook pumpkin pieces in boiling water for 30 minutes until tender. Drain. Puree cooked pumpkin by forcing through a food mill. Beat egg yolks until thick and creamy. In a double boiler, combine pumpkin puree, beaten egg yolks, sugar, salt, cinnamon, nutmeg, and ginger. Cook, stirring until well-blended and thickened. Cool. Lightly whip heavy cream and add cream to the cooled mixture. Churn and freeze.

CASHEW NUT ICE CREAM

1/2	pound unsalted cashew nuts, skinned and chopped
1	pound strained honey
3	egg yolks, beaten
1/8	teaspoon salt
3	egg whites, stiffly beaten
1-1/2	cups heavy cream, lightly whipped

Combine cashew nuts and honey, mixing well. Add beaten egg yolks, salt, stiffly beaten egg whites and lightly-whipped heavy cream to the nut-honey mixture. Churn and freeze.

PEACH ICE CREAM

3	cups canned peaches
2	tablespoons unflavored gelatin
1	cup granulated sugar
1/4	teaspoon salt
1	teaspoon almond extract
1	teaspoon vanilla extract
1/4	teaspoon red food coloring
3	cups heavy cream, lightly whipped

Drain the peaches and then puree them in an electric blender. Add gelatin to 1/4 cup of the peach puree. Let stand for 5 minutes. In a sauce pan, combine remaining peach puree, sugar and salt. Heat to a boil, stirring occasionally. Add the gelatin-peach puree mixture to the hot peach mixture. Stir and cool. Add almond and vanilla extracts, food coloring and lightly whipped cream to the cooled mixture. Churn-freeze.

PAPAYA ICE CREAM

1	ripe papaya
1/2	cup orange juice
3	tablespoons lemon juice
1/2	pint cream
1/2	cup sugar

Peel papaya, remove seeds and blend in blender to make fine puree. To 1-1/2 cups puree, mix all other ingredients well. Put in 2 ice cube trays and freeze until firm.

CHOCOLATE CHIP ICE CREAM

6	cups heavy cream
3	tablespoons cornstarch
3/4	cup milk
4	eggs, beaten
1	cup granulated sugar
1	tablespoon vanilla extract
12	ounces semi-sweet chocolate bits

In top of double boiler, heat heavy cream. Dissolve cornstarch in the milk and add to the hot cream. Cook, stirring occasionally, until slightly thickened. Beat a tablespoon of the hot custard into the beaten eggs and then stir eggs into custard. Continue to cook until thick. Remove from heat. Add sugar to custard and beat until smooth. Cool. Add vanilla and chocolate to the cooled custard. Churn-freeze.

ORANGE SHERBET

1-1/2	cups granulated sugar
1/2	cup light corn syrup
3	cups water
1/4	teaspoon salt
1/2	cup fresh lemon juice
2	cups fresh orange juice

In a sauce pan, mix together sugar, corn syrup, water and salt. Cook, stirring on low heat for 5 minutes. Cool. Add lemon juice and orange juice to the cooled mixture. Churn-freeze.

CANTALOUPE SHERBET

3	cups water
1-1/2	cups granulated sugar
4	cups fresh cantaloupe pulp (about 2 medium-sized melons, 2-1/4 pounds each
2	tablespoons fresh lemon juice

In a sauce pan combine water and sugar. Boil for 5 minutes. Cool. Remove cantaloupe from shell and puree in an electric blender on high speed. Add cantaloupe pulp and lemon juice to sugar syrup. Churn-freeze.

APRICOT SHERBET

4	cups water
1	cup granulated sugar
2-1/2	cups canned apricot nectar
2	tablespoons fresh lemon juice

In a sauce pan combine water and sugar. Boil for 5 minutes. Cool. Add apricot nectar and lemon juice to sugar syrup. Churn-freeze.

CREAMY LIME SHERBET

1	(3 ounce) package lime flavored gelatin
1-1/4	cups sugar
1	(6 ounce) can frozen limeade concentrate
4	cups milk
1	cup boiling water
3/4	tablespoon salt
8	drops green food coloring
2	cups light cream

Dissolve gelatin in boiling water. Add sugar and salt. Add limeade, stirring until thawed. Stir in food coloring, milk and light cream. Pour into 1-gallon freezer container, filling about 3/4 full. Freeze following usual procedure for crank or electric ice cream freezer. Makes 1 gallon.

Apples

SOUR CREAM APPLE PIE

1	cup sour cream
3/4	cup white sugar
2	tablespoons flour
1/4	teaspoon salt
1	teaspoon vanilla
1	egg
2	cups canned apple pie slices, diced
1	unbaked 9 inch pie shell
1/2	cup brown sugar, packed
1/3	cup flour
1/4	cup butter, softened

Beat together sour cream, white sugar, 2 tablespoons flour, salt, vanilla and egg. Mix in diced apples and turn into pie shell. Bake at 425 degrees for 25 minutes. Remove from oven and spread with mixture of brown sugar, 1/3 cup flour and butter. Return to oven and bake 20 more minutes. This recipe is simply delicious!

ENID'S WASHINGTON STATE GOLDEN APPLE CRISP

6	Golden Delicious apples, pared and sliced
1/2	cup sugar
1/2	teaspoon cinnamon
1/4	teaspoon cloves
2	teaspoons lemon juice

Combine sugar, cinnamon, cloves and lemon juice. Mix with apples. Pour into 8 inch square baking dish.

Topping:

1/2	cup sugar
3/4	cup sifted flour
1/2	teaspoon salt
1/2	cup margarine
1/2	cup chopped nuts

Crumble together sugar, flour, salt and margarine. Mix with nuts. Crumble over apples. Bake at 375 degrees for 45 minutes. Serve warm topped with whipped cream. Makes 6 to 8 servings. This Washington State golden apple crisp is one that I make for special occasions. I entered it in the fair and won the Golden Apple Award.

APPLE DESSERT

4	cups chopped apples
1/2	cup sugar
2	tablespoons flour
1/4	teaspoon salt
1	teaspoon cinnamon

Mix above ingredients together and put in a pan. Mix topping ingredients before adding to top of apple mixture.

Topping:

1	cup oatmeal
1	cup flour
1	cup brown sugar
1/4	teaspoon baking soda
1/4	teaspoon baking powder
1	cube butter

Bake at 300 degrees until apples are done, about 45 minutes.

APPLE DUMPLINGS

Cut 4 inch squares from biscuit dough or pie crust. Place in the center of each, 2 slices of apple (peeled) sprinkled with sugar and nutmeg. Fold corners to center and pinch all edges. Place in pan and cover with the following syrup:

1	cup sugar
1	tablespoon flour
	juice of 1 lemon and grated rind
1-1/4	cups boiling water

Mix flour and sugar, stir together with water, lemon juice and rind. Pour over dumplings. Bake 45 minutes at 350 degrees.

BAKED APPLE DUMPLINGS

4	cups sifted flour
4	teaspoons baking powder
1	cup butter
1-1/2	cup milk
4-5	apples (peeled, cored and quartered)

Mix sifted flour and baking powder together with butter. Add milk to make a stiff dough. Roll out and cut into large rounds. Fold apple in each round. Bake in syrup.

Syrup:

3	cups water
1	cup sugar
1	tablespoon butter
	dash of nutmeg

Bake at 350 degrees for about 30 minutes or until apples are done.

APPLE DOUGHNUTS

2	eggs
1	cup sugar
2	tablespoons salad oil
2	cups applesauce
1	teaspoon salt
4-1/2	teaspoons baking powder
1	cup buttermilk
5	cups flour
1	teaspoon baking soda
1	teaspoon nutmeg
1/2	teaspoon cinnamon

Beat eggs, sugar, oil, applesauce and milk. Add dry ingredients. Mix together and chill for 1/2 to 1 hour. Roll out and cut. Fry in deep fat heated to 375 degrees.

APPLE CANDY

2	tablespoons gelatin
1	cup unsweetened applesauce
1	tablespoon vanilla
2	cups sugar
1/2	cup walnuts

Soak gelatin in 1/4 cup applesauce for 10 minutes. Mix sugar into remaining applesauce. Combine and boil for 15 minutes. Stir in nuts and vanilla. Pour into buttered pan and let stand a day or overnight. Cut in squares and roll in powdered sugar.

APPLE CRISP TOPPING (nice for tops of pies)

1	cup quick oats
2	tablespoons butter
4	tablespoons wheat germ

Mix well and put on.

APPLESAUCE CAKE

1/2	cup shortening
1	cup granulated sugar
1	egg, beaten
1-1/2	cups all-purpose flour
1/2	teaspoon salt
1/2	teaspoon cloves
1/2	teaspoon cinnamon
1	teaspoon soda
1	cup applesauce, unsweetened (if sweetened, decrease sugar)

Cream shortening. Add sugar and cream till well blended. Add beaten egg and blend well. Sift flour with salt, cloves and cinnamon. Stir soda into applesauce. Add alternately with flour to creamed mixture. Combine well. Turn into 13 x 9 inch pan and bake at 350 degrees for about 40 minutes or until done. Will make about 16 cupcakes. Bake for 20 to 25 minutes. Some can be frozen without frosting. Make butter cream frosting. I use half vanilla and lemon flavoring and whip it. Very good!

EDITH'S APPLESAUCE CAKE

1	cup butter
2	cups sugar
2	eggs, beaten
2-1/2	cups flour
1	teaspoon salt
2	teaspoons cinnamon
2	teaspoons soda
1	teaspoon cloves
2	cups raisins
2	cups nuts, chopped
2	cups hot applesauce

Cream butter. Add sugar gradually. Beat until smooth and creamy. Add eggs and blend well. Mix and sift dry ingredients. Add to first mixture and mix well. Add raisins and nuts (which have been floured to keep from sinking). When well blended, add hot applesauce. Bake in tube pan or 9 x 13 inch pan at 350 degrees for about 1 hour. Top with this topping if you wish, (we like it plain). Take from oven and spread the following topping on cake.

1 pound box brown sugar, enough cream or milk to make thin enough to spread easily and 2 cups shredded coconut. Mix and spread on cake. Put under broiler a few minutes until bubbly, being careful not to burn.

FRESH APPLE CAKE

4	cups diced apples (not too fine)
2	cups sugar

Mix together and add:

1/2	cup salad oil
1	cup chopped nuts
2	eggs, well beaten
2	teaspoons vanilla

Mix dry ingredients and add to above:

2	teaspoons cinnamon
2	teaspoons soda
1	teaspoon salt
2	cups flour

Bake at 350 degrees for 1 hour in 9 x 13 x 2 inch pan or loaf pan.

Glaze:

1	tablespoon vinegar
1	cup water
2	tablespoons cornstarch
1	cup sugar
2	tablespoons butter
1	teaspoon cinnamon

Cook until thick and pour on the cake while cake is still hot.

APPLE CAKE

2	eggs
2	cups sugar
2	teaspoons soda
	pinch of salt
2	teaspoons cinnamon
1	teaspoon vanilla
2	cups cake flour, sifted
4	cups diced apples (raw)
1/2	cup salad oil
1	cup broken nuts

Cream eggs and sugar. Add remaining ingredients. Pour into a greased and floured 9 x 12 inch pan Bake at 350 degrees for 45 minutes then frost.

Frosting:

1-1/2	cups powdered sugar
1	(6 ounce) package cream cheese
3	tablespoons butter
1/4	teaspoon salt
1/2	teaspoon vanilla

Mix all ingredients together to a creamy stage. You may add nuts to the frosting if desired. This cake is real moist.

RAW APPLE CAKE

2	cups raw apples (cut up)
1	cup brown sugar
1	cup white sugar
1	cup shortening
2	eggs
1	cup strong black coffee
2	cups flour
1-1/2	teaspoons soda
1/2	teaspoon nutmeg
2	teaspoons cinnamon
1/2	teaspoon salt
1	cup raisins and nuts

In a mixer, cream shortening and sugar. Add eggs. Beat well. Alternate flour and coffee beating continually. Mix spices in flour. Add raisins, nuts and apples. Bake at 375 degrees about 45 minutes or until center of cake is done. This cake is more moist the second day.

APPLESAUCE FRUITCAKE

2	cups glazed fruit mix
1	cup broken walnut meats
4	cups sifted flour
1	teaspoon salt
1	teaspoon cinnamon
1	teaspoon nutmeg
1/2	teaspoon ginger
1/2	teaspoon cloves
2-1/2	cups (#2 can) applesauce
3/4	cup salad oil
2	cups sugar

Oil and flour bottom of tube pan. Preheat oven to 350 degrees. Mix fruit, nuts and about 1/2 the flour. Sift spices and remaining flour. Heat the applesauce. Mix soda, oil and sugar in large bowl. Add hot applesauce; then flour with spices; then floured fruit and nut mixture. Blend well after each addition. Pour into tube pan and lay paper over the cake during the first 1/2 hour of baking. Bake for 1-1/4 hours or until straw comes out clean. Cool in the pan 15 to 20 minutes. Loosen sides and remove cake carefully. Serve with a light sprinkling of powdered sugar or a simple glaze: 1 cup powdered sugar; 1 tablespoon milk; 1/4 teaspoon of your favorite flavoring.

APPLESAUCE FRUIT CAKE

Combine and boil 5 minutes:

3	cups plain or sweetened applesauce
2	cups sugar
1	cup shortening

Cool to room temperature.

In a large bowl put the following fruit and nuts:

1-1/2	cups candied fruit mix
1/2	cup halved candied cherries
1/2	cup candied pineapple
3	cups raisins
1	pound pitted dates, cut up
1	cup broken walnuts

Sift dry ingredients over fruit and mix well.

4-1/2	cups flour
4	teaspoons soda
1	teaspoon salt
2-1/2	teaspoons cinnamon
1	teaspoon nutmeg
1/2	teaspoon cloves

Add cooled applesauce and mix well.

Line 3 breadpans with well greased foil. Bake at 250 degrees for 2-1/2 hours. Cool on rack with foil on. Wrap well and store in refrigerator to ripen for a month. Then freeze. If desired, every 3 days open and lace with rum or brandy. Do this 3 times.

HONEY APPLE COOKIES

3/4	cup honey
1/2	cup shortening
1/2	teaspoon vanilla
2	eggs
2	cups whole wheat flour
1	teaspoon soda
1-1/2	teaspoons cinnamon
1/2	teaspoon allspice
1-1/2	cups finely chopped apples
1	cup chopped raisins
1	cup chopped nuts

Cream shortening and sugar. Add eggs and vanilla. Beat well. Add apples and mix well. Sift dry ingredients together and add to creamed mixture. Beat well by hand or use dough hooks on electric mixer. Add raisins and nuts. Drop by teaspoon onto greased cookie sheet. Bake at 350 degrees for 12 to 15 minutes.

GLAZED APPLE KNOCKERS COOKIES

2	cups all-purpose flour
1	teaspoon soda
1/2	teaspoon salt
1/2	cup soft shortening
1/2	teaspoon cinnamon
1	teaspoon cloves
1-1/3	cups brown sugar (firmly packed)
1/2	teaspoon nutmeg
1	cup finely chopped apples
1	egg, unbeaten
1	cup raisins, chopped
1/4	cup apple juice or milk
1/4	cup chopped walnuts

Sift flour with soda. Mix shortening, sugar, salt, cinnamon, cloves, nutmeg and egg until well blended. Stir in half the flour mixture, then nuts, apples and raisins. Blend in apple juice or milk, then remaining flour mixture. Drop by rounded teaspoon, two inches apart on baking sheet and bake at 400 degrees for 11 to 14 minutes. While cookies are still hot, spread thinly with vanilla glaze. Makes 3-1/2 dozen.

Vanilla glaze:

1-1/2	cups powdered sugar
1	tablespoon soft butter
1/4	teaspoon vanilla
1/8	teaspoon salt
2-1/2	tablespoons light cream

Blend above ingredients together in small bowl.

APPLESAUCE COOKIES

1/2	cup shortening
1-1/2	teaspoons soda
1	cup sugar
1/2	teaspoon nutmeg
1	egg, beaten
1/2	cup chopped nuts
1	cup thick applesauce, unsweetened
2	cups flour
1	cup raisins
1/2	teaspoon salt
3/4	teaspoon allspice

Method: cream shortening and sugar. Add egg and applesauce. Sift together dry ingredients and add creamed mixture. Blend well. Add nuts and raisins. Drop by teaspoon onto greased cookie sheet and bake at 350 degrees for 12 to 15 minutes, until brown. Frost with powdered sugar frosting if desired. Makes 3 dozen large cookies.

APPLESAUCE BANANA BREAD

1/2	cup shortening
2	eggs, well beaten
3/4	cup sugar
3	tablespoons buttermilk
1/2	cup ripe bananas, mashed
1/2	cup applesauce
2	cups sifted flour
3/4	teaspoon soda
1	teaspoon salt

Cream shortening and sugar. Add the liquid ingredients, then the dry. Pour into a greased loaf pan and bake at 350 degrees 45 - 60 minutes. 1/2 cup chopped nuts can be added if desired.

CRUNCH-TOP APPLESAUCE BARS

1	cup sugar
1/2	cup shortening
1	cup unsweetened applesauce
2	cups flour
1	teaspoon soda
1-1/2	teaspoons cinnamon
1	teaspoon nutmeg
	dash of cloves
1/4	teaspoon salt
1	cup raisins
1/4	cup nuts
1	teaspoon vanilla

Cream sugar, shortening and applesauce. Add flour, soda, cinnamon, nutmeg and salt. Mix well. Add raisins, nuts and vanilla. Spread in 15-1/2 x 10-1/2 inch pan.

Topping:

2/3	cup crushed cornflakes
1/4	cup sugar
1/2	cup nuts
2	tablespoons soft butter

Mix well and sprinkle over batter. Bake at 350 degrees for 30 minutes.

MOM'S APPLE NUT BREAD

1/2	cup shortening
2/3	cup sugar
2	eggs
2	cups flour
1	teaspoon salt
1	teaspoon soda
1	teaspoon baking powder
1	cup chopped raw apples
1/2	cup chopped nuts
1/2	cup glazed fruit

Cream shortening and sugar. Add eggs, one at a time and mix well after each egg. Combine flour, salt, baking powder and soda and add to mixture. Add apples. Stir until well blended, then add nuts and fruit. Do not beat. Pour into 2 greased loaf pans, 1 large and 1 small. Bake at 350 degrees for 1 hour. Take from pan and cool. Spread with topping.

Topping:

Mix 1 cup powdered sugar with small amount of milk. Drizzle over the top. Then place small pieces of glazed fruit, nuts or more sugar on top.

PUMPKIN-APPLE BREAD

4	cups sugar
1	cup oil
3	cups fresh pumpkin
1	teaspoon cloves
1	teaspoon cinnamon
1	teaspoon salt
4	teaspoons soda
2	cups chopped apples
1	cup raisins
1	cup chopped nuts
5-1/2	cups flour (if using canned pumpkin, use 5 cups flour)

Grease 2 loaf pans, line with paper and grease again. Mix together first 3 ingredients. Add and stir in spices, salt, soda and apples. Then add remaining ingredients and stir in. Pour into pans and bake at 350 degrees for 1-1/2 hours. Cool for at least 15 minutes.

APPLE COOKIES

1-1/2	cups flour
1	teaspoon baking powder
1/2	teaspoon soda
1/2	teaspoon salt
1	teaspoon cinnamon
1/4	teaspoon nutmeg
3/4	cup shortening
3/4	cup brown sugar
1	egg
1/4	teaspoon instant coffee
1	tablespoon water
1	teaspoon vanilla
1	cup grated apple
1	cup oats
1/2	cup crunchy granola
1/2	cup raisins

Sift first 6 ingredients. Add shortening, brown sugar and egg. Beat at medium speed. Blend in coffee, water and vanilla. Stir in apple, oats, granola and raisins. Chill dough 1/2 hour. Shape into small balls and dip in sugar. Bake on greased cookie sheet at 375 degrees 12 to 15 minutes.

WASHINGTON STATE APPLE MUFFINS

1	egg
1/2	cup milk
1/4	cup oil
1/2	cup sugar
1-1/2	cups flour
2	teaspoons baking powder
1/2	teaspoon salt
1	cup chopped apples
1/2	teaspoon cinnamon

Topping:

1/3	cup brown sugar
1/3	cup chopped nuts
1/2	teaspoon cinnamon

Beat together egg, sugar, milk and oil. Add to dry ingredients and then mix in the apples. Put on topping and bake for 20 - 25 minutes at 350 degrees.

HOMEMADE WINE

Making wine in your own home can be approached from two different points of view. You can be very exacting and precise and even come very close to reproducing your favorite commercially-bottled wines. Or you can approach it from a recreational viewpoint and make wine as a seasonal or part-time hobby. I tend to favor the latter approach for a couple of reasons. Much of the excitement comes from trying a new recipe and not knowing beforehand what it will, taste like. I also feel that, at least in some cases, one can take the real fun out of something by getting too complex and exacting in its completion.

The following, then, is simply an overview of the wine-making process. It is by no means the "final word" on the subject nor is it meant to cover everything.

Permit requirements (if any) vary from state to state. Be sure to check for any laws that might apply or any permits that are required where you live.

Basic equipment is readily available and fairly cheap, especially when you consider that your wine will cost about 25 to 30 cents per quart. Wine can be made in almost any container that has a tight-fitting lid. Gallon glass jugs work very well, but I strongly recommend using five-gallon plastic buckets with a snap locking top. These containers usually start out in bakeries filled with icing or pie filling and are then sold or sometimes given away. Ask at the bakery department of any large grocery store. The advantages of the larger containers are many. The time involved in making five gallons of wine is not that much greater than in making only one gallon. Also, the larger amount enables you to sample the product at various stages in its development and still have something left when it has aged and mellowed properly.

We will also need the following items that can be purchased from a store selling wine-making supplies. First, we need some type of air lock that allows the gasses produced by fermentation to escape without letting any air back in. Air locks usually employ the method of bubbling the gasses through a small container of water and act as a very effective one-way valve. This lock should be accompanied by a rubber cork or stopper with a hole in it. The stem of the air lock is inserted through the hole in the stopper and then the stopper is inserted in a hole drilled in the top of the container.

Also we will need approximately six feet of flexible, clear plastic tubing to use as a syphon hose. A 3/8-inch inside diameter tubing works well. It will be used to transfer wine from one container to another.

Then purchase any good all-purpose wine yeast. There are specific yeasts for particular wines, and you may want to get into that as your skills develop. But for our purposes, the all-purpose yeast will be the best.

A short word on other additives and chemicals sold in wine-making departments. Most of these are overpriced to the point of being a rip-off. If you know the name of a specific chemical, run down to your friendly neighborhood drugstore and buy it there at half the price.

I would also recommend one other purchase. Buy a book on wine-making. There are several choices in any good book store and are usually written for various levels of expertise in the art. Find one with recipes for different types of wine. This book should be a valuable reference tool for uses of chemicals like campden or bisulphide and for the use of hydrometers and some of the other more sophisticated measuring instruments.

Before we walk into the kitchen to get started, we should discuss probably the single most important aspect in wine-making, and that is cleanliness. All the utensils, containers and materials that come into contact with the wine must be sterile to avoid fermenting something other than alcohol. This is very important. Winemaking is a sort of controlled decay. The process of fermenting sugar, fruit and water has to be strictly controlled in order to grow only those things that you want to grow. If you get the wrong thing growing in your wine, you went through a lot of time and effort for nothing.

Now pick a recipe that sounds good and get the proper fruit or juices needed. Gather your materials in the kitchen and wash everything squeaky clean. Take a 1-1/2 gallon pan, fill it with one gallon of water and bring it to a boil. At this point I always add my sugar to the water so that it will be completely dissolved. Pour the boiling water into the container that you are making the wine in and repeat the boiling process until you have the proper amount of sugar and water in the wine container. Stir in the fruit or juice and allow the mixture to cool until it is lukewarm or even cold. Then add the yeast and cover the container with the lid and air lock. Make sure you don't get the container too full, as the yeast action will produce a foamy head above the level of the liquid. Four gallons is about the right amount of liquid for a five-gallon container.

Locate the container in a warm, draft-free spot in the house. Try to find a place with a consistent temperature and get it up off the floor if drafts can occur. The fermentation process will be faster and more complete if this method is used.

After the first day, things will start to happen. If you are using a crushed fruit mixture, the bubbling action will float the fruit to the top of the container. This should be stirred so that it will sink back into the liquid. You may have to do this two or three times a day and should be done regularly to get the flavor and natural sugar from the fruit into the liquid.

Strong fermentation will continue for approximately 21 days. At this time the bubbling will be reduced greatly and it is time to go from the primary to the secondary stage. Strain the liquid through a collander, strainer jelly bag or whatever is clean and handy. This will remove the big pieces of fruit. Also try to leave out as much of the sediment in the bottom of the container and then sterilize the same container and return the wine to it. Put the lid and the air lock back on and leave it alone until all fermentation stops. The time this takes varies with the type of wine and can take from 2 weeks to 2 months.

Now that fermentation has stopped, it is time to settle out all the yeast and small particles in the wine. One of the easiest ways is to drop the temperature of the wine about 40 degrees. You can put it in the refrigerator, or if space won't allow this, put it in the garage or basement in the coldest corner you can find.

Another method used to clear wine is to save your breakfast egg shells. Wash them off and crush them up finely. Gently stir the crushed egg shells into the wine and try not to stir the sediment on the bottom.

After a week or so, the wine will start to clear and it is time to transfer the wine into another container. Use the clear plastic siphon hose for this step. Put the hose in the top of the container and siphon the wine from the top down until you start drawing the sediment on the bottom. Stop at this time. The wine can then be bottled in your favorite container.

The wine can probably be consumed at this time but usually imparts a yeasty or "green" taste. Even though it takes a large amount of will power, I would recommend that you let it age for at least six months or, better yet, for a full year. The wine will improve remarkably with age and the wait is well worth the finished product.

Finally, I would suggest that as you complete each step in the wine-making process, write down everything you did. Note such things as variations in the original recipe, dates the wine was started, transferred and bottled. The reason for this is that if you get an excellent wine, you will be able to duplicate the exact recipe at a later date. Or on the other hand, if you have a recipe that bombs, you can study your notes and try a different variation on the next batch.

In closing, I would like to list a potpourri of things that may save you a little trouble or help make your drinking more pleasurable. Here goes ... Yeast can be frozen solid but too much heat will kill it dead. Never pour yeast into hot liquid. Never use orange drink or grape drink in wine-making. Make sure it is pure juice. The "drinks" have preservatives and artificial things that will not allow a ferment. Stay away from fruit juices that have a high acid content unless you are a chemist. Go into partners with someone and buy bulk sugar, yeast and chemicals. It's cheaper. One of my friends makes what he calls a 30-day Wunderwine. He runs a 21-day primary ferment, then kills the yeast with sodium metabisulphide. He racks it off and throws the jugs into the nearest snowbank for nine days. It's some dynamite stuff!!

With a wine yeast, alcohol content at 16 or 17 percent is not unheard of. To boost your alcohol content, run an additional primary ferment. To do this you add more yeast and sugar at the end of the first 21 days. Sometimes a batch of wine doesn't want to quit fermenting. I've had some carry on for four months. You can either kill the yeast with chemicals or try cooling it down in the same manner you would settle or clear it out.

DANDELION WINE

1	gallon blossoms
1	gallon sugar
1	gallon water
1	yeast cake or package
1	lemon
1	orange

Pinch all stems off blossoms. Pack them down a little in the pail. Put the blossoms, sugar and sliced lemon and orange in a crock. Pour boiling water; when lukewarm, add yeast that has been soaked in warm water. Let stand three days; stir each day, strain. Put in jugs or bottles; fill each day with sugar water. Let ferment 4 to 6 weeks in a warm place. Strain through cloth and bottle.

RHUBARB WINE

12   pounds rhubarb
2   gallons water
8   pounds sugar

Cut rhubarb in small pieces. Put in crock; let soak for 3 days; stir each day. Strain through cloth; add sugar; put in bottles. Fill each day with sugar water. Let ferment 4 to 6 weeks in a warm place. Strain through cloth and bottle. Do not put corks on too tight.

WILD CHOKECHERRY WINE

Fill a crock within about 3 inches from the top with cherries. Cover with cold water. Let stand about 12 days. Stir each day. As the water goes down, pour on enough water to cover cherries. Strain; add 1/2 as much sugar as juice. Let ferment 4 to 6 weeks in a warm place. Strain through cloth and bottle. If sweeter wine is desired, more sugar can be added after the wine is through fermenting.

BEET-GRAPE WINE

6   pounds beetroot
1   gallon water
       wine yeast
1   lemon
3-1/2 pounds sugar
1/2   cup grape concentrate (bottled or frozen)

Wash beets (do not peel); cut in slices and cook in water until tender. Strain onto the sugar and stir until dissolved. Add juice from lemon. When cooled, add yeast. Cover with plastic and leave for 24 hours. Put into fermenting bottle and fit air lock; ferment out. Rack in three weeks. When clear and stable, bottle. Keep 6 to 8 months.

BEET WINE

Cook 5 pounds of beets just enough to remove the skins. Drain off juice and add enough water to make 1 gallon.

Add:

3   pounds sugar
1   pound raisins
1   orange, sliced
1   lemon, sliced
1/3   cake yeast

Combine well. Let stand for 28 days, stirring every morning. Strain and then let set for 6 days. Do not stir. It is then ready to bottle. Makes 1 gallon of wine.

SWEET CHERRY WINE

9   pounds fruit
1   pound raisins
1   package yeast
8-1/2 pounds sugar
2   gallons boiling water
       juice of lemon

Put fruit in one-half of the boiling water. Let come to boil; add sugar; stir well to dissolve. Add remaining water. Set aside to cool until lukewarm. Add yeast; stir well. Strain and let ferment.

METHODS OF COOKING

MRS. BOYLE'S EGG FREEZING METHOD

It is **very important** that you use clean, fresh, well-chilled eggs for freezing.

Label should include:

Name; whole egg, yolk or white amounts (how many or measurement); added ingredients and amount (salt or sugar); date of freezing.

Containers:

Use moisture-vapor proof plastic freezer containers or glass jars. Do not use milk cartons, cottage cheese cartons or other paper board containers. These waxed cartons are not moisture-vapor proof enough.

Whole eggs:

Break into a bowl (do not freeze eggs which have odor or blood spots). Stir with a fork (beater at low speed) until whites and yolks are thoroughly mixed. Do not beat air into them. Add ingredients to make smoother when thawed. To 1 cup eggs add: 1/2 teaspoon salt (use for salad dressing or main dish) or 1/2 tablespoon sugar, corn syrup or honey (use for cakes or desserts).

Egg whites:

Separate whites from yolks and measure amount for each container. Seal, label and freeze. No ingredients are needed.

Egg yolks:

Separate yolks from whites and break yolks by stirring. Do not beat in air. Add ingredients. To 1 cup egg yolks add: 1/2 teaspoon salt or 1/2 tablespoon sugar or sweetening.

Recommended storage time for frozen eggs is 6 to 8 months.

Measurements for frozen eggs: 1 to 1-1/2 tablespoons frozen yolks equals 1 egg yolk. 2 tablespoons whites equals 1 egg white. 3 tablespoons yolks and whites equals 1 whole egg. 1 cup equals 5 whole eggs, 12 yolks or 8 whites.

Thawing frozen eggs: the safest place to thaw eggs is in the refrigerator, overnight or under cold running water. **Do not** let them wait for longer than 24 hours. **Do not** re-freeze. Frozen eggs sour very quickly. Stir before using.

PREPARING WILD FOODS

Always use extreme caution when eating wild foods. If you are not sure it is best not to fool with it. Of particular concern in Washington is the Night Shade plant. For more information on this plant, please call your local County Extension Office.

Edibility Rule:

1. Prepare sample. Eat 1 teaspoonful.
2. After 2 hours, if no ill effects, prepare and eat 1 tablespoonful.
3. If no ill effects, plant may be considered edible.

Berry Rule:

White: Poison
Red: Danger
Blue: Edible
Black: Edible

Star on flower end of berry — Good.
Dot on flower end of berry — Caution.

SALADS AND GREENS

1. Asparagus, Wild (shoots)
2. Cabbage, Skunk (Leaves): Boil thrice.
3. Cattail (Shoot, Root, Stalk): Boil raw.
4. Curly Dock: Boil.
5. Dandelion (Roots, Leaves): Boil raw.
6. Daisy (Petals): Raw.
7. Fern, Bracken
8. Milkweed
9. Mustard, Wild
10. Nettle
11. Onion, Wild: Boil raw.
12. Plantain (Leaf): Raw.
13. Rose Apple, Wild (Fruit)
14. Water Cress (Leaves)

POT HERBS (Cooked like Spinach)

1. Nettle: Drain water thrice.
2. Skunk Cabbage (Leaf)
3. Solomon's Seal (Shoots)

VEGETABLES (Usually boiled)

1. Arrowhead
2. Bellwort (shoots)
3. Bullrush
4. Cattail (roots, flower)
5. Milkweed (young pods)
6. Yellow Pond Lily

COFFEE (Roots dried and roasted)

1. Dandelion
2. Goat's Beard
3. Goldenrod (flowers)
4. Wild Coffee (fruit, orange)

TEA (Dried leaves steeped in water)

1. Bass wood (flowers)
2. Bergamot (leaves)
3. Elderberry (flowers)
4. Labrador Tea (leaves)
5. Plaintain (leaves)
6. Spearmint (leaves)
7. Spice Bush (twigs)
8. Spruce (needles)
9. Staghorn Sumac (cones)
10. Strawberry (leaves)
11. Winter green (leaves)

FLOUR (Dried and crushed tubers, roots, nuts or seeds)

1. Cattails (roots)
2. Oak (acorns)

NUTS — SEEDS

1. Hazel (nut)
2. Hickory (nut)
3. Oak (acorn)
4. Sunflower (seeds)
5. Walnuts (nut)

AVOID

1. Seeds of fruit (cyanide poison)
2. Plants with milk sap (except figs, dandelion and lettuce)
3. Soapy-tasting plants
4. Bulbs with fairly large flower
5. Plant resembling:
   a. Dill
   b. Parsley
   c. Parsnip
   d. Carrot-like foliage
6. **ALL** mushrooms must be considered poisonous
7. Bitter-tasting fruit
8. Smoke from toxic or poisonous plants (poison oak, ivy and sumac)
9. Wood of laurel and rhododendrons in cooking spits, etc.

POISONOUS PLANTS COMMON TO THE NORTHWEST

1. False Hellebore
2. Lupine Pea
3. Water Hemlock
4. Death Camas
5. Bane Berry
6. Fox Glove
7. Night Shade
8. Jack-in-the-Pulpit

MISCELLANEOUS USE OF PLANTS

1. Salt (ashes of sunflower)
2. Pepper (smartweed leaves)
3. Tobacco (inner bark of osier dogwood)
4. Soap (yucca)
5. Scouring pad (scouring rush)
6. Thread (nettles and inner bark)
7. Seasoning (wild ginger and onions)
8. Twine (spruce roots)
9. Containers (bark of birch, elm and bamboo sections)
10. Yarrow (seasoning)

EXTREME STARVATION FOODS

1.   Aspen (inner bark and buds)
2.   Maple (inner bark)
3.   Pine (inner bark and pine nuts)
4.   Willow (inner bark and young leaves)

TABLE OF WEIGHTS AND MEASURES

3	teaspoons	= 1 tablespoon	= 15 milliliters
2	tablespoons	= 1 ounce	= 30 milliliters
16	tablespoons	= 1 cup	= 250 milliliters
8	ounces	= 1 cup	= 250 milliliters
32	ounces	= 1 quart	= .9463 liters
2	cups	= 1 pint	= .4732 liters
4	quarts	= 1 gallon	= 3.785 liters

DRY MEASURE

2	pints = 1 quart
8	quarts = 1 peck
4	pecks = 1 bushel
36	bushels = 1 chaldron

LIQUID MEASURE

4	gills = 1 pint
2	pints = 1 quart
4	quarts = 1 gallon
31-1/2	gallons = 1 barrel
2	barrels = 1 hogshead

FREEZING AND BOILING POINTS

Milk.. freezes at 30° above zero
Water .... freezes at 32° above zero
Olive oil .... freezes at 36° above zero
Wine .... freezes at 20° above zero
Vinegar .... freezes at 28° above zero
Alcohol... boils at 173° above zero
Water .... boils at 212° above zero
Petrol. (av.).. boils at 306° above zero
Blood heat..98.4° above zero
Eggs hatch.. 104° above zero

FOOD EQUIVALENTS

Cheese:

1   pound = 2-2/3 cup cubed

Chocolate:

1   square unsweetened = 3 tablespoons cocoa plus 1 tablespoon fat

Chocolate chips:

1   6-ounce package = 1 cup
1   12-ounce package = 2 cups
1   pound cocoa = 4 cups

Coffee:

1   pound = 5 cups ground

Cracker Crumbs:

23   soda crackers = 1 cup
15   graham crackers = 1 cup

Dates:

1   pound pitted = 1-3/4 cup cut up

Eggs:

1   egg = 4 tablespoons liquid or 1/4 cup
4-5   whole eggs = 1 cup
7-9   whites = 1 cup
2   whites = 1/4 cup
12-14 yolks = 1 cup
3   yolks = 1/4 cup
1   whole = 2 yolks plus 1 tablespoon water

Flour:

1   pound all-purpose = 4 cups
1   pound cake = 4-1/2 cups

Macaroni:

1   cup broken, uncooked = 2-2/3 cups cooked

Nuts:

1   pound shelled almonds = 3-1/2 cups nutmeats
1   pound shelled pecans = 4 cups nutmeats
1   pound shelled peanuts = 3 cups nutmeats
1   pound walnuts = 4 cups nutmeats

Rice:

1   cup uncooked = 3 cups cooked

Shortening or Butter:

1   pound = 2 cups

Spaghetti:

1   cup broken, uncooked = 2 cups cooked

Sugar:

1   pound brown = 2-1/4 cups firmly-packed
1   pound granulated = 2 cups
1   pound powdered = 3-1/2 cups sifted

BASIC FACTS ABOUT COOKING WITH HERBS

1. Use herbs sparingly; it is better to have too little than too much.
2. Don't use herbs in every dish; use only for variety and accent.
3. When using blends of herbs, have only one strong flavored herb in the mixture with the remaining herbs having a less pronounced flavor. Blends should be very subtle.
4. If you use fresh savory leaves of herbs, chop them exceedingly fine. The more the cut surface is exposed, the more aromatic herb oils are released. When using dried leaf herbs, crush the leaves as you add to foods.
5. 1/2 teaspoon of dried herb leaves is the equivalent of 1 teaspoon of fresh chopped leaves.
6. To help bring out the flavor of herbs, try soaking them in a few drops of water or lemon juice about 30 minutes before using.
7. To draw out the flavor and permit storage for longer periods of time, blend herbs into butter, fats or oils, and then heat the mixture gently.
8. Herb vinegars are excellent in soups, chopped meats, on salads, sauces and for basting roast meats and poultry.
9. When using herbs in soups and gravies, tie sprigs of fresh herbs in tiny bundles and place them in the foods during their last 20 minutes of cooking. If dry herbs are used, place them in a cheesecloth bag and add them to the food during the last part of their cooking period.
10. If herbs are cooked for too long a period in foods, they will lose their aroma and can give the foods a bitter flavor.
11. The amount of herbs used in a dish will depend on the freshness of the dried herbs being used. The fresher the dried herbs, the stronger they are.

DIFFERENT HERBS FOR DIFFERENT DISHES

BREADS, CAKES, PASTRIES: caraway, coriander, sesame, anise, cumin
CHEESE: basil, sweet marjoram, thyme, tarragon
CREAM OR COTTAGE CHEESE: chives, mint, dill, sage, sweet basil, marjoram, thyme, French tarragon
CONFECTIONARY: mint, sesame, caraway, coriander, borage flowers
EGG DISHES: chives, tarragon, basil, chervil, parsley
DESSERTS: mint, sweet marjoram, anise
FRUIT CUP and COLD BEVERAGES: mint, borage, lemon balm, salad burnet, thyme, rosemary, anise
JAMS & JELLIES: mint, rosemary, lemon verbena

MEATS, POULTRY, FISH

BEEF: basil, sweet marjoram, summer savory, thyme, rosemary
PORK: sage, basil, rosemary, sweet marjoram, chives
LAMB: sweet marjoram, summer savory, thyme, sage
VEAL: rosemary, summer savory, thyme, sage
POULTRY: summer savory, tarragon, thyme, marjoram, sage
FISH: fennel, sage, thyme, basil, chervil, parsley

SAUCES

MEAT & POULTRY SAUCE: dill, mint, tarragon, thyme, chervil, marjoram
FISH SAUCE: fennel, parsley, chervil, thyme, mint, tarragon
BEEF VEGETABLE SOUP OR STEWS: basil, sweet marjoram, summer savory, parsley, thyme, chives, chervil

VEGETABLES

BEETS: basil, summer savory, fennel, caraway, coriander

CABBAGE: mint caraway, fennel

CARROTS: summer savory, mint, basil, parsley, thyme

ONIONS: tarragon, thyme

PEAS: mint, summer savory, basil, chives, rosemary

SPINACH: sweet marjoram, mint

STRING BEANS: summer savory, sweet marjoram, sage

TOMATOES: sweet basil, sweet marjoram, sage, thyme

POTATOES: parsley, basil, chives

PICKLES & CONDIMENTS

dill, mint, tarragon, burnet, sage, rosemary, borage, fennel, anise

VINEGARS:

tarragon, burnet, dill, basil, mint, lemon balm, sweet marjoram

TEAS:

mint, sage, lemon balm, sweet marjoram, catnip, thyme, anise, chamomile, lemon verbena

DIFFERENT HERBS FOR DIFFERENT VEGETABLES

ASPARAGUS: sweet basil, dry mustard, nutmeg, savory, tarragon, thyme

AVOCADO: cayenne pepper, chili powder, paprika

BEANS (Green): basil, curry powder, dry mustard, nutmeg, oregano, savory, marjoram

BEETS: allspice, cloves, basil, dry mustard, nutmeg, paprika, thyme, fennel

BROCCOLI: basil, curry powder, nutmeg

BRUSSEL SPROUTS: basil, curry powder, dry mustard, nutmeg

CABBAGE: mint, caraway, fennel, basil, tarragon

CARROTS: basil, summer savory, mint, parsley, thyme, ginger, nutmeg

CAULIFLOWER: rosemary, sage

CELERY: basil, marjoram, curry powder, dry mustard

CUCUMBER: basil, tarragon, thyme

LETTUCE: marjoram, chili powder

MUSHROOMS: rosemary, thyme

ONIONS: marjoram, tarragon, thyme, rosemary

PEAS (Green): mint, summer savory, basil, rosemary, ginger

POTATOES (White): basil, parsley, chives, mint

POTATOES (Sweet): cinnamon, ginger, nutmeg

RUTABAGAS: basil, rosemary, savory, thyme

SPINACH: sweet marjoram, mint, rosemary

SQUASH (Summer): basil, marjoram, rosemary, sage

SQUASH (Winter): allspice, cinnamon, cloves, nutmeg

TOMATOES: sweet basil, sweet marjoram, oregano, sage, tarragon, thyme

TURNIPS: allspice, basil, nutmeg

DIFFERENT HERBS FOR DIFFERENT SOUPS

Herbs make good soups even better. A spice garnish adds a finishing touch.

ASPARAGUS: chives, curry powder, mace, paprika, sage

BEAN: allspice, basil, oregano, savory, tarragon BEEF: celery seed, chili powder, curry powder

BEEF CONSOMME: bay leaf, whole cloves, oregano, garlic, marjoram, tarragon

BORSCHT (Beet): bay leaf, whole cloves, oregano, thyme

CHICKEN: celery salt, nutmeg, sage, rosemary

CHICKEN GUMBO: bay leaf, cayenne, oregano, parsley

CHICKEN NOODLE: marjoram, nutmeg

CHOWDERS: basil, bay leaf, caraway seed, celery seed, paprika, tarragon, thyme

MINESTRONE: basil, garlic, oregano, parsley, sage

MULLIGATAWNY: cloves, curry powder, mace, parsley

ONION: marjoram, thyme

OXTAIL: bay leaf, marjoram, thyme

PEA SOUP: allspice, basil, cardamom seed, cloves, rosemary, savory

TOMATO: basil, cloves, curry powder, marjoram, oregano, thyme

VEGETABLE: basil, celery salt, cloves, marjoram, sage, rosemary, savory, thyme

VICHYSSOISE OR POTATO: basil, caraway, chives, cloves, curry, nutmeg

HERBS FOR SALADS AND SALAD DRESSING

The seasoning makes the salad. Experiment with some of the suggestions below. They will give you some delightful results.

Egg Salads: cayenne pepper, curry powder, chili powder, garlic, dry mustard, celery salt, capers, sesame seed, chopped chives, summer savory, tarragon, chervil, basil

Chicken Salads: use all the seasonings that egg salads require with the exception of chili powder

Seafood Salad: caraway seed, cayenne pepper, celery salt, sweet marjoram, thyme, basil, sage, crushed seeds of fennel

Tossed Green Salads: sweet basil, summer savory, lovage leaves, marjoram

Fruit Salad (in the dressing): caraway seed, curry powder, nutmeg, paprika, sesame, mint, cinnamon

SALAD DRESSINGS (with Herb & Spice Seasoning)

HERB FRENCH DRESSING

3	tablespoons salad oil
1	tablespoon salad burnet vinegar
1	teaspoon mixture of equal parts of marjoram, basil, summer savory

Blend all ingredients by shaking well. Refrigerate.

MINT-SOUR CREAM DRESSING

1/2	cup sour cream
1	tablespoon fine chopped mint; use 12 teaspoon if dried mint used
1/2	teaspoon sugar
1/2	teaspoon lemon juice
1/4	teaspoon salt
	pinch allspice

Mix the ingredients 24 hours before use and store in refrigerator. Serve with fruit salad or mixed greens.

HONEY DRESSING FOR FRUIT SALADS

1	large package cream cheese
2	tablespoons honey
2	tablespoons lemon juice
2	tablespoons orange juice
1	tablespoon sugar
	dash each nutmeg and sesame seeds

Blend the above ingredients and keep in the refrigerator. Optional to add some candied ginger.

HERB DRESSING

3	heaping tablespoons mayonnaise
1	teaspoon Worcestershire sauce
1	teaspoon herb vinegar, your choice
1	teaspoon mustard
	salt and pepper to taste

Blend all ingredients by shaking vigorously in a closed bottle. Good in tossed green salads or over hard boiled eggs. Add a little to the next potato salad you make.

HOW TO MAKE HERB VINEGAR

When making herb vinegar, it is essential to use fresh herb foliage in full flavor, and to be sure that it has lost none of its aromatic oils. Use the leafy tips of the foliage and cut before the plants come into flower. Wash the foliage clean of dirt and foreign matter and place immediately in a clean crock. Bruise the foliage with a wooden spoon or pestel. Avoid using any metal material when making herb vinegar. Pour boiling vinegar over the bruised foliage. Cover the crock with a lid, put in a warm place and allow to infuse for 8 to 10 days. Stir the herbs and vinegar every 24 hours. After the 8-10 days, strain out the leaves with a cheesecloth and pour the liquid into bottles. Seal tightly and store in a cool, dark place.

Foliage herbs for making vinegars: mint, sweet basil, French tarragon, dill, salad burnet and caraway.

Recommended combinations of herb vinegars:

1. thyme, basil and chives in equal parts
2. tarragon, lemon, thyme, basil, chives, burnet
3. basil, burnet, young borage leaves
4. thyme, chives

HERB BUTTER

Cream 1/2 cup slightly soft butter or margarine until fluffy, using electric mixer or wooden spoon. Stir in 1 teaspoon dried rosemary, crushed, (or 4 teaspoons fresh rosemary, chopped), and 1/2 teaspoon dried marjoram, crushed (or 2 teaspoons marjoram, chopped).

Herbs that go well with pork and ham: sage, basil, chives, rosemary, thyme and sweet marjoram.

Herbs that go well with poultry: summer savory, thyme, tarragon, sweet marjoram and sage.

Herbs that go well with fish: fennel, sage, thyme, basil, chives, chervil, parsley and tarragon.

HERB TEAS

Both fresh and dried herb leaves can be used to make tea. When using dried leaves, use only 1/4 as much material. When using fresh herbs, pick off only the leafy tips. Do not use the old foliage at the base of the plant.

Foliage herbs for teas: lemon balm, costmary, lemon verbena, pennyroyal, bergamot, feverfew, marjoram, wintergreen, calamint, horehound, rosemary, yarrow, catnip, sage, thyme, lemon, lovage, thyme garden and all the mints.

HOME DRYING FRUITS AND VEGETABLES

Drying foods is one of the oldest methods of preservation known to man. It preserves food by removing water. When food is sufficiently dry and properly protected from contamination, it will keep for some time.

Drying is one of the simplest methods of preservation, requiring little outlay of equipment and expense. It can be done out-of-doors or indoors, in an oven or specially-built dehydrator. This publication will cover only the "sun-dried" and "oven-dried" methods.

Either method takes time. Both require attention, especially at the beginning and at the end of the drying process. Stirring the food on drying trays — once a day when sun drying and every half hour under controlled heat conditions — is necessary for an evenly dried product.

Whichever method you use, drying should be done as quickly as possible at a temperature that does not seriously affect the texture, color and flavor of the vegetable or fruit. If the temperature is too high and humidity too low, there is danger that moisture will be removed from the surface of the food more rapidly than water can diffuse from the interior and a hard crust will form on the food. This layer will not permit free diffusion of moisture from the inside and the product will not dry properly.

Under controlled conditions, drying time for fruits varies from 6 to 24 hours, and for vegetables from 3 to 15 hours. Sun drying takes much longer — up to a week or 10 days, depending on the product, the heat of the sun and amount of moisture in the air. Once started, drying should be continuous until enough moisture is removed to keep the food from spoiling.

What to Dry

Fruits and vegetables selected for drying should be fresh, firm, and ripe. Immature or over-mature fruits or vegetables will not be satisfactory products when dried. "Speed" is your watchword. The faster you work from harvest to completion of the drying process, the better the product.

Wash all fresh produce thoroughly. Cleanliness is essential in order to remove all traces of dirt, spray or insecticide. Sort and remove any defective or spoiled product.

PREPARING THE PRODUCT

Vegetables:

Corn, mature beans and celery are the best vegetables for drying. Select the vegetables in prime eating condition. Vegetables that are not mature lose flavor. Over-mature vegetables are often tough and fibrous. Blanching before drying helps preserve the quality of the product.

Steam Blanching:

1. Use a kettle with a close-fitting wire basket or sieve placed so that the steam will circulate freely among the vegetables. Water should not touch the product.

2. Have the water boiling briskly before putting the prepared vegetable into the kettle.

3. Layer vegetables in the steamer not more than 2-1/2 inches deep.

4. Steam the vegetables until each piece is heated through and thoroughly wilted.

5. Test by removing a piece from the center of the steamer and pressing it. It should feel tender but not completely cooked.

Fruit:

Fruits are easier to dry than most vegetables. The higher sugar content makes them easier to preserve and they give up water more easily than vegetables. Apples, pears, peaches, apricots, cherries, plums and berries are satisfactory for drying.

To prevent discoloration, pare all foods with all stainless steel knives. Cut food into thin, even pieces for easier drying.

Sulfuring of fruits is recommended to preserve color and to decrease loss of Vitamin A and C.

Sulfuring — Outdoors:

1. Place fruit in single layers of wooden trays with wooden slats. Place the fruit with the skin side down to prevent the loss of juices. (Metal will react with the sulfur so it is important that wooden trays are used.)

2. Stack the trays about 1-1/2 inches apart to permit the sulfur fumes to circulate.

3. Use a tight wooden box or heavy carton to cover the trays. It should be slightly larger than the stacked trays.

4. Cut a small opening at the bottom of the box for lighting the sulfur and for ventilation.

5. Place sulfur in a clean metal container such as a tin can, shallow but deep enough to prevent overflow. To each pound of prepared fruit, use 2 teaspoons of sulfur if sulfuring time is less than 3 hours; 3 teaspoons of sulfur if the sulfuring time is 3 hours or longer. You can buy sulfur at the drugstore or the lumberyard.

Other Less Effective Treatments:

1. Dip fruit in a bath of 4 to 6 tablespoons of salt to 1 gallon of water for 10 minutes.

2. Ascorbic acid solution — immerse fruit and stir gently in an ascorbic acid solution (1 to 1-1/2 tablespoons ascorbic acid to 1 gallon water). This preparation retards oxidation, and prevents darkening of light-colored fruits to some extent.

3. Steam — follow the method for vegetables. Have only one layer of fruit in the basket or steamer.

DRYING THE PRODUCT

Sun Drying

Fruit:

1. Sulfur—spread as previously directed in trays. Air circulation below as well as above fruit will speed up drying.

2. Place in direct sun. Turn occasionally. A light covering of cheesecloth or screen will keep food from insects.

3. Several days in direct sun are sufficient to make fruit about two-thirds dry. At this stage, stack the trays in the shade where there is good air circulation and continue drying until leathery.

Vegetables:

1. Steam vegetables and spread in a thin layer (not over 1/2 inch deep) on trays as previously directed.

2. Place in direct sun. Turn occasionally.

3. Expose the trays to the sun. Vegetables should not be exposed to the sun long enough to produce sunburn or scorching. Generally, two days or less is sufficient time in the sun. Drying can be completed in the shade.

Oven Drying:

Fruits and vegetables can also be dried in the oven. Trays should have outside dimensions at least 1-1/2 inches smaller than the inside width and depth of the oven for air circulation.

1. Do not put more than 4 to 6 pounds of fresh food in the oven at one time.

2. Use 2 to 4 trays. Have the trays at least 2-1/2 inches apart. Two trays may be stacked by using wooden blocks at each corner of the lower tray which is placed on the oven rack.

3. Allow at least a 3-inch space at the top and bottom of the oven.

4. Place a thermometer on the top tray toward the back.

5. Hold the temperature at 140-150 degrees.

Don't turn on the top unit in an electric oven. If necessary, remove it. Turn on the current or light the gas burner 15 minutes before drying time. If there is a regulator, set it at 150 degrees, 200 degrees, or 250 degrees, whichever is the lowest. If a gas stove has no regulator, turn the flame very low. Be careful that the flame does not go out.

Leave the oven door ajar at least 8 inches when using a gas oven, less if using an electric. Prop an electric oven door open by tucking a folded potholder in the top corner to make about a half-inch crack. Prop a gas oven door open with an 8-inch stick. The right opening helps control heat and lets out moist air.

6.   Examine the food and turn and rotate the trays frequently to prevent scorching.

7.   Keep the room well ventilated.

Most vegetables take 4 to 12 hours to dry; fruits, 6 hours or longer.

PACKAGING AND STORING

All products dried in air or sun should be given a final brief heating at 165 to 170 degrees before being stored to kill any micro-organism that may be adhering to the surface. This may be accomplished by spreading the food on trays and reheating it in an oven for 10 to 15 minutes.

Pack the food into dry, insect-proof containers which are as nearly moisture-proof as possible. The products should be packed tightly into the cans or jars without crushing. Store in a cool place, preferably dark. Glass jars may be wrapped in paper to keep out light.

All dried vegetables and fruits deteriorate in flavor, color, texture and odor while in storage. They should not be kept for more than a year, preferably less.

DRYING TABLE FOR FRUITS AND VEGETABLES

1. Spread in single layers on trays unless otherwise noted.
2. Usual drying temperature is 140 to 150 degrees.

FOOD	PREPARATION FOR DRYING	DRYNESS TEST
Apples	Pare, core and cut in one-fourth inch slices or rings. Sulfur outdoors 30 minutes or dip in solution. Spread not more than one-half inch deep on trays.	Pliable, springy feel, creamy white
Apricots	Same as peaches.	Pliable and leathery
Berries	No pretreatment. Leave whole, except cut strawberries in half.	No visible moisture when crushed
Cherries	Remove stems and pits. If juicy, drain about an hour.	Leathery, but sticky

FOOD	PREPARATION FOR DRYING	DRYNESS TEST
Grapes	Leave whole, remove pits. IF juicy, drain about 1 hour.	Pliable, dark brown
Peaches	Peel if desired. Cut in halves, remove pits. Sulfur outdoors, peeled 30 minutes. unpeeled 2 to 3 hours; or dip in solution; or precook. Dry pit side up.	Pliable and leathery
Pears	Pare and remove core and woody tissue. Cut into one-fourth inch slices or rings, or into quarters or eighths. Sulfur outdoors 2 to 4 hours, according to size of pieces; or dip in solution; or precook.	Leathery, springy feel
Prunes	Cut ini halves and remove pits or leave whole. Halves: no pretreatment. Whole: to soften and crack skins and to help fruit dry better, hold in steam or boiling water for 2 minutes, or dip in boiling water lye bath (3 tablespoons lye to 1 gallon of water) for one-half minute.	Pliable and leathery

VEGETABLES

FOOD	PREPARATION FOR DRYING	DRYNESS TEST
Beans, Green Lima	Shell. Steam 15 to 20 minutes, or until tender but firm.	Shatter when hit with hammer
Beans, Snap	Trim and slice lengthwise or cut in 1 inch pieces. Steam about 20 minutes or until tender, but firm. Spread about one-half inch deep on trays.	Brittle, dark green to brownish
Beets	Trim off all but 1 inch of tops and roots. Steam whole about 30 to 60 minutes depending on size , or until cooked through. Cool and peel. Cut in one-fourth inch cubes or slice one-eighth inch thick. Spread not more than one-fourth inch deep on trays.	Brittle, dark red
Carrots, Parsnips	Steam whole about 20 minutes, or until tender but firm. Scrape or peel. Slice crosswise one-eighth inch thick or dice in one-fourth inch cubes. Or shred before.	Very brittle, deep orange
Mushrooms	Peel the larger mushrooms. Dry whole or sliced, depending on size. No precooking necessary. If stems are tender, slice for drying; if tough, discard. Spread not more than one-half inch deep on trays.	Leathery or brittle
Peas, Green	Steam shelled peas 15 minutes, until tender but firm. Stir frequently during the first few hours of drying.	shatter when hit with hammer
Peppers & Pimientos	Cut in one-half inch strips or rings. Remove seeds. Steam 10 minutes. Spread rings 2 layers deep – strips not more than on-half inch deep.	Pliable
Pumpkin & Squash	Quarter, remove seeds and pith; cut in one-inch strips and peel. Slice strips clockwise one-fourth inch thick. Steam 8 to 13 minutes until slightly soft, but not sticky.	Leathery

LEAVES FOR SEASONING

FOOD	PREPARATION FOR DRYING	DRYNESS TEST
Celery	Wash.	Brittle
Parsley	Wash.	Brittle
Tomatoes for Stewing	Select tomatoes of good color. Steam or dip in boiling water to loosen skins. Chill in cold cold water. Peel. Cut into sections not over 3/4 inches wide. Cut small pear or plum tomatoes in half. Dry to to 20 minutes.	Leathery
Powdered Vegetables	For use in soups or puree. Powder leafy vegetables after drying by grinding in a blender or osterizer.	
Soup Mixture	Combine and store dried vegetables in combination for soups.	

BEEF ROASTING CHART

	Approximate Weight (Pounds)	Internal Temperature on Removal from Oven		Approximate Cooking Time (Total Time)
Roast meat at constant oven temperature at 325 degrees unless otherwise noted.				
Standing Rib	4 to 6	140	(rare)	2 1/4 to 2 3/4 Hrs.
		160	(medium)	2 3/4 to 3 1/4 Hrs.
		170	(well done)	3 1/4 to 3 1/2 Hrs.
Standing Rib	6 to 8	140	(rare)	2 3/4 to 3 Hrs.
		160	(medium)	3 to 3 1/2 Hrs.
		170	(well done)	3 3/4 to 4 Hrs.
Rolled Rib		140	(rare)	2 to 2 1/2 Hrs.
		160	(medium)	3 1/4 to 3 1/2 Hrs.
		170	(well done)	3 3/4 to 4 Hrs.
Rolled Rump	4 to 6	150 to 170		2 to 2 1/2 Hrs.
Sirloin Tip	3 1/2 to 4	150 to 170		2 to 2 3/4 Hrs.
Rib Eye or Delmonico	4 to 6	140	(rare)	1 1/2 to 1 3/4 Hrs.
		160	(medium)	1 3/4 Hrs.
		170	(well done)	2 Hrs.
Tenderloin, Whole (Roast at 425)	4 to 6	140	(rare)	45 min – 1 Hr.
Tenderloin, Half (Roast at 425)	2 to 3	140	(rare)	45 to 50 min

POULTRY ROASTING CHART

	Ready to Cook Weight (pounds)	Oven Temperature	Roasting Time Stuffed & Un-stuffed
Chicken	1 1/2 to 2	375	3/4 to 1 Hr.
	2 to 2 1/2	375	1 to 1 1/4 Hrs.
	2 1/2 to 3	375	1 1/4 to 1 1/2 Hrs.
	3 to 4	375	1 1/2 to 2 Hrs.
Capon	4 to 7	375	1 1/2 to 2 Hrs.
Turkey	6 to 8	325	3 1/2 to 4 Hrs.
	8 to 12	325	4 to 4 1/2 Hrs.
	12 to 16	325	3 to 3 1/4 Hrs.
	16 to 20	325	5 1/2 to 6 1/2 Hrs.
	22 to 24	325	6 1/2 to 7 1/2 Hrs.
Foil-wrapped Turkey	8 to 10	450	2 1/4 to 2 1/2 Hrs.
	10 to 12	450	2 1/2 to 3 Hrs.
	14 to 16	450	3 to 3 1/4 Hrs.
	18 to 20	450	3 1/4 to 3 1/2 Hrs.
	22 to 24	450	3 1/2 to 3 3/4 Hrs.
Domestic Duck	3 to 5	325 then 425	1 1/2 to 2 Hrs. 15 min.
Domestic Goose	4 to 6	325	2 3/4 to 3 Hrs.
	6 to 8	325	3 to 3 1/2 Hrs.
	8 to 10	325	3 1/2 to 3 3/4 Hrs.
	10 to 12	325	3 3/4 to 4 1/4 Hrs.
	12 to 14	325	4 1/4 to 4 3/4 Hrs.
Cornish Game Hen	1 to 1 1/2	375	1 1/2 Hrs.
Guinea Hen	1 to 2	375	3/4 to 1 Hr.
	2 to 2 1/2	375	1 to 1 1/2 Hrs.

HAM ROASTING CHART

	Approximate Weight (Pounds)	Internal Temperature on Removal from Oven	Approximate Cooking Time (Total Time)
Roast meat at constant oven temperature at 325 degrees.			
Ham (fully cooked)			
Half, boneless	4 to 5	135 to 140	1 1/2 to 2 Hrs.
Whole, boneless	8 to 10	135 to 140	2 to 2 1/4 Hrs.
Half	5 to 7	135 to 140	1 3/4 to 2 1/4 Hrs.
Whole	10 to 14	135 to 140	2 1/2 to 3 Hrs.
Ham (cook before eating)			
Shank or Butt	3 to 4	160	2 to 2 1/4 Hrs.
Half	5 to 7	160	2 1/2 to 3 Hrs.
Whole	10 to 14	160	3 1/2 to 4 Hrs.

TO BROIL* OR PAN FRY FULLY COOKED HAM SLICES

Ham Slices, Bone-in	1 to 1 1/4		Broil 10 to 12 minutes
3/4-inch thick			Pan fry 12 to 15 minutes
1-inch thick	1 1/4 to 1 3/4		Broil 14 to 16 minutes
3/8-inch thick			Pan fry 4 to 5 minutes
1/4-inch thick	2 ounces		Broil 3 to 4 minutes
			Pan fry 3 to 4 minutes

TO BROIL* OR PAN FRY COOK BEFORE EATING HAM SLICES

Ham Slices, Bone-in	1 to 1 1/4		Broil 13 to 14 minutes
3/4-inch thick			Pan fry 15 to 20 minutes
1-inch thick	1 1/4 to 1 3/4		Broil 18 to 20 minutes
			Pan fry 20 to 22 minutes

*Broil 3 inches from heat.

FRESH AND SMOKED PORK ROASTING CHART

	Approximate Weight (pounds)	Internal Temperature on Removal from Oven	Approximate Cooking Time (Total Time)
Roast meat at constant oven temperature at 325 degrees.			
Loin, Center	3 to 5	170	2 1/2 to 3 Hrs.
Loin, Half	5 to 7	170	3 1/2 to 4 1/4 Hrs.
Loin, Blade or Sirloin	3 to 4	170	2 1/4 to 2 3/4 Hrs.
Loin, Center – rolled	3 to 4	170	2 1/2 to 3 Hrs.
Boston Shoulder	4 to 6	170	3 to 4 Hrs.
Boston Shoulder Roll	3 to 5	170	2 to 3 Hrs.
Leg (Fresh Ham)	12 to 16	170	5 to 6 Hrs.
Leg, Half (Fresh Ham)	5 to 7	170	3 1/2 to 4 1/2 Hrs.
Picnic (Smoked, cook before eating)	5 to 8	170	3 to 4 Hrs.

VEAL ROASTING CHART

Leg	5 to 8	170	2 3/4 to 3 3/4 Hrs.
Loin	4 to 6	170	2 1/2 to 3 Hrs.
Rolled Shoulder	4 to 6	170	3 1/2 to 3 3/4 Hrs.
	12 to 16	325	3 to 3 1/4 Hrs.
	16 to 20	325	5 1/2 to 6 1/2 Hrs.
	22 to 24	325	6 1/2 to 7 1/2 Hrs.

ROASTING CHART FOR GAME BIRDS

(The temperature listed in this section refers to oven temperature not internal temperature.)

Wild Duck	1 to 2	400	1 to 1 1/2 Hrs.
Wild Goose	2 to 4	400	1 1/2 to 3 Hrs.
	4 to 6	400	3 to 4 Hrs.
Partridge	1/2 to 1	450	30 to 45 minutes
Pheasant	1 to 3	350	1 to 2 1/2 Hrs.
Quail	4 to 6 ounces	400	30 to 45 minutes
Squab	12 to 14 ounces	400	40 to 50 minutes

REFRIGERATOR STORAGE

Refrigerator Temperature at 36 to 40 degrees.

BEEF

Standing Rib Roast...5 to 8 days
Steaks ....3 to 5 days
Pot Roast..5 to 6 days
Stew Meat .... 2 days
Ground Beef .... 2 days

VEAL

Roasts...5 to 6 days
Chops .... 4 days

PORK

Roasts..2 to 3 days
Chops .... 3 days
Spareribs.. 3 days
Bulk Pork Sausage ....2 to 3 days

SMOKED MEAT

Ham or Picnic Shoulder
    Whole or Half... 7 days
    Slices .... 3 days
Bacon...5 to 7 days
Dried Beef ....10 to 12 days
Corned Beef ....5 to 7 days

LAMB

Roasts .... 5 days
Chops .... 3 days

VARIETY MEATS

Liver, sliced... 2 days
Heart... 2 days
Sweetbreads, cooked .... 2 days
Smoked Tongue ....6 to 7 days

FISH .... 1 to 2 days

POULTRY

Chicken, whole..2 days
Chicken, cut up...2 days
Turkey, whole...2 days
Ducklings, whole ....2 days

COOKED MEATS

Leftover Cooked Meats ....4 days
Ham or Picnic Shoulder ....7 days
Cooked Fish..3 to 4 days
Cooked Poultry ....3 to 4 days
Poultry Gravy and Stuffing..3 to 4 days
Frankfurters ....4 to 5 days
Sliced Luncheon Meats..3 days
Unsliced Bologna...4 to 6 days

FREEZING UNCOOKED MEAT

Storage time at 0 degrees.

BEEF

Roasts..8 to 12 months
Steaks ....8 to 12 months

LAMB

Roasts..8 to 12 months
Chops...3 to 4 months

PORK

Roasts..4 to 8 months
Chops...3 to 4 months

VEAL

Roasts..4 to 8 months
Chops...3 to 4 months

GROUND MEAT ....2 to 3 months

POULTRY

Chicken	12 months
Turkey	6 months
Duck	6 months
Goose	6 months
Giblets	3 months

FISH .... 1 to 2 days

SHELLFISH

Oysters	3 months
Clams	3 months
Scallops	3 months
Crabs	1 month
Lobsters	1 month
Shrimp	3 months

INDEX

WILD FOODS

BREADS

YEAST BREADS AND ROLLS:

SOURDOUGH:

SEAFOODS

OTHER LANDS

The Washington Cookbook makes a great gift for a friend, loved one or for yourself. The form below can be used to order a book to be sent as a gift or directly to you. We will include a gift card if you desire. Shipping is FREE anywhere in the continental United States. Books are $27.95 each. Washington residents please add sales tax of $2.00 per book. That is less than current rates anywhere in the state. We will make up the difference.

Please make check or money order payable to SDH Company. Send order to PO Box 923, Spokane, WA 99210

We pride ourselves on excellent customer service and will ship your book(s) out right away. Guaranteed.

PLEASE SEND _____ BOOK(S) TO: ENCLOSED $_____

_____

_____

                                        STATE   ZIP

email address *(not required)*

(Send us your email address if you would like shipping confirmation)

☐   **THIS IS A GIFT. PLEASE INCLUDE THE FOLLOWING MESSAGE.**

_____

_____

_____

Books can also be ordered online @ **www.thewashingtoncookbook.com**